Voyages and Discoveries
of the Companions of Columbus

Voyages and Discoveries
of the Companions of Columbus

By WASHINGTON IRVING *With an Intro-duction by the Author a Foreword by* VAN WYCK BROOKS *and a Decoration by* EDWARD A. WILSON

FREDERICK UNGAR PUBLISHING CO.
NEW YORK

Printed in the United States of America

Library of Congress Catalog Card Number 59-11667

To declare my opinion herein,
whatsoever hath heretofore been discovered by the famous travels of Saturnus
and Hercules, with such other whom the
Antiquitie for their heroical acts honoured as gods, seemeth but little and ob-
scure, if it be compared to the victorious
labours of the Spanyards.

P. Martyr, Decad. III. *c.*4.
Lock's translation

FOREWORD

THE VOYAGES AND DISCOVERIES OF THE COMPANIONS OF COLUMBUS *was issued in* 1831, *three years after the publication of the* HISTORY OF THE LIFE AND VOYAGES OF CHRISTOPHER COLUMBUS. *Irving had spent seven years in Spain, delving in the national archives at Madrid and corresponding with Spanish scholars, and had mastered his subject as no previous writer, whether English or Spanish, had been able to do before him, for he was animated by a fervor that had its roots in the profound nationalistic enthusiasm that followed the American War of Independence.*

His first intention, when he settled in Madrid, had been to translate the Coleccion de los Viajes y Descubrimientos *of Martin Fernandez de Navarrete, which had just appeared; but he soon found that this consisted rather of raw materials than a biography proper, and he determined to write his own life of Columbus, which was published in four volumes with marked success. This had naturally led him to investigate the travels of those hardly less romantic worthies who followed in the train of the great navigator, Alonzo de Ojeda, Diego de Nicuesa and the far better known Balboa and Ponce de Leon, with results that have an even more distinguished charm. They were all,*

vii

as Irving says, enkindled by the zeal of the Admiral and instructed by his example, and they fulfilled in various ways the
hopes and intentions with which he had set out on his voyages.
"It is a curious fact," Irving remarks again, "that the spirit of
chivalry entered largely into the early expeditions of the Spanish
discoverers, giving them a character wholly distinct from similar
enterprises undertaken by other nations." These chapters are
chips from the workshop that produced the great History, but
they are chips of the rarest material.

There is something exceedingly attractive, perhaps because so
extravagant, in the characters of these chivalric adventurers.
Alonzo de Ojeda, we are told, was a bold and graceful horseman,
dextrous with every weapon, and noted for his extraordinary
skill and adroitness in all feats of agility. He had accompanied
Columbus on his second voyage, and in 1499, having previously
undertaken an expedition with the Florentine merchant Amerigo
Vespucci, he set sail on the journey that led him to the discovery
of Venezuela. He penetrated to the Indian village of Maracaibo,
sending a detachment of twenty-seven of his followers on a visit
to the interior, and was received with kindness and even honor
by the native population that poured forth to receive him. This
hospitality he scarcely requited, for he crowded his ships with
captives, whom he subsequently sold into slavery in Spain. His
second voyage was marked by no special adventures, but on the
third he explored the coast of Cartagena, founded the colony of

Saint Sebastian, explored Cuba and visited Jamaica and San Domingo, desperate undertakings in some instances and leading only, as in the case of Columbus himself, to "the obscurity which gathers round a ruined man." For it is one of the most appealing facts about these adventurers that in so many cases their lives terminated in the abysses of tragedy.

This was certainly the case with Nicuesa and Balboa, if not Ponce de Leon, who died honorably from the wound of an arrow in the thigh. Nicuesa was driven from the coast of Darien in a crazy brigantine and disappeared in the Caribbean Sea, while Balboa was beheaded in his native country, the victim of the jealousy of his rival Pedrarias. Such turbulent lives were almost bound, it seems, to end in some equal violence. But there were gay and pleasant episodes all along the way, islands abounding with flowers and brilliant birds, gentle savages who came bearing exotic gifts, fountains of youth, gold mines and treasuries of precious stones. There was the marvellous discovery of the Pacific from that peak in Darien, treks over magical mountains and in quest of golden temples and fabulous seas. "The imagination," says our sympathetic chronicler, "delights to picture forth the splendid confusion of their thoughts." And Irving does full justice to these innumerable wonders. Although his own imagination never rises to any great intensity, it plays with a charming zest over the thoughts, speculations, and discoveries of his heroes, in the most ferociously cruel of whom he always finds

some redeeming qualities. For they were, after all, to a man, full of
daring, resolution, vigor, and devotion to some cause greater than
their own personal advancement. Difficult and dangerous all their
enterprises were, abounding in every kind of peril both on land
and on sea, and if they were avaricious, greedy and reckless of
the rights of the primitive peoples among whom they found them-
selves, it must be said that they were lured on by the most romantic
prospect of the most extraordinary prizes that has ever dazzled
the human imagination. For what prize has history ever dangled
before men comparable with the prize of the Western hemisphere
as it dimly appeared before men's eyes in the days of the Con-
quistadors? And what race was ever so prepared by the inborn
qualities of its character to be dazzled by this prospect and the hope
of this prize? The courage of the Spaniards was always equal
to their cruelty, and it is written large over all the pages of this
book, for Irving had a prodigious admiration for his heroes, as he
had an intimate, first-hand knowledge of their descendants in less
glorious times. The commanders were called upon again and
again to cheer and reanimate their men, worn down by despair,
hunger, and thirst, in islands without springs or streams of
fresh water, inhabited by foes occasionally, at least, as ferocious
as themselves. And they worked for the glory of Spain, and they
perished through the treachery of their fellow Spaniards.

The high points of the book are, of course, the sudden dis-
covery of the Pacific Ocean and the cruise of Juan Ponce in

search of the Fountain of Youth; and here Irving's mood rises to a mild ecstasy. "Here was the dream of the alchemist realized!" he exclaims over the reflections of Juan Ponce. "One had but to find this gifted land, and revel in the enjoyment of boundless riches and perennial youth! . . . Juan Ponce de Leon listened to these tales with fond credulity. He was advancing in life, and the ordinary term of existence seemed insufficient for his mighty plans. Could he but plunge into this marvellous fountain or gifted river, and come out with his battered war-worn body restored to the strength and freshness and suppleness of youth, and his head still retaining the wisdom and knowledge of age, what enterprises might he not accomplish in the additional course of vigorous years assured to him!" Fairyland itself was no more marvellous than these islands and mainlands of the West as they appeared partly in the imagination of the Spaniards and partly in the realities they found.

The great Admiral, the forerunner of all these lesser adventurers, has received of late an extraordinary amount of attention from biographers and historians. No doubt Ponce de Leon and Balboa will also come in for their share in this revival of interest in the origins of our Western history, for the recent growth of interest in all things American, an interest almost, if not quite, unprecedented, is bound to extend backward until it has covered the whole course of our history. Meanwhile it has been a happy thought to revive for a fresh generation of readers the glowing chapters of Washington Irving, which ma᷎ well be surpassed in erudition by future writers, but can hardly be excelled in human feeling and romantic enthusiasm.

VAN WYCK BROOKS.

Westport, Connecticut
   January, 1929

CONTENTS

VICENTE YAÑEZ PINZON

DIEGO DE LEPE AND RODRIGO DE BASTIDES

ALONZO DE OJEDA
SECOND VOYAGE

ALONZO DE OJEDA
THIRD VOYAGE

DIEGO DE NICUESA

VASCO NUÑEZ DE BALBOA

DISCOVERER OF THE PACIFIC OCEAN

PAGE

JUAN PONCE DE LEON

CONQUEROR OF PORTO RICO, AND DISCOVERER OF FLORIDA

APPENDIX

NOTES ON THE TEXT

INTRODUCTION

THE first discovery of the western hemisphere has already been related by the author in his History of Columbus. It is proposed by him, in the present work, to narrate the enterprises of certain of the companions and disciples of the admiral, who, enkindled by his zeal, and instructed by his example, sallied forth separately in the vast region of adventure to which he had led the way. Many of them sought merely to skirt the continent which he had partially visited, and to secure the first fruits of the pearl fisheries of Paria and Cubaga, or to explore the coast of Veragua, which he had represented as the Aurea Chersonesus of the Ancients. Others aspired to accomplish a grand discovery which he had meditated toward the close of his career. In the course of his expeditions along the coast of Terra Firma, Columbus had repeatedly received information of the existence of a vast sea to the south. He supposed it to be the great Indian Ocean, the region of the Oriental spice islands, and that it must communicate by a strait with the Caribbean Sea. His last and most disastrous voyage was made for the express purpose of discovering that imaginary strait, and making his way into this Southern Ocean. The illustrious navigator, however, was doomed to die, as it were, upon the threshold of his discoveries. It was reserved for one of his followers, Vasco Nuñez de Balboa, to obtain the first view of the promised ocean, from the lofty mountains of Darien, some years after the eyes of the venerable admiral had been closed in death.

The expeditions herein narrated, therefore, may be considered as springing immediately out of the voyages of Columbus, and fulfilling some of his grand designs. They may be compared to the attempts of adventurous knights errant to achieve the enterprise left unfinished by some illustrious predecessor. Neither is this comparison entirely fanciful. On the contrary, it is a curious fact, well worthy of notice, that the spirit of chivalry entered largely into the early expeditions of the Spanish discoverers, giving them a character wholly distinct from similar enterprises undertaken by other nations. It will not, perhaps, be considered far sought, if we trace the cause of this peculiarity to the domestic history of the Spaniards during the middle ages.

Eight centuries of incessant warfare with the Moorish usurpers of the peninsula produced a deep and lasting effect upon the Spanish character and manners. The war, being ever close at home, mingled itself with the domestic habits and concerns of the Spaniard. He was born a soldier. The wild and predatory nature of the war, also, made him a kind of chivalrous marauder. His horse and weapon were always ready for the field. His delight was in roving incursions and extravagant exploits, and no gain was so glorious in his eyes as the cavalgada of spoils and captives, driven home in triumph from a plundered province. Religion, which has ever held great empire in the Spanish mind, lent its aid to sanctify these roving and ravaging propensities, and the Castilian cavalier, as he sacked the towns and laid waste the fields of his Moslem neighbour, piously believed he was doing God service.

The conquest of Granada put an end to the peninsular wars between christian and infidel; the spirit of Spanish chivalry was thus suddenly deprived of its wonted sphere of action; but it had been too long fostered and excited to be as suddenly appeased. The youth of the nation, bred up to daring adventure and heroic achievement, could not brook the tranquil and regular pursuits of common life, but panted for some new field of romantic enterprise.

It was at this juncture that the grand project of Columbus was carried into effect. His treaty with the sovereigns was, in a manner, signed with the same pen that had subscribed the capitulation of the Moorish capital, and his first expedition may almost be said to have departed from beneath the walls of Granada. Many of the youthful cavaliers who had fleshed their swords in that memorable war, crowded the ships of the discoverers, thinking a new career of arms was to be opened to them—a kind of crusade into splendid and unknown regions of infidels. The very weapons and armour that had been used against the Moors, were drawn from the arsenals to equip the discoverers, and some of the most noted of the early commanders in the new world will be found to have made their first essay in arms under the banner of Ferdinand and Isabella, in their romantic campaigns among the mountains of Andalusia.

To these circumstances may, in a great measure, be ascribed that swelling chivalrous spirit which will be found continually mingling, or rather warring, with the technical habits of the seaman, and the sordid schemes of the mercenary adventurer; in these early Spanish discoveries, chivalry had left the land and launched upon the deep. The Spanish cavalier had embarked in the Caravel of the discoverer; he carried among the trackless wildernesses of the new world, the same contempt of danger and fortitude under suffering, the same restless roaming spirit, the same passion for inroad and ravage, and vain-glorious exploit, and the same fervent, and often bigoted, zeal for the propagation of his faith that had distinguished him during his warfare with the Moors. Instances in point will be found in the extravagant career of the daring Ojeda, particularly in his adventures along the coast of Terra Firma and the wild shores of Cuba. In the sad story of the "unfortunate Nicuesa;" graced as it is with occasional touches of high-bred courtesy; in the singular cruise of that brave, but credulous, old cavalier, Juan Ponce de Leon, who fell upon the flowery coast of Florida, in his search after an imaginary fountain of youth; and above all in the chequered fortunes of Vasco Nuñez de Balboa, whose discovery of the Pacific ocean forms one of the most beautiful and striking incidents in the history of the new world, and whose fate might furnish a theme of wonderful interest for a poem or a drama.

The extraordinary actions and adventures of these men, while they rival the exploits recorded in chivalric tale, have the additional interest of verity. They leave us in admiration of the bold and heroic qualities inherent in the Spanish character, which led that nation to so high a pitch of power and glory, and which are still discernible in the great mass of that gallant people, by those who have an opportunity of judging of them rightly.

Before concluding these prefatory remarks, the author would acknowledge how much he has been indebted to the third volume of the invaluable Historical collection of Don Martin Fernandez de Navarrete, wherein he has exhibited his usual industry, accuracy and critical acumen. He has likewise profited greatly by the second volume of Oviedo's general history, which only exists in manuscript, and a copy of which he found in the Columbian library of the Cathedral of Seville.

He has had some assistance also from the documents of the law case between Don Diego Columbus and the Crown, which exists in the archives of the Indies; and for an inspection of which he is much indebted to the permission of the Spanish Government and the kind attentions of Don Josef de La Higuera Lara, the keeper of the archives. These, with the historical works of Las Casas, Herrera Gomera, and Peter Martyr, have been his authorities for the facts contained in the following work; though he has not thought proper to refer to them continually at the bottom of his page.

While his work was going through the press he received a volume of Spanish Biography, written with great elegance and accuracy, by Don Manuel Josef Quintana, and containing a life of Vasco Nuñez de Balboa. He was gratified to find that his ·arrangement of facts were generally corroborated by this work; though he was enabled to correct his dates in several instances, and to make a few other emendations from the volume of Señor Quintana, whose position in Spain gave him the means of attaining superior exactness on these points.

WASHINGTON IRVING.

ALONZO DE OJEDA

His First Voyage

IN WHICH HE WAS ACCOMPANIED BY
AMERIGO VESPUCCI[1]

CHAPTER I

Some Accounts of Ojeda—of Juan de la Cosa—of Amerigo Vespucci.—Preparations for the Voyage.—[1499.]

THOSE who have read the History of Columbus will, doubtless, remember the character and exploits of Alonzo de Ojeda[2]; as some of the readers of the following pages, however, may not have perused that work, and as it is proposed at present to trace the subsequent fortunes of this youthful adventurer, a brief sketch of him may not be deemed superfluous.

Alonzo de Ojeda was a native of Cuenca, in New Castile, and of a respectable family. He was brought up as a page or esquire, in the service of Don Luis de Cerda, Duke of Medina Celi, one of the most powerful nobles of Spain; the same who for some time patronised Columbus during his application to the Spanish court.[3]

In those warlike days, when the peninsula was distracted by contests between the christian kingdoms, by feuds between the nobles and the crown, and by the incessant and marauding warfare with the Moors, the household of a Spanish nobleman was a complete school of arms, where the youth of the country were sent to be trained up in all kinds of hardy exercises, and to be led to battle under an illustrious banner. Such was especially the case with the service of the Duke of Medina Celi, who possessed princely domains, whose household was a petty court, who led legions of armed retainers to the field, and who appeared in splendid state and with an immense retinue, more as an ally of Ferdinand and Isabella, than as a subject. He engaged in many of the roughest expeditions of the memorable war of Granada, always insisting on leading his own troops in person, when the service was of peculiar difficulty and danger. Alonzo de Ojeda was formed to signalize himself in such a school. Though small of stature, he was well made, and of wonderful force and activity, with a towering spirit and a daring eye that seemed to make up for deficiency of height. He was a bold and graceful horseman, an excellent foot soldier, dexterous with every weapon, and noted for his extraordinary skill and adroitness in all feats of strength and agility.

He must have been quite young when he followed the
duke of Medina Celi, as page, to the Moorish wars; for he
was but about twenty-one years of age when he accompanied
Columbus in his second voyage; he had already, however,
distinguished himself by his enterprizing spirit and headlong
valour; and his exploits during that voyage contributed to
enhance his reputation. He returned to Spain with Columbus, but did not accompany him in his third voyage, in the
spring of 1498. He was probably impatient of subordination,
and ambitious of a separate employment or command, which
the influence of his connexions gave him a great chance of
obtaining. He had a cousin german of his own name, the
reverend Padre Alonzo de Ojeda, a Dominican friar, who
was one of the first inquisitors of Spain, and a great favourite
with the Catholic sovereigns.[4] This father inquisitor was,
moreover, an intimate friend of the bishop Don Juan
Rodriguez Fonseca, who had the chief management of the
affairs of the Indies, under which general name were com-
prehended all the countries discovered in the new world.
Through the good offices of his cousin inquisitor, therefore,
Ojeda had been introduced to the notice of the bishop, who
took him into his especial favour and patronage. Mention has
already been made, in the History of Columbus, of a present
made by the bishop of Ojeda of a small Flemish painting of
the Holy Virgin. This the young adventurer carried about

with him as a protecting relic, invoking it at all times of
peril, whether by sea or land; and to the special care of the
Virgin he attributed the remarkable circumstance that he
had never been wounded in any of the innumerable brawls
and battles into which he was continually betrayed by his
rash and fiery temperament.

While Ojeda was lingering about the court, letters were
received from Columbus, giving an account of the events of
his third voyage, especially of his discovery of the coast of
Paria, which he described as abounding with drugs and
spices, with gold and silver, and precious stones, and, above
all, with oriental pearls, and which he supposed to be the
borders of that vast and unknown region of the East, wherein, according to certain learned theorists, was situated the
terrestrial paradise. Specimens of the pearls, procured in
considerable quantities from the natives, accompanied his
epistle, together with charts descriptive of his route. These
tidings caused a great sensation among the maritime adventurers of Spain; but no one was more excited by them
than Alonzo de Ojeda, who, from his intimacy with the
bishop, had full access to the charts and correspondence of
Columbus. He immediately conceived the project of making
a voyage in the route thus marked out by the admiral, and
of seizing upon the first fruits of discovery which he had left
ungathered. His scheme met with ready encouragement

from Fonseca, who, as has heretofore been shown, was an implacable enemy to Columbus, and willing to promote any measure that might injure or molest him. The bishop accordingly granted a commission to Ojeda, authorizing him to fit out an armament and proceed on a voyage of discovery, with the proviso merely that he should not visit any territories appertaining to Portugal, or any of the lands discovered in the name of Spain previous to the year 1495. The latter part of this provision appears to have been craftily worded by the bishop, so as to leave the coast of Paria and its pearl fisheries open to Ojeda, they having been recently discovered by Columbus in 1498.

The commission was signed by Fonseca alone, in virtue of general powers vested in him for such purposes, but the signature of the sovereigns did not appear on the instrument, and it is doubtful whether their sanction was sought on the occasion. He knew that Columbus had recently remonstrated against a royal mandate issued in 1495, permitting voyages of discovery, by private adventurers, and that the sovereigns had in consequence revoked their mandate wherever it might be deemed prejudicial to the stipulated privileges of the admiral.[5] It is probable, therefore, that the bishop avoided raising any question that might impede the enterprize; being confident of the ultimate approbation of Ferdinand, who would be well pleased to have his dominions in the new world

extended by the discoveries of private adventurers, undertaken at their own expense. It was stipulated in this, as well
as in subsequent licenses for private expeditions, that a certain proportion of the profits, generally a fourth or fifth,
should be reserved for the crown.

Having thus obtained permission to make the voyage, the
next consideration with Ojeda was to find the means. He was
a young adventurer, a mere soldier of fortune, and destitute
of wealth; but he had a high reputation for courage and
enterprise, and with these, it was thought, would soon make
his way to the richest parts of the newly discovered lands,
and have the wealth of the Indies at his disposal. He had no
difficulty, therefore, in finding monied associates among the
rich merchants of Seville, who, in that age of discovery, were
ever ready to stake their property upon the schemes of roving
navigators. With such assistance he soon equipped a squadron of four vessels at Port St. Mary, opposite Cadiz. Among
the seamen who engaged with him were several who had just
returned from accompanying Columbus in his voyage to
this very coast of Paria. The principal associate of Ojeda,
and one on whom he placed great reliance, was Juan de la
Cosa; who accompanied him as first mate, or, as it was
termed, chief pilot. This was a bold Biscayan, who may be
regarded as a disciple of Columbus, with whom he had sailed
in his second voyage, when he coasted Cuba and Jamaica,

and he had since accompanied Rodrigo de Bastides, in an expedition along the coast of Terra Firma. The hardy veteran was looked up to by his contemporaries as an oracle of the seas, and was pronounced one of the most able mariners of the day; he may be excused, therefore, if in his harmless vanity, he considered himself on a par even with Columbus.[6]

Another conspicuous associate of Ojeda, in this voyage, was Amerigo Vespucci, a Florentine merchant, induced by broken fortunes and a rambling disposition to seek adventures in the new world. Whether he had any pecuniary interest in the expedition, and in what capacity he sailed, does not appear. His importance has entirely arisen from subsequent circumstances; from his having written and published a narrative of his voyages, and from his name having eventually been given to the new world.

CHAPTER II

*Departure from Spain.—Arrival on the Coast of Paria.—
Customs of the Natives.*

OJEDA sailed from Port St. Mary on the 20th of
May, 1499, and, having touched for supplies at
the Canaries, took a departure from Gomara,
pursuing the route of Columbus, in his third voyage, being guided by the chart he had sent home, as well as by
the mariners who had accompanied him on that occasion. At
the end of twenty-four days he reached the continent of the
new world, about two hundred leagues farther south than
the part discovered by Columbus, being, as it is supposed,
the coast of Surinam.[7]

From thence he ran along the coast of the Gulf of Paria,
passing the mouths of many rivers, but especially those of
the Esquivo and the Oronoko. These, to the astonishment of
the Spaniards, unaccustomed as yet to the mighty rivers
of the new world, poured forth such a prodigious volume of
water, as to freshen the sea for a great extent. They beheld
none of the natives until they arrived at the Island of
Trinidad, on which island they met with traces of the recent
visit of Columbus.

Vespucci, in his letters, gives a long description of the people of this island and of the coast of Paria, who were of the Carib race, tall, well made and vigorous, and expert with the bow, the lance and the buckler. His description, in general, resembles those which have frequently been given of the Aboriginals of the new world; there are two or three particulars, however, worthy of citation.

They appeared, he said, to believe in no religious creed, to have no place of worship, and to make no prayers or sacrifices; but, he adds, from the voluptuousness of their lives, they might be considered Epicureans.[8] Their habitations were built in the shape of bells; of the trunks of trees, thatched with palm leaves, and were proof against wind and weather. They appeared to be in common, and some of them were of such magnitude as to contain six hundred persons: in one place there were eight principal houses capable of sheltering nearly ten thousand inhabitants. Every seven or eight years the natives were obliged to change their residence, from the maladies engendered by the heat of the climate in their crowded habitations.

Their riches consisted in beads and ornaments made from the bones of fishes; in small white and green stones strung like rosaries, with which they adorned their persons, and in the beautiful plumes of various colours for which the tropical birds are noted.

The Spaniards smiled at their simplicity in attaching an extraordinary value to such worthless trifles; while the savages, in all probability, were equally surprised at beholding the strangers so eager after gold, and pearls and precious stones, which to themselves were objects of indifference.

Their manner of treating the dead was similar to that observed among the natives of some of the islands. Having deposited the corpse in a cavern or sepulchre, they placed a jar of water and a few eatables at its head, and then abandoned it without moan or lamentation. In some parts of the coast, when a person was considered near his end, his nearest relatives bore him to the woods and laid him in a hammock suspended to the trees. They then danced round him until evening, when, having left within his reach sufficient meat and drink to sustain him for four days, they repaired to their habitations. If he recovered and returned home, he was received with much ceremony and rejoicing; if he died of his malady or of famine, nothing more was thought of him.

Their mode of treating a fever is also worthy of mention. In the height of the malady they plunged the patient in a bath of the coldest water, after which they obliged him to make many evolutions round a great fire, until he was in a violent heat, when they put him to bed, that he might sleep: a treatment, adds Amerigo Vespucci, by which we saw many cured.

CHAPTER III

Coasting of Terra Firma.—Military Expedition of Ojeda.

AFTER touching at various parts of Trinidad and the Gulf of Paria, Ojeda passed through the strait of the Boca del Drago, or Dragon's Mouth, which Columbus had found so formidable, and then steered his course along the coast of Terra Firma, landing occasionally until he arrived at Curiana, or the Gulf of Pearls. From hence he stood to the opposite island of Margarita, previously discovered by Columbus, and since renowned for its pearl fishery. This, as well as several adjacent islands, he visited and explored; after which he returned to the main land, and touched at Cumana and Maracapana, where he found the rivers infested with alligators resembling the crocodiles of the Nile.

Finding a convenient harbour at Maracapana he unloaded and careened his vessels there, and built a small brigantine. The natives came to him in great numbers, bringing abundance of venison, fish, and cassava bread, and aiding the seamen in their labours. Their hospitality was not certainly disinterested, for they sought to gain the protection of the

Spaniards, whom they reverenced as superhuman beings. When they thought they had sufficiently secured their favour, they represented to Ojeda that their coast was subject to invasion from a distant island, the inhabitants of which were cannibals, who carried their people into captivity, to be devoured at their unnatural banquets. They besought Ojeda, therefore, to avenge them upon these ferocious enemies.

The request was gratifying to the fighting propensities of Alonzo de Ojeda, and to his love of adventure, and was readily granted. Taking seven of the natives on board of his vessels, therefore, as guides, he set sail in quest of the cannibals. After sailing for seven days he came to a chain of islands, some of which were peopled, others uninhabited, and which are supposed to have been the Carribee islands. One of these was pointed out by his guides as the habitation of their foes. On running near the shore he beheld it thronged with savage warriors, decorated with coronets of gaudy plumes, their bodies painted with a variety of colours. They were armed with bows and arrows, with darts, lances, and bucklers, and seemed prepared to defend their island from invasion.

This show of war was calculated to rouse the martial spirit of Ojeda. He brought his ships to anchor, ordered out his boats, and provided each with a paterero or small cannon. Beside the oarsmen, each boat contained a number of soldiers, who were told to crouch out of sight in the bottom. The boats then pulled in steadily for the shore. As they approached the Indians let fly a cloud of arrows, but without much effect. Seeing the boats continue to advance, the savages threw themselves into the sea, and brandished their lances to prevent their landing. Upon this, the soldiers sprang up in the boats and discharged the patereroes. At the sound and smoke of these unknown weapons the savages abandoned the water in affright, while Ojeda and his men leaped on shore and pursued them. The Carib warriors rallied on the banks, and fought for a long time with that courage peculiar to their race, but were at length driven to the woods, at the edge of the sword, leaving many killed and wounded on the field of battle.

On the following day the savages were seen on the shore in still greater numbers, armed and painted, and decorated with war plumes, and sounding defiance with their conchs and drums. Ojeda again landed with fifty-seven men, whom he separated into four companies, and ordered them to charge the enemy from different directions. The Caribs fought for a time hand to hand, displaying great dexterity in covering themselves with their bucklers, but were at length entirely routed and driven, with great slaughter, to the forests. The Spaniards had but one man killed and twenty-one wounded in these combats,—such superior advantage did their armour give them over the naked savages. Having plundered and set fire to the houses they returned triumphantly to their ships, with a number of Carib captives; and made sail for the main land. Ojeda bestowed a part of the spoil upon the seven Indians who had accompanied him as guides, and sent them exulting to their homes, to relate to their countrymen the signal vengeance that had been wreaked upon their foes. He then anchored in a bay where he remained for twenty days, until his men had recovered from their wounds.[9]

CHAPTER IV

Discovery of the Gulf of Venezuela.—Transactions there.—
Ojeda explores the Gulf.—Penetrates to Maracaibo

IS crew being refreshed and the wounded sufficiently recovered, Ojeda made sail, and
touched at the island of Curazao, which, according to the accounts of Vespucci, was inhabited by a race of giants, "every woman appearing a
Penthesilea, and every man an Antæus."[10] As Vespucci was
a scholar, and as he supposed himself exploring the regions
of the extreme East, the ancient realm of fable, it is probable,
his imagination deceived him, and construed the formidable
accounts given by the Indians of their cannibal neighbours
of the islands, into something according with his recollections
of classic fable. Certain it is, that the reports of subsequent
voyagers proved the inhabitants of the island to be of the
ordinary size.

Proceeding along the coast, he arrived at a vast deep gulf,
resembling a tranquil lake; entering which, he beheld on the
eastern side a village, the construction of which struck him
with surprise. It consisted of twenty large houses, shaped

like bells, and built on piles driven into the bottom of the lake, which, in this part was limpid and of but little depth. Each house was provided with a drawbridge, and with canoes by which the communication was carried on. From these resemblances to the Italian city, Ojeda gave to the bay the name of the Gulf of Venice: and it is called at the present day Venezuela, or little Venice: the Indian name was Coquibacoa.

When the inhabitants beheld the ships standing into the bay, looking like wonderful and unknown apparitions from the deep, they fled with terror to their houses, and raised the drawbridges. The Spaniards remained for a time gazing with admiration at this amphibious village, when a squadron of canoes entered the harbour from the sea. On beholding the ships they paused in mute amazement, and on the Spaniards attempting to approach them, paddled swiftly to shore, and plunged into the forest. They soon returned with sixteen young girls, whom they conveyed in their canoes to the ships, distributing four on board of each, either as peace-offerings or as tokens of amity and confidence. The best of understanding now seemed to be established; and the inhabitants of the village came swarming about the ships in their canoes, and others swimming in great numbers from the shores.

The friendship of the savages, however, was all delusive. On a sudden several old women at the doors of the houses uttered loud shrieks, tearing their hair in fury. It appeared to be a signal for hostility. The sixteen nymphs plunged into the sea and made for shore; the Indians in the canoes caught up their bows and discharged a flight of arrows, and even those who were swimming brandished darts and lances, which they had hitherto concealed beneath the water.

Ojeda was for a moment surprised at seeing war thus starting up on every side, and the very sea bristling with weapons. Manning his boats, he immediately charged amongst the thickest of the enemy, shattered and sunk several of their canoes, killed twenty Indians and wounded many more, and spread such a panic among them, that most of the survivors flung themselves into the sea and swam to shore. Three of them were taken prisoners, and two of the fugitive girls, and were conveyed on board of the ships, where the men were put in irons. One of them, however, and the two girls, succeeded in dexterously escaping the same night.

Ojeda had but five men wounded in the affray; all of whom recovered. He visited the houses, but found them abandoned and destitute of booty; notwithstanding the unprovoked hostility of the inhabitants, he spared the buildings, that he might not cause useless irritation along the coast.

Continuing to explore this gulf, Ojeda penetrated to a port or harbour, to which he gave the name of St. Bartholomew, but which is supposed to be the same at present known by the original Indian name of Maracaibo. Here, in compliance with the entreaties of the natives, he sent a detachment of twenty-seven Spaniards on a visit to the interior. For nine days they were conducted from town to town, and feasted and almost idolized by the Indians, who regarded them as angelic beings, performing their national dances and games, and chanting their traditional ballads for their entertainment.

The natives of this part were distinguished for the symmetry of their forms; the females in particular appeared to the Spaniards to surpass all others that they had yet beheld in the new world for grace and beauty; neither did the men evince, in the least degree, that jealousy which prevailed in other parts of the coast; but, on the contrary, permitted the most frank and intimate intercourse with their wives and daughters.

By the time the Spaniards set out on their return to the ship, the whole country was aroused, pouring forth its population, male and female, to do them honour. Some bore them in litters or hammocks, that they might not be fatigued with the journey, and happy was the Indian who had the honour of bearing a Spaniard on his shoulders across a river. Others loaded themselves with the presents that had been bestowed on their guests, consisting of rich plumes, weapons of various

kinds, and tropical birds and animals. In this way they returned in triumphant procession to the ships, the woods and
shores resounding with their songs and shouts.

Many of the Indians crowded into the boats that took the
detachment to the ships; others put off in canoes, or swam
from shore, so that in a little while the vessels were thronged
with upwards of a thousand wondering natives. While gazing
and marvelling at the strange objects around them, Ojeda
ordered the cannon to be discharged, at the sound of which,
says Vespucci, the Indians "plunged into the water like so
many frogs from a bank." Perceiving, however, that it was
done in harmless mirth, they returned on board, and passed
the rest of the day in great festivity. The Spaniards brought
away with them several of the beautiful and hospitable
females from this place, one of whom, named by them Isabel,
was much prized by Ojeda, and accompanied him in a subsequent voyage.[11]

CHAPTER V

Prosecution of the Voyage.—Return to Spain.

LEAVING the friendly port of Coquibacoa, Ojeda continued along the western shores of the gulf of Venezuela, and standing out to sea, and doubling Cape Maracaibo, he pursued his coasting voyage from port to port, and promontory to promontory, of this unknown continent, until he reached that long stretching headland called Cape de la Vela. There the state of his vessels, and perhaps the disappointment of his hopes at not meeting with abundant sources of immediate wealth, induced him to abandon all further voyaging along the coast, and changing his course, he stood across the Caribbean Sea for Hispaniola. The tenor of his commission forbade his visiting that island; but Ojeda was not a man to stand upon trifles when his interest or inclination prompted the contrary. He trusted to excuse the infraction of his orders by the alleged necessity of touching at the island to caulk and refit his vessels, and to procure provisions. His true object, however, is supposed to have been to cut dye-wood, which abounds in the western part of Hispaniola.

He accordingly anchored at Yaquimo in September, and landed with a large party of his men. Columbus at that time held command of the island, and, hearing of this unlicensed intrusion, despatched Francesco Roldan, the quondam rebel, to call Ojeda to account. The contest of stratagem and management that took place between these two adroit and daring adventurers, has been already detailed in the History of Columbus. Roldan was eventually successful, and Ojeda, being obliged to leave Hispaniola, resumed his rambling voyage, visiting various islands, from whence he carried off numbers of the natives. He at length arrived at Cadiz in June, 1500, with his ships crowded with captives, whom he sold as slaves. So meagre, however, was the result of this expedition, that we are told, when all the expenses were deducted, but five hundred ducats remained to be divided between fifty-five adventurers. What made this result the more mortifying was, that a petty armament which had sailed sometime after that of Ojeda, had returned two months before him, rich with the spoils of the New World. A brief account of this latter expedition is necessary to connect this series of minor discoveries.

PEDRO ALONZO NIÑO
And
CHRISTOVAL GUERRA
[1499.]

THE permission granted by Bishop Fonseca to Alonzo de Ojeda, to undertake a private expedition to the New World, roused the emulation of others of the followers of Columbus. Among these was Pedro Alonzo Niño,[12] a hardy seaman, native of Moguer in the vicinity of Palos, who had sailed with Columbus, as a pilot, in his first voyage, and also in his cruisings along the coasts of Cuba and Paria.[13] He soon obtained from the bishop a similar license to that given to Ojeda, and like the latter, sought for some monied confederate among the rich merchants of Seville. One of these, named Luis Guerra, offered to fit out a caravel for the expedition; but on condition that his brother, Christoval Guerra, should have the command. The poverty of Niño compelled him to assent to the stipulations of the man of wealth, and he sailed as subaltern in his own enterprise; but his nautical skill and knowledge soon gained him the ascendancy, he became virtually the captain, and ultimately enjoyed the whole credit of the voyage.

The bark of these two adventurers was but of fifty tons burthen, and the crew thirty-three souls all told. With this slender armament they undertook to traverse unknown and dangerous seas, and to explore the barbarous shores of that vast continent recently discovered by Columbus;—such was the daring spirit of the Spanish voyagers of those days.

It was about the beginning of June, 1499, and but a few days after the departure of Ojeda, that they put to sea. They sailed from the little port of Palos, the original cradle of American discovery, whose brave and skilful mariners long continued foremost in all enterprises to the New World. Being guided by the chart of Columbus, they followed his route, and reached the southern continent, a little beyond Paria, about fifteen days after the same coast had been visited by Ojeda.

They then proceeded to the gulf of Paria, where they landed to cut dye-wood, and were amicably entertained by the natives. Shortly after, sallying from the gulf by the Boca del Drago, they encountered eighteen canoes of Caribs, the pirate rovers of these seas, and the terror of the bordering lands. This savage armada, instead of being daunted, as usual, by the sight of a European ship, with swelling sails, resembling some winged monster of the deep, considered it only as an object of plunder or hostility, and assailed it with showers of arrows. The sudden burst of artillery, however, from the sides of the caravel, and the havoc made among the Caribs by this seeming thunder, struck them with dismay, and they fled in all directions. The Spaniards succeeded in capturing one of the canoes, with one of the warriors who had manned it. In the bottom of the canoe lay an Indian prisoner, bound hand and foot. On being liberated he informed the Spaniards by signs that these Caribs had been on a marauding expedition along the neighbouring coasts, shutting themselves up at night in a stockade which they carried with them, and issuing forth by day to plunder the villages and to make captives. He had been one of seven prisoners; his companions had been devoured before his eyes at the cannibal banquets of these savages, and he had been awaiting the same miserable fate. Honest Niño and his confederates were so indignant at this recital, that, receiving it as established fact, they performed what they considered an act of equitable justice, by abandoning the Carib to the discretion of his late captive. The latter fell upon the defenceless warrior with fist and foot and cudgel; nor did his rage subside even after the breath had been mauled out of his victim, but, tearing the grim head from the body, he placed it on a pole, as a trophy of his vengeance.

Niño and his fellow-adventurers now steered for the island of Margarita, where they obtained a considerable quantity of pearls by barter. They afterwards skirted the opposite coast of Cumana, trading cautiously and shrewdly, from port to port; sometimes remaining on board of their little bark, and obliging the savages to come off to them, when the latter appeared too numerous, at other times venturing on shore, and even into the interior. They were invariably treated with amity by the natives, who were perfectly naked, excepting that they were adorned with necklaces and bracelets of pearls. These they sometimes gave freely to the Spaniards, at other times they exchanged them for glass beads and other trinkets, and smiled at the folly of the strangers in making such silly bargains.[14]

The Spaniards were struck with the grandeur and density of the forests along this coast, for in these regions of heat and moisture, vegetation appears in its utmost magnificence. They heard also the cries and roarings of wild and unknown animals in the woodlands, which, however, appeared not to be very dangerous, as the Indians went about the forest armed solely with bows and arrows. From meeting with deer and rabbits, they were convinced that that was a part of Terra Firma, not having found any animals of the kind on the islands.[15]

Niño and Guerra were so well pleased with the hospitality

of the natives of Cumana, and with the profitable traffic for pearls, by which they obtained many of great size and beauty, that they remained upwards of three months on the coast.

They then proceeded westward to a country called Cauchieto, trading, as usual, for pearls, and for the inferior kind of gold called guanin. At length they arrived at a place where there was a kind of fortress protecting a number of houses and gardens situated on a river, the whole forming, to the eyes of the Spaniards, one of the most delicious abodes imaginable. They were about to land and enjoy the pleasures of this fancied paradise, when they beheld upwards of a thousand Indians, armed with bows and arrows, and war clubs, preparing to give them a warm reception; having been probably incensed by the recent visit of Ojeda. As Niño and Guerra had not the fighting propensities of Ojeda, and were in quest of profit rather than renown, having moreover, in all probability, the fear of the rich merchant of Seville before their eyes, they prudently abstained from landing, and, abandoning this hostile coast, returned forthwith to Cumana, to resume their trade for pearls. They soon amassed a great number, many of which were equal in size and beauty, to the most celebrated of the East, though they had been injured in boring from a want of proper implements.

Satisfied with their success, they now set sail for Spain, and piloted their little bark safely to Bayonne in Gallicia, where they anchored about the middle of April, 1500, nearly two months before the arrival of Ojeda and his associates, La Cosa and Vespucci.[16]

The most successful voyagers to the New World were doomed to trouble from their very success. The ample amount of pearls paid to the treasury, as the royal portion of the profits of this expedition, drew suspicion instead of favour upon the two adventurers. They were accused of having concealed a great part of the pearls collected by them, thus defrauding their companions and the crown. Pedro Alonzo Niño was actually thrown into prison on this accusation, but, nothing being proved against him, was eventually set free, and enjoyed the enviable reputation of having performed the richest voyage that had yet been made to the New World.[17]

VICENTE YAÑEZ PINZON
[1499.]

AMONG the maritime adventurers of renown who were roused to action by the licenses granted for private expeditions of discovery, we find conspicuous the name of Vicente Yañez Pinzon of Palos, one of the three brave brothers who aided Columbus in his first voyage, and risked life and fortune with him in his doubtful and perilous enterprise.

Of Martin Alonzo Pinzon, the eldest and most important of these three brothers, particular mention has been made in the History of Columbus, and of the unfortunate error in conduct which severed him from the admiral, brought on him the displeasure of the sovereigns, and probably contributed to his premature and melancholy death.

Whatever cloud of disgrace may have overshadowed his family, it was but temporary. The death of Martin Alonzo, as usual, atoned for his faults, and his good deeds lived after him. The merits and services of himself and his brothers were acknowledged, and the survivers of the family were restored to royal confidence. A feeling of jealous hostility prevented

28

them from taking a part in the subsequent voyages of Columbus; but the moment the door was thrown open for individual enterprise, they pressed forward for permission to engage in it at their own risk and expense—and it was readily granted. In fact, their supposed hostility to Columbus was one of the surest recommendations they could have to the favour of the Bishop Fonseca, by whom the license was issued for their expedition.

Vicente Yañez Pinzon was the leader of this new enterprise, and he was accompanied by two nephews, named Arias Perez and Diego Fernandez, sons of his late brother, Martin Alonzo Pinzon. Several of his sailors had sailed with Columbus in his recent voyage to Paria, as had also his three principal pilots, Juan Quintero, Juan de Umbria, and Juan de Jerez. Thus these minor voyages seemed all to emanate from the great expeditions of Columbus, and to aim at realizing the ideas and speculations contained in the papers transmitted by him to Spain.

The armament consisted of four caravels, and was fitted out at the port of Palos. The funds of Vicente Yañez were completely exhausted before he had fitted out his little squadron; he was obliged therefore to purchase on credit the sea stores and articles of traffic necessary for the enterprise. The merchants of Palos seem to have known how to profit by the careless nature of sailors and the sanguine spirit of discoverers. In their bargains they charged honest Pinzon eighty and a hundred per cent. above the market value of their merchandise, and in the hurry and urgency of the moment he was obliged to submit to the imposition.[18]

The squadron put to sea in the beginning of December, 1499, and after passing the Canary and Cape de Verde Islands, stood to the south-west. Having sailed about seven hundred leagues, they crossed the equator and lost sight of the north star. They had scarcely passed the equinoctial line when they encountered a terrible tempest, which had well nigh swallowed up their slender barks. The storm passed away, and the firmament was again serene; but the mariners remained tossing about in confusion, dismayed by the turbulence of the waves and the strange aspect of the heavens. They looked in vain to the south for some polar star by which to shape their course, and fancied that some swelling prominence of the globe concealed it from their view. They knew nothing as yet of the firmament of that hemisphere, nor of that beautiful constellation the southern cross, but expected to find a guiding star at the opposite pole, similar to the cynosure of the north.

Pinzon, however, who was of an intrepid spirit, pursued his course resolutely to the west, and after sailing about two hundred and forty leagues, and being in the eighth degree of southern latitude, he beheld land afar off on the 28th of

January, to which he gave the name of *Santa Maria de la Consolacion*, from the sight of it having consoled him in the midst of doubts and perplexities. It is now called Cape St. Augustine, and forms the most prominent part of the immense empire of Brazil.

The sea was turbid and discoloured as in rivers, and on sounding they had sixteen fathoms water. Pinzon landed, accompanied by a notary and witnesses, and took formal possession of the territory for the Castilian crown; no one appeared to dispute his pretensions, but he observed the print of footsteps on the beach which seemed of gigantic size.

At night there were fires lighted upon a neighbouring part of the coast, which induced Pinzon on the following morning to send forty men well armed to the spot. A band of Indians, of about equal number, sallied forth to encounter them, armed with bows and arrows, and seemingly of extraordinary stature. A still greater number were seen in the distance hastening to the support of their companions. The Indians arrayed themselves for combat, and the two parties remained for a short time eyeing each other with mutual curiosity and distrust. The Spaniards now displayed looking glasses, beads and other trinkets, and jingled strings of hawks' bells, in general so captivating to an Indian ear; but the haughty savages treated all their overtures with contempt, regarding these offerings carelessly for a short time, and then stalking off with stoic gravity. They were ferocious of feature, and apparently warlike in disposition, and are supposed to have been a wandering race of unusual size, who roamed about in the night, and were of the most fierce untractable nature. By nightfall there was not an Indian to be seen in the neighbourhood.

Discouraged by the inhospitable character of the coast, Pinzon made sail and stood to the north-west, until he came to the mouth of a river too shallow to receive his ships. Here he sent his boats on shore with a number of men well armed. They landed on the river banks, and beheld a multitude of naked Indians on a neighbouring hill. A single Spaniard armed simply with sword and buckler, was sent to invite them to friendly intercourse. He approached them with signs of amity, and threw to them a hawks' bell. They replied to him with similar signs, and threw to him a small gilded wand. The soldier stooped to pick it up, when suddenly a troop of savages rushed down to seize him; he threw himself immediately upon the defensive, with sword and target, and though but a small man, and far from robust, he handled his weapons with such dexterity and fierceness, that he kept the savages at bay, making a clear circle round him, and wounding several who attempted to break it. His unlooked-for prowess surprised and confounded his assailants, and gave time for his comrades to come to his assistance.

The Indians then made a general assault, with such a galling discharge of darts and arrows that almost immediately eight or ten Spaniards were slain, and many more wounded. The latter were compelled to retreat to their boats disputing every inch of ground. The Indians pursued them even into the water, surrounding the boats and seizing hold of the oars. The Spaniards made a desperate defence, thrusting many through with their lances, and cutting down and ripping up others with their swords, but such was the ferocity of the survivers, that they persisted in their attack until they overpowered the crew of one of the boats, and bore it off in triumph. With this they retired from the combat, and the Spaniards returned defeated and disheartened to their ships, having met with the roughest reception that the Europeans had yet experienced in the New World.

Pinzon now stood forty leagues to the north-west, until he arrived in the neighbourhood of the equinoctial line. Here he found the water of the sea so fresh that he was enabled to replenish his casks with it. Astonished at so singular a phenomenon he stood in for the land, and arrived among a number of fresh and verdant islands inhabited by a gentle and hospitable race of people, gaily painted, who came off to the ships with the most frank and fearless confidence. Pinzon soon found that these islands lay in the mouth of an immense river, more than thirty leagues in breadth, the water of which entered upwards of forty leagues into the sea before losing its sweetness. It was in fact, the renowned Maranon, since known as the Orellana and the Amazon. While lying in the mouth of this river there was a sudden swelling of the stream which, being opposed by the current of the sea, and straitened by the narrow channels of the islands, rose more than five fathoms, with mountain waves, and a tremendous noise, threatening the destruction of the ships. Pinzon extricated his little squadron with great difficulty from this perilous situation, and finding there was but little gold, or any thing else of value to be found among the simple natives, he requited their hospitality, in the mode too common among the early discoverers, by carrying off thirty-six of them captive.

Having regained the sight of the polar star, Pinzon pursued his course along the coast, passing the mouths of the Oronoko, and entering the Gulf of Paria, where he landed and cut Brazil wood. Sallying forth by the Boca del Drago, he reached the island of Hispaniola about the 23d of June, from whence he sailed for the Bahamas. Here, in the month of July, while at anchor, there came such a tremendous hurricane that two of the caravels were swallowed up with all their crews in the sight of their terrified companions: a third parted her cables and was driven out to sea, while the fourth was so furiously beaten by the tempest that the crew threw themselves into the boats and made for shore. Here

they found a few naked Indians, who offered them no moles-
tation; but, fearing that they might spread the tidings of a
handful of shipwrecked Spaniards being upon the coast, and
thus bring the savages of the neighbouring islands upon them
a council of war was held whether it would not be a wise
precaution to put these Indians to death. Fortunately for the
latter, the vessel which had been driven from her anchors
returned and put an end to the alarm, and to the council of
war. The other caravel also rode out the storm uninjured,
and the sea subsiding, the Spaniards returned on board, and
made the best of their way to the Island of Hispaniola. Having repaired the damages sustained in the gale, they again
made sail for Spain, and came to anchor in the river before
Palos, about the end of September.

Thus ended one of the most chequered and disastrous
voyages that had yet been made to the New World. Yañez
Pinzon had lost two of his ships, and many of his men; what
made the loss of the latter more grievous was that they had
been enlisted from among his neighbours, his friends, and
relatives. In fact, the expeditions to the New World must
have realized the terrors and apprehensions of the people of
Palos by filling that little community with widows and or-
phans. When the rich merchants, who had sold goods to
Pinzon, at a hundred per cent. advance, beheld him return
in this sorry condition, with two shattered barks and a handful

of poor, tattered, weatherbeaten seamen, they began to tremble for their money. No sooner, therefore, had he and his nephews departed to Granada, to give an account of their discoveries to the sovereigns, than the merchants seized upon their caravels and cargoes, and began to sell them, to repay themselves. Honest Pinzon immediately addressed a petition to the government, stating the imposition that had been practised upon him, and the danger he was in of imprisonment and utter ruin, should his creditors be allowed to sacrifice his goods at a public sale. He petitioned that they might be compelled to return the property thus seized, and that he might be enabled to sell three hundred and fifty quintals of Brazil wood, which he had brought back with him, and which would be sufficient to satisfy the demands of his creditors. The sovereigns granted his prayer. They issued an order to the civil authorities of Palos to interfere in the matter, with all possible promptness and brevity, allowing no vexatious delay, and administering justice so impartially that neither of the parties should have cause to complain.

Pinzon escaped from the fangs of his creditors, but, of course, must have suffered in purse from the expenses of the law; which, in Spain is apt to bury even a successful client, under an overwhelming mountain of documents and writings. We infer this in respect to Pinzon from a royal order issued in the following year, allowing him to export a quantity of grain, in consideration of the heavy losses he had sustained in his voyage of discovery. He did but share the usual lot of the Spanish discoverers, whose golden anticipations too frequently ended in penury; but he is distinguished from among the crowd of them by being the first European who crossed the equinoctial line, on the western ocean, and by discovering the great kingdom of Brazil.[19]

DIEGO DE LEPE

And

RODRIGO DE BASTIDES [1500.]

NOTWITHSTANDING the hardships and disasters that had beset the voyagers to the New World, and the penury in which their golden anticipations had too frequently terminated, adventurers continued to press forward, excited by fresh reports of newly discovered regions, each of which, in its turn, was represented as the real land of promise. Scarcely had Vicente Yañez Pinzon departed on the voyage recently narrated, when his townsman Diego de Lepe likewise set sail with two vessels from the busy little port of Palos, on a like expedition. No particulars of importance are known of this voyage, excepting that Lepe doubled Cape St. Augustine, and beheld the southern continent stretching far to the south-west. On returning to Spain he drew a chart of the coast for the Bishop Fonseca, and enjoyed the reputation, for upwards of ten years afterwards, of having extended his discoveries further south than any other voyager.

38

Another contemporary adventurer to the New World was Rodrigo de Bastides, a wealthy notary of Triana, the suburb of Seville inhabited by the maritime part of its population. Being sanctioned by the sovereigns, to whom he engaged to yield a fourth of his profits, he fitted out two caravels in October, 1500, to go in quest of gold and pearls.

Prudently distrusting his own judgment in nautical matters, this adventurous notary associated with him the veteran pilot Juan de la Cosa, the same hardy Biscayan who had sailed with Columbus and Ojeda. A general outline of their voyage has already been given in the life of Columbus; it extended the discoveries of the coast of Terra Firma from Cape de la Vela, where Ojeda had left off, quite to the port of Nombre de Dios.

Bastides distinguished himself from the mass of discoverers by his kind treatment of the natives, and Juan de la Cosa by his sound discretion and his able seamanship. Their voyage had been extremely successful, and they had collected, by barter, a great amount of gold and pearls, when their prosperous career was checked by an unlooked-for evil. Their vessels to their surprise became leaky in every part, and they discovered to their dismay, that the bottoms were pierced in innumerable places by the broma, or worm, which abounds in the waters of the torrid zone, but of which they, as yet, had scarcely any knowledge. It was with great difficulty they

could keep afloat until they reached a small islet on the coast
of Hispaniola. Here they repaired their ships as well as they
were able, and again put to sea to return to Cadiz. A succession of gales drove them back to port; the ravages of the
worms continued, the leaks broke out afresh; they landed the
most portable and precious part of their wealthy cargoes,
and the vessels foundered with the remainder. Bastides lost,
moreover, the arms and ammunition saved from the wreck,
being obliged to destroy them lest they should fall into the
hands of the Indians.

Distributing his men into three bands, two of them headed
by La Cosa and himself, they set off for San Domingo by
three several routes, as the country was not able to furnish
provisions for so large a body. Each band was provided with
a coffer stored with trinkets and other articles of Indian
traffic, with which to buy provisions on the road.

Francesco de Bobadilla, the wrong-headed oppressor and
superseder of Columbus, was at that time governor of San
Domingo. The report reached him that a crew of adventurers
had landed on the island, and were marching through the
country in three bands, each provided with a coffer of gold,
and carrying on illicit trade with the natives. The moment
Bastides made his appearance, therefore, he was seized and
thrown into prison, and an investigation commenced. In his
defence he maintained that his only traffic with the natives

was for the purpose of procuring provisions for his followers, or guides for his journey. It was determined, however, to send him to Spain for trial, with the written testimony and the other documents of his examination.

He was accordingly conveyed in the same fleet in which Bobadilla embarked for Spain, and which experienced such an awful shipwreck in the sight of Columbus. The ship of Rodrigo Bastides was one of the few that outlived the tempest: it arrived safe at Cadiz in September, 1502. Bastides was ultimately acquitted of the charges advanced against him. So lucrative had been his voyage, that, notwithstanding the losses sustained by the foundering of his vessels, he was enabled to pay a large sum to the crown as a fourth of his profits, and to retain a great amount for himself. In reward of his services and discoveries the sovereigns granted him an annual revenue for life, to arise from the proceeds of the province of Uraba, which he had discovered. An equal pension was likewise assigned to the hardy Juan de la Cosa, to result from the same territory, of which he was appointed Alguazil Mayor.[20] Such was the economical generosity of King Ferdinand, who rewarded the past toils of his adventurous discoverers out of the expected produce of their future labours.

Second Voyage of
ALONZO DE OJEDA
[1502.]

THE first voyage of Alonzo de Ojeda to the coast of Paria, and its meagre termination in June, 1500, has been related. He gained nothing in wealth by that expedition, but he added to his celebrity as a bold and skilful adventurer. His youthful fire, his sanguine and swelling spirit, and the wonderful stories that were told of his activity and prowess, made him extremely popular, so that his patron, the Bishop Fonseca, found it an easy matter to secure for him the royal favour. In consideration of his past services and of others expected from him, a grant was made to him of six leagues of land on the southern part of Hispaniola, and the government of the province of Coquibacoa which he had discovered. He was, furthermore, authorized to fit out any number of ships, not exceeding ten, at his own expense, and to prosecute the discovery of the coast of Terra Firma. He was not to touch or traffic on the pearl coast of Paria; extending as far as a bay in the vicinity of the

island of Margarita. Beyond this he had a right to trade in
all kinds of merchandise, whether of pearls, jewels, metals, or
precious stones; paying one fifth of the profits to the crown,
and abstaining from making slaves of the Indians without a
special license from the sovereigns. He was to colonize Coquibacoa, and, as a recompense, was to enjoy one half of the
proceeds of his territory, provided the half did not exceed
300,000 maravedies: all beyond that amount was to go to the
crown.

A principal reason, however, for granting this government
and those privileges to Ojeda, was that, in his previous
voyage, he had met with English adventurers on a voyage of
discovery in the neighbourhood of Coquibacoa, at which the
jealousy of the sovereigns had taken the alarm. They were
anxious, therefore, to establish a resolute and fighting commander like Ojeda upon this outpost, and they instructed
him to set up the arms of Castile and Leon in every place he
visited, as a signal of discovery and possession, and to put a
stop to the intrusions of the English.[21]

With this commission in his pocket, and the government
of an Indian territory in the perspective, Ojeda soon found
associates to aid him in fitting out an armament. These were
Juan de Vergara, a servant of a rich canon of the cathedral of
Seville, and Garcia de Campos, commonly called Ocampo.
They made a contract of partnership to last for two years,

according to which the expenses and profits of the expedition, and of the government of Coquibacoa were to be shared equally between them. The purses of the confederates were not ample enough to afford ten ships, but they fitted out four. 1st, The Santa Maria de la Antigua, commanded by Garcia del Campo; 2d, The Santa Maria de la Granada, commanded by Juan de Vergara; 3d, The Caravel Magdalena, commanded by Pedro de Ojeda, nephew to Alonzo; and 4th, The Caravel Santa Ana, commanded by Hernando de Guevara. The whole was under the command of Alonzo de Ojeda. The expedition set sail in 1502, touched at the Canaries, according to custom, to take in provisions, and then proceeded westward for the shores of the New World.

After traversing the Gulf of Paria, and before reaching the Island of Margarita, the caravel Santa Ana, commanded by Hernando de Guevara, was separated from them, and for several days the ships were mutually seeking each other, in these silent and trackless seas. After they were all reunited they found their provisions growing scanty; they landed therefore at a part of the coast called Cumana by the natives, to which, from its beauty and fertility, Ojeda gave the name of Valfermoso. While foraging here for their immediate supplies, the idea occurred to Ojeda that he should want furniture and utensils of all kinds for his proposed colony, and that it would be better to pillage them from a country where he was a mere transient visitor, than to wrest them from his neighbours in the territory where he was to set up his government. His companions were struck with the policy, if not the justice, of this idea, and they all set to work to carry it into execution. Dispersing themselves, therefore, in ambush in various directions, they at a concerted signal rushed forth from their concealment, and set upon the natives. Ojeda had issued orders to do as little injury and damage as possible, and on no account to destroy the habitations of the Indians. His followers, however, in their great zeal, transcended his orders. Seven or eight Indians were killed and many wounded in the skirmish which took place, and a number of their cabins were wrapped in flames. A great quantity of hammocks, of cotton, and of utensils of various kinds, fell into the hands of the conquerors; they also captured several female Indians, some of whom were ransomed with the kind of gold called guanin; some were retained by Vergara for himself and his friend Ocampo, others were distributed among the crews, the rest, probably the old and ugly, were set at liberty. As to Ojeda, he reserved nothing for himself of the spoil excepting a single hammock.

The ransom paid by the poor Indians for some of their effects and some of their women, yielded the Spaniards a trifling quantity of gold, but they found the place destitute of provisions, and Ojeda was obliged to despatch Vergara in a caravel to the island of Jamaica to forage for supplies, with instructions to rejoin him at Maracaibo or Cape de la Vela.

Ojeda at length arrived at Coquibacoa, at the port destined for his seat of government. He found the country, however, so poor and sterile, that he proceeded along the coast to a bay which he named Santa Cruz, but which is supposed to be the same at present called Bahia Honda, where he found a Spaniard who had been left in the province of Citarma by Bastides in his late voyage about thirteen months before, and had remained ever since among the Indians, so that he had acquired their language.

Ojeda determined to form his settlement at this place; but the natives seemed disposed to defend their territory, for, the moment a party landed to procure water, they were assailed by a galling shower of arrows, and driven back to the ships. Upon this Ojeda landed with all his force, and struck such terror into the Indians, that they came forward with signs of amity, and brought a considerable quantity of gold as a peace offering, which was graciously accepted.

Ojeda, with the concurrence of his associates, now set to work to establish a settlement, cutting down trees, and commencing a fortress. They had scarce begun, when they were attacked by a neighbouring cacique, but Ojeda sallied forth upon him with such intrepidity and effect as not merely to defeat, but to drive him from the neighbourhood. He then proceeded quietly to finish his fortress, which was defended by lombards, and contained the magazine of provisions and the treasure amassed in the expedition. The provisions were dealt out twice a day, under the inspection of proper officers; the treasure gained by barter, by ransom, or by plunder, was deposited in a strong box secured by two locks, one key being kept by the royal supervisor, the other by Ocampo.

In the mean time provisions became scarce. The Indians never appeared in the neighbourhood of the fortress, except to harass it with repeated though ineffectual assaults. Vergara did not appear with the expected supplies from Jamaica and a caravel was despatched in search of him. The people, worn out with labour and privations of various kinds, and disgusted with the situation of a settlement, which was in a poor and unhealthy country, grew discontented and factious. They began to fear that they should lose the means of departing, as their vessels were in danger of being destroyed by the broma or worms. Ojeda led them forth repeatedly upon foraging parties about the adjacent country, and collected some provisions and booty in the Indian villages. The provision he deposited in the magazine, part of the spoils he divided among his followers, and the gold he locked up in the strong box, the keys of which he took possession of, to the great displeasure of the supervisor and his associate Ocampo. The murmurs of the people grew loud as their sufferings increased. They insinuated that Ojeda had no authority over this part of the coast, having passed the boundaries of his government, and formed his settlement in the country discovered by Bastides. By the time Vergara arrived from Jamaica, the factions of this petty colony had risen to an alarming height. Ocampo had a personal enmity to the governor, arising probably from some feud about the strong box; being a particular friend of Vergara, he held a private conference with him, and laid a plan to entrap the doughty Ojeda. In pursuance of this the latter was invited on board of the caravel of Vergara, to see the provisions he had brought from Jamaica, but no sooner was he on board than they charged him with having transgressed the limits of his government, with having provoked the hostility of the Indians, and needlessly sacrificed the lives of his followers, and above all with having taken possession of the strong box, in contempt of the authority of the royal supervisor, and with the intention of appropriating to himself all the gains of the enterprise; they informed him therefore of their intention to convey him a prisoner to Hispaniola, to answer to the Governor for his offences. Ojeda finding himself thus entrapped, proposed to Vergara and Ocampo that they should return to Spain with such of the crews as chose to accompany them, leaving him with the remainder to prosecute his enterprise. The two recreant partners at first consented, for they were disgusted with the enterprise which offered little profit and severe hardships. They agreed to leave Ojeda the smallest of the caravels, with a third of the provisions and of their gains, and to build a row boat for him. They actually began to labour upon the boat. Before ten days had elapsed, however, they repented of the arrangement, the ship-carpenters were ill, there were no caulkers, and moreover they recollected that as Ojeda, according to their representations, was a defaulter to the crown, they would be liable as his sureties, should they return to Spain without him. They concluded, therefore, that the wisest plan was to give him nothing, but to carry him off prisoner.

When Ojeda learned the determination of his wary partners, he attempted to make his escape and get off to St. Domingo, but he was seized, thrown in irons, and conveyed on board of the caravel. The two partners then set sail from Santa Cruz, bearing off the whole community, its captive governor, and the litigated strong box.

They put to sea about the beginning of September, and arrived at the western part of the island of Hispaniola. While at anchor within a stone's throw of the land, Ojeda, confident in his strength and skill as a swimmer, let himself quietly slide down the side of the ship into the water during the night, and attempted to swim for the shore. His arms were free, but his feet were shackled, and the weight of his irons threatened to sink him. He was obliged to shout for help; a boat was sent from the vessel to his relief, and the unfortunate governor was brought back half drowned to his unrelenting partners.[22]

The latter now landed and delivered their prisoner into the hands of Gallego, the commander of the place, to be put at the disposal of the governor of the island. In the mean time the strong box, which appears to have been at the bottom of all these feuds, remained in the possession of Vergara and Ocampo, who, Ojeda says, took from it whatever they thought proper, without regard to the royal dues, or the consent of the royal supervisor. They were all together, prisoner and accusers, in the city of San Domingo, about the end of September, 1502, when the chief judge of the island, after hearing both parties, gave a verdict against Ojeda that stripped him of all his effects, and brought him into debt to the crown for the royal proportion of the profits of the voyage. Ojeda appealed to the sovereign, and, after some time was honourably acquitted, by the royal council, from all the charges, and a mandate was issued in 1503, ordering a restitution of his property. It appears, however, that the costs of justice, or rather of the law, consumed his share of the treasure of the strong box, and that a royal order was necessary to liberate him from the hands of the governor; so that like too many other litigants, he finally emerged from the labyrinths of the law a triumphant client, but a ruined man.

Third Voyage of
ALONZO DE OJEDA

CHAPTER I

*Ojeda applies for a Command.—Has a rival Candidate in
Diego de Nicuesa.—His success.*

FOR several years after his ruinous, though successful lawsuit, we lose all traces of Alonzo de Ojeda, excepting that we are told he made another voyage to the vicinity of Coquibacoa, in 1505. No record remains of this expedition, which seems to have been equally unprofitable with the preceding, for we find him in 1508, in the island of Hispaniola, as poor in purse, though as proud in spirit, as ever. In fact, however fortune might have favoured him, he had a heedless squandering disposition that would always have kept him poor.

About this time the cupidity of King Ferdinand was greatly excited by the accounts which had been given by Columbus, of the gold mines of Veragua, in which the admiral fancied he had discovered the Aurea Chersonesus of the ancients, from whence King Solomon procured the gold, used in building the temple of Jerusalem. Subsequent voyagers had corroborated the opinion of Columbus as to the general riches of the coast of Terra Firma; King Ferdinand resolved, therefore, to found regular colonies along that coast and to place the whole under some capable commander. A project of the kind had been conceived by Columbus, when he discovered that region in the course of his last voyage, and the reader may remember the disasters experienced by his brother Don Bartholomew and himself, in endeavouring to establish a colony on the hostile shores of Veragua. The admiral being dead, the person who should naturally have presented himself to the mind of the sovereign for this particular service was Don Bartholomew, but the wary and selfish monarch knew the Adelantado to be as lofty in his terms as his late brother, and preferred to accomplish his purposes by cheaper agents. He was unwilling, also, to increase the consequence of a family, whose vast, but just, claims were already a cause of repining to his sordid and jealous spirit. He looked round, therefore, among the crowd of adventurers, who had sprung up in the school of Columbus, for some individual who might be ready to serve him on more accommodating terms. Among those, considered by their friends as most fitted for this purpose, was Alonzo de Ojeda, for his roving voyages and daring exploits had made him famous among the voyagers; and it was thought that an application on his part would be attended with success, for he was known to possess a staunch friend at court in the Bishop Fonseca. Unfortunately he was too far distant to urge his suit to the bishop, and what was worse, he was destitute of money. At this juncture there happened to be at Hispaniola the veteran navigator and pilot Juan de la Cosa, who was a kind of Nestor in all nautical affairs.[23] The hardy Biscayan had sailed with Ojeda, and had conceived a great opinion of the courage and talents of the youthful adventurer. He had contrived, also, to fill his purse in the course of his cruising, and now, in the generous spirit of a sailor, offered to aid Ojeda with it in the prosecution of his wishes.

His offer was gladly accepted; it was agreed that Juan de la Cosa should depart for Spain, to promote the appointment of Ojeda to the command of Terra Firma, and, in case of success, should fit out, with his own funds, the necessary armament.

La Cosa departed on his embassy; he called on the Bishop Fonseca, who, as had been expected, entered warmly into the views of his favourite Ojeda, and recommended him to the ambitious and bigot king, as a man well fitted to promote his empire in the wilderness, and to dispense the blessings of Christianity among the savages.

The recommendation of the bishop was usually effectual

in the affairs of the New World, and the opinion of the veteran de la Cosa had great weight even with the sovereign; but a rival candidate to Ojeda had presented himself, and one who had the advantage of higher connexions and greater pecuniary means. This was Diego de Nicuesa, an accomplished courtier of noble birth, who had filled the post of grand carver to Don Enrique Enriquez, uncle of the king. Nature, education, and habit seemed to have combined to form Nicuesa as a complete rival of Ojeda. Like him he was small of stature, but remarkable for symmetry and compactness of form and for bodily strength and activity; like him he was master at all kinds of weapons, and skilled, not merely in feats of agility, but in those graceful and chivalrous exercises, which the Spanish cavaliers of those days had inherited from the Moors; being noted for his vigour and address in the jousts or tilting matches after the Moresco fashion. Ojeda himself could not surpass him in feats of horsemanship, and particular mention is made of a favourite mare, which he could make caper and caracol in strict cadence to the sound of a viol; beside all this, he was versed in the legendary ballads or romances of his country, and was renowned as a capital performer on the guitar! Such were the qualifications of this candidate for a command in the wilderness, as enumerated by the reverend Bishop Las Casas. It is probable, however, that he had given evidence of qualities more adapted to the desired post; having already been out to Hispaniola in the military train of the late Governor Ovando.

Where merits were so singularly balanced as those of Ojeda and Nicuesa, it might have been difficult to decide; King Ferdinand avoided the dilemma by favouring both of the candidates; not indeed by furnishing them with ships and money, but by granting patents and dignities which cost nothing, and might bring rich returns.

He divided that part of the continent which lies along the Isthmus of Darien into two provinces, the boundary line running through the Gulf of Uraba. The eastern part, extending to Cape de la Vela was called New Andalusia, and the government of it given to Ojeda. The other to the west, including Veragua, and reaching to Cape Gracias á Dios, was assigned to Nicuesa. The island of Jamaica was given to the two governors in common, as a place from whence to draw supplies of provisions. Each of the governors was to erect two fortresses in his district, and to enjoy for ten years the profits of all the mines he should discover, paying to the crown one tenth part the first year, one ninth the second, one eighth the third, one seventh the fourth, and one fifth part in each of the remaining years.

Juan de la Cosa, who had been indefatigable in promoting the suit of Ojeda, was appointed his lieutenant in the government, with the post of Alguazil Mayor of the province. He immediately freighted a ship and two brigantines, in which he embarked with about two hundred men. It was a slender armament, but the purse of the honest voyager was not very deep, and that of Ojeda was empty. Nicuesa, having ampler means, armed four large vessels and two brigantines, furnished them with abundant munitions and supplies, both for the voyage and the projected colony, enlisted a much greater force, and set sail in gay and vaunting style, for the golden shores of Veragua, the Aurea Chersonesus of his imagination.

CHAPTER II

Feud between the Rival Governors Ojeda and Nicuesa.—
A Challenge.—[1509.]

THE two rival armaments arrived at San Domingo about the same time. Nicuesa had experienced what was doubtless considered a pleasant little turn of fortune by the way. Touching at Santa Cruz, one of the Carribee islands, he had succeeded in capturing a hundred of the natives, whom he had borne off in his ships to be sold as slaves at Hispaniola. This was deemed justifiable in those days, even by the most scrupulous divines from the belief that the Caribs were all anthropophagi, or man-eaters; fortunately the opinion of mankind, in this more enlightened age, makes but little difference in atrocity between the cannibal and the kidnapper.

Alonzo de Ojeda welcomed with joy the arrival of his nautical friend and future lieutenant in the government, the worthy Juan de la Cosa; still he could not but feel some mortification at the inferiority of his armament to that of his rival Nicuesa, whose stately ships rode proudly at anchor in the harbor of San Domingo. He felt, too, that his means were

57

inadequate to the establishment of his intended colony. Ojeda, however, was not long at a loss for pecuniary assistance. Like many free spirited men, who are careless and squandering of their own purses, he had a facility at commanding the purses of his neighbours. Among the motley population of San Domingo there was a lawyer of some abilities, the Bachelor Martin Fernandez de Enciso, who had made two thousand castillanos by his pleading;[24] for it would appear that the spirit of litigation was one of the first fruits of civilized life transplanted to the New World, and flourished surprisingly among the Spanish colonists.

Alonzo de Ojeda became acquainted with the Bachelor, and finding him to be of a restless and speculative character, soon succeeded in inspiring him with a contempt for the dull but secure and profitable routine of his office in San Domingo, and imbuing him with his own passion for adventure. Above all he dazzled him with the offer to make him Alcalde Mayor, or chief judge of the provincial government he was about to establish in the wilderness.

In an evil hour the aspiring Bachelor yielded to the temptation, and agreed to invest all his money in the enterprise. It was agreed that Ojeda should depart with the armament which had arrived from Spain, while the Bachelor should remain at Hispaniola to beat up for recruits and provide supplies; with these he was to embark in a ship purchased by himself, and proceed to join his high-mettled friend at the seat of his intended colony. Two rival governors, so well matched as Ojeda and Nicuesa, and both possessed of swelling spirits, pent up in small but active bodies, could not remain long in a little place like San Domingo without some collision. The island of Jamaica which had been assigned to them in common, furnished the first ground of contention; the province of Darien furnished another, each pretending to include it within the limits of his jurisdiction. Their disputes on these points ran so high that the whole place resounded with them. In talking, however, Nicuesa had the advantage; having been brought up in the court he was more polished and ceremonious, had greater self-command, and probably perplexed his rival governor in argument. Ojeda was no great casuist, but he was an excellent swordsman, and always ready to fight his way through any question of right or dignity which he could not clearly argue with the tongue; so he proposed to settle the dispute by single combat. Nicuesa, though equally brave was more a man of the world, and saw the folly of such arbitrament. Secretly smiling at the heat of his antagonist, he proposed as a preliminary to the duel, and to furnish something worth fighting for, that each should deposit five thousand castillanos, to be the prize of the victor. This, as he foresaw, was a temporary check upon the fiery valour of his rival, who did not possess a pistole in his treasury; but probably was too proud to confess it.

It is not likely, however, that the impetuous spirit of Ojeda would long have remained in check, had not the discreet Juan de la Cosa interposed to calm it. It is interesting to notice the great ascendency possessed by this veteran navigator over his fiery associate. Juan de la Cosa was a man whose strong natural good sense had been quickened by long and hard experience; whose courage was above all question, but tempered by time and trial. He seems to have been personally attached to Ojeda, as veterans who have outlived the rash impulse of youthful valour, are apt to love the fiery quality in their younger associates. So long as he accompanied Ojeda in his enterprises he stood by him as a Mentor in council, and a devoted partisan in danger.

In the present instance the interference of this veteran of the seas had the most salutary effect: he prevented the impending duel of the rival governors, and persuaded them to agree that the river Darien should be the boundary line between their respective jurisdictions.

The dispute relative to Jamaica was settled by the admiral, Don Diego Columbus himself. He had already felt aggrieved by the distribution of these governments by the king without his consent or even knowledge, being contrary to the privileges which he inherited from his father, the discoverer. It was in vain to contend, however, when the matter was beyond his reach and involved in technical disputes. But as to the island of Jamaica, it in a manner lay at his own door, and he could not brook its being made a matter of gift to these brawling governors. Without waiting the slow and uncertain course of making remonstrances to the king, he took the affair, as a matter of plain right, into his own hands, and ordered a brave officer, Juan de Esquibel, the same who had subjugated the province of Higuey, to take possession of that island, with seventy men, and to hold it subject to his command.

Ojeda did not hear of this arrangement until he was on the point of embarking to make sail. In the heat of the moment he loudly defied the power of the admiral, and swore that if he ever found Juan de Esquibel on the island of Jamaica he would strike off his head. The populace present heard this menace, and had too thorough an idea of the fiery and daring character of Ojeda to doubt that he would carry it into effect. Notwithstanding his bravado, however, Juan de Esquibel proceeded according to his orders to take possession of the island of Jamaica.

The squadron of Nicuesa lingered for some time after the sailing of his rival. His courteous and engaging manners, aided by the rumour of great riches in the province of Veragua, where he intended to found his colony, had drawn numerous volunteers to his standard, insomuch that he had to purchase another ship to convey them.

Nicuesa was more of the courtier and the cavalier, than

the man of business, and had no skill in managing his pecuniary affairs. He had expended his funds with a free and lavish hand, and involved himself in debts which he had not the immediate means of paying. Many of his creditors knew that his expedition was regarded with an evil eye by the admiral, Don Diego Columbus; to gain favour with the latter, therefore, they threw all kinds of impediments in the way of Nicuesa. Never was an unfortunate gentleman more harassed and distracted by duns and demands, one plucking at his skirts as soon as the other was satisfied. He succeeded, however, in getting all his forces embarked. He had seven hundred men, well chosen and well armed, together with six horses. He chose Lope de Olano to be his captain general, a seemingly impolitic appointment, as this Olano had been concerned with the notorious Roldan in his rebellion against Columbus.

The squadron sailed out of the harbour and put to sea, excepting one ship, which, with anchor a-trip and sails unfurled waited to receive Nicuesa, who was detained on shore until the last moment by the perplexities which had been artfully multiplied around him.

Just as he was on the point of stepping into his boat he was arrested by the harpies of the law, and carried before the Alcalde Mayor to answer a demand for five hundred ducats, which he was ordered to pay on the spot, or prepare to go to prison.

This was a thunderstroke to the unfortunate cavalier. In vain he represented his utter incapacity to furnish such a sum at the moment; in vain he represented the ruin that would accrue to himself and the vast injury to the public service, should he be prevented from joining his expedition. The Alcalde Mayor was inflexible, and Nicuesa was reduced to despair. At this critical moment relief came from a most unexpected quarter. The heart of a public notary was melted by his distress! He stepped forward in court and declared that rather than see so gallant a gentleman reduced to extremity he himself would pay down the money. Nicuesa gazed at him with astonishment, and could scarcely believe his senses, but when he saw him actually pay off the debt and found himself suddenly released from this dreadful embarrassment, he embraced his deliverer with tears of gratitude, and hastened with all speed to embark, lest some other legal spell should be laid upon his person.

CHAPTER III

Exploits and Disasters of Ojeda on the Coast of Carthagena.—
Fate of the veteran Juan de la Cosa.—[1509.]

I T was on the 10th of November, 1509, that Alonzo
de Ojeda set sail from San Domingo with two ships,
two brigantines, and three hundred men. He took
with him also twelve brood mares. Among the remarkable adventurers who embarked with him was Francisco
Pizarro, who was afterwards renowned as the conqueror of
Peru.[25] Hernando Cortez had likewise intended to sail in the
expedition, but was prevented by an inflammation in one of
his knees.

The voyage was speedy and prosperous, and they arrived
late in the autumn in the harbour of Carthagena. The veteran
Juan de la Cosa was well acquainted with this place, having
sailed as pilot with Rodrigo de Bastides, at the time he discovered it in 1501. He warned Alonzo de Ojeda to be upon
his guard, as the natives were a brave and warlike race of
Carib origin, far different from the soft and gentle inhabitants of the islands. They wielded great swords of palm wood,
defended themselves with osier targets, and dipped their

64

arrows in a subtle poison. The women, as well as the men, mingled in battle, being expert in drawing the bow and throwing a species of lance called the azagay. The warning was well timed, for the Indians of these parts had been irritated by the misconduct of previous adventurers, and flew to arms on the first appearance of the ships.

Juan de la Cosa now feared for the safety of the enterprise in which he had person, fortune, and official dignity at stake. He earnestly advised Ojeda to abandon this dangerous neighbourhood, and to commence a settlement in the gulf of Uraba, where the people were less ferocious, and did not use poisoned weapons. Ojeda was too proud of spirit to alter his plans through fear of a naked foe. It is thought, too, that he had no objection to a skirmish, being desirous of a pretext to make slaves to be sent to Hispaniola in discharge of the debts he had left unpaid.[26] He landed, therefore, with a considerable part of his force, and a number of friars, who had been sent out to convert the Indians. His faithful lieutenant, being unable to keep him out of danger, stood by to second him.

Ojeda advanced towards the savages, and ordered the friars to read aloud a certain formula which had recently been digested by profound jurists and divines in Spain. It began in stately form. "I, Alonzo de Ojeda, servant of the most high and mighty sovereigns of Castile and Leon, conquerors of barbarous nations, their messenger and captain, do notify unto you, and make you know, in the best way I can, that God our Lord, one and eternal, created the heaven and the earth, and one man and one woman, from whom you and we, and all the people of the earth proceeded, and are descendants, as well as all those who shall come hereafter." The formula then went on to declare the fundamental principles of the Catholic Faith; the supreme power given to St. Peter over the world and all the human race, and exercised by his representative the pope; the donation made by a late pope of all this part of the world and all its inhabitants, to the Catholic sovereigns of Castile; and the ready obedience which had already been paid by many of its lands and islands and people to the agents and representatives of those sovereigns. It called upon those savages present, therefore, to do the same, to acknowledge the truth of the Christian doctrines, the supremacy of the pope, and the sovereignty of the Catholic King, but, in case of refusal, it denounced upon them all the horrors of war, the desolation of their dwelling, the seizure of their property, and the slavery of their wives and children. Such was the extraordinary document, which, from this time forward, was read by the Spanish discoverers to the wondering savages of any newly-found country, as a prelude to sanctify the violence about to be inflicted on them.[27]

When the friars had read this pious manifesto, Ojeda made signs of amity to the natives, and held up glittering

presents; they had already suffered, however, from the cruelties of the white men, and were not to be won by kindness.
On the contrary they brandished their weapons, sounded
their conchs, and prepared to make battle.

Juan de la Cosa saw the rising choler of Ojeda, and knew
his fiery impatience. He again intreated him to abandon
these hostile shores, and reminded him of the venomous
weapons of the enemy. It was all in vain: Ojeda confided
blindly in the protection of the Virgin. Putting up, as usual,
a short prayer to his patroness, he drew his weapon, braced
his buckler, and charged furiously upon the savages. Juan
de la Cosa followed as heartily as if the battle had been of
his own seeking. The Indians were soon routed, a number
killed, and several taken prisoners; on their persons were
found plates of gold, but of an inferior quality. Flushed by
this triumph, Ojeda took several of the prisoners as guides,
and pursued the flying enemy four leagues into the interior.
He was followed, as usual, by his faithful lieutenant, the
veteran La Cosa, continually remonstrating against his useless temerity, but hardily seconding him in the most hare-
brained perils. Having penetrated far into the forest, they
came to a stronghold of the enemy, where a numerous force
was ready to receive them, armed with clubs, lances, arrows
and bucklers. Ojeda led his men to the charge with the old
Castilian war cry, "Santiago!" The savages soon took to
flight. Eight of their bravest warriors threw themselves into

a cabin, and plied their bows and arrows so vigorously, that the Spaniards were kept at bay. Ojeda cried shame upon his followers to be daunted by eight naked men. Stung by this reproach, an old Castilian soldier rushed through a shower of arrows, and forced the door of the cabin, but received a shaft through the heart, and fell dead on the threshold. Ojeda, furious at the sight, ordered fire to be set to the combustible edifice; in a moment it was in a blaze, and the eight warriors perished in the flames.

Seventy Indians were made captive and sent to the ships, and Ojeda, regardless of the remonstrances of Juan de la Cosa, continued his rash pursuit of the fugitives through the forest. In the dusk of the evening they arrived at a village called Yurbaco; the inhabitants of which had fled to the mountains with their wives and children and principal effects. The Spaniards, imagining that the Indians were completely terrified and dispersed, now roved in quest of booty among the deserted houses, which stood distant from each other, buried among the trees. While they were thus scattered, troops of savages rushed forth, with furious yells, from all parts of the forest. The Spaniards endeavoured to gather together and support each other, but every little party was surrounded by a host of foes. They fought with desperate bravery, but for once their valour and their iron armour were of no avail; they were overwhelmed by numbers, and sank beneath war clubs and poisoned arrows.

Ojeda on the first alarm collected a few soldiers and en-sconced himself within a small enclosure, surrounded by palisades. Here he was closely besieged and galled by flights of arrows. He threw himself on his knees, covered himself with his buckler, and, being small and active, managed to protect himself from the deadly shower, but all his com-panions were slain by his side, some of them perishing in frightful agonies. At this fearful moment the veteran La Cosa, having heard of the peril of his commander, arrived, with a few followers, to his assistance. Stationing himself at the gate of the palisades, the brave Biscayan kept the sav-ages at bay until most of his men were slain and he himself was severely wounded. Just then Ojeda sprang forth like a tiger into the midst of the enemy, dealing his blows on every side. La Cosa would have seconded him, but was crippled by his wounds. He took refuge with the remnant of his men in an Indian cabin; the straw roof of which, he aided them to throw off, lest the enemy should set it on fire. Here he defended himself until all his comrades, but one, were destroyed. The subtle poison of his wounds at length overpowered him, and he sank to the ground. Feeling death at hand, he called to his only surviving companion. "Brother," said he, "since God hath protected thee from harm, sally forth and fly, and if ever thou shouldst see Alonzo de Ojeda, tell him of my fate!"

Thus fell the hardy Juan de la Cosa, faithful and devoted

to the very last; nor can we refrain from pausing to pay a passing tribute to his memory. He was acknowledged by his contemporaries to be one of the ablest of those gallant Spanish navigators who first explored the way to the New World. But it is by the honest and kindly qualities of his heart that his memory is most endeared to us; it is, above all, by that loyalty in friendship displayed in this his last and fatal expedition. Warmed by his attachment for a more youthful and a hot-headed adventurer, we see this wary veteran of the seas forgetting his usual prudence and the lessons of his experience, and embarking heart and hand, purse and person, in the wild enterprises of his favourite. We behold him watching over him as a parent, remonstrating with him as a counsellor, but fighting by him as a partisan; following him, without hesitation, into known and needless danger, to certain death itself, and showing no other solicitude in his dying moments, but to be remembered by his friend.

The history of these Spanish discoveries abounds in noble and generous traits of character, but few have charmed us more than this instance of loyalty to the last gasp, in the death of the staunch Juan de la Cosa. The Spaniard who escaped to tell the story of his end was the only surviver of seventy that had followed Ojeda in this rash and headlong inroad.

CHAPTER IV

Arrival of Nicuesa.—Vengeance taken on the Indians.

WHILE these disastrous occurrences happened on shore, great alarm began to be felt on board of the ships. Days had elapsed since the party had adventured so rashly into the wilderness; yet nothing had been seen or heard of them, and the forest spread a mystery over their fate. Some of the Spaniards ventured a little distance into the woods, but were deterred by the distant shouts and yells of the savages, and the noise of their conchs and drums. Armed detachments then coasted the shore in boats, landing occasionally, climbing the rocks and promontories, firing signal guns, and sounding trumpets. It was all in vain; they heard nothing but the echoes of their own noises, or perhaps the wild whoop of an Indian from the bosom of the forest. At length, when they were about to give up the search in despair, they came to a great thicket of mangrove trees on the margin of the sea. These trees grow within the water, but their roots rise, and are intertwined, above the surface. In this entangled and almost impervious grove, they caught

71

a glimpse of a man in Spanish attire. They entered, and, to their astonishment, found it to be Alonzo de Ojeda. He was lying on the matted roots of the mangroves, his buckler on his shoulder, and his sword in his hand; but so wasted with hunger and fatigue that he could not speak. They bore him to the firm land; made a fire on the shore to warm him, for he was chilled with the damp and cold of his hiding place, and when he was a little revived they gave him food and wine. In this way he gradually recovered strength to tell his doleful story.[28]

He had succeeded in cutting his way through the host of savages, and attaining the woody skirts of the mountains; but when he found himself alone, and that all his brave men had been cut off, he was ready to yield up in despair. Bitterly did he reproach himself for having disregarded the advice of the veteran La Cosa, and deeply did he deplore the loss of that loyal follower, who had fallen a victim to his devotion. He scarce knew which way to bend his course, but continued on, in the darkness of the night and of the forest, until out of hearing of the yells of triumph uttered by the savages over the bodies of his men. When the day broke, he sought the rudest parts of the mountains, and hid himself until the night; then struggling forward among rocks, and precipices and matted forests, he made his way to the sea side, but was too much exhausted to reach the ships. Indeed it was wonderful that one, so small of frame, should have been able to endure such great hardships; but he was of admirable strength and hardihood. His followers considered his escape from death as little less than miraculous, and he himself regarded it as another proof of the special protection of the Virgin; for, though he had, as usual, received no wound, yet it is said his buckler bore the dints of upwards of three hundred arrows.[29]

While the Spaniards were yet on the shore, administering to the recovery of their commander, they beheld a squadron of ships standing towards the harbour of Carthagena, and soon perceived them to be the ships of Nicuesa. Ojeda was troubled in mind at the sight, recollecting his late intemperate defiance of that cavalier; and, reflecting that, should he seek him in enmity, he was in no situation to maintain his challenge or defend himself. He ordered his men, therefore, to return on board the ships and leave him alone on the shore, and not to reveal the place of his retreat while Nicuesa should remain in the harbour.

As the squadron entered the harbour, the boats sallied forth to meet it. The first inquiry of Nicuesa was concerning Ojeda. The followers of the latter replied, mournfully, that their commander had gone on a warlike expedition into the country, but days had elapsed without his return, so that they feared some misfortune had befallen him. They entreated Nicuesa, therefore, to give his word, as a cavalier, that should Ojeda really be in distress, he would not take advantage of his misfortunes to revenge himself for their late disputes.

Nicuesa, who was a gentleman of noble and generous spirit, blushed with indignation at such a request. "Seek your commander instantly," said he; "bring him to me if he be alive; and I pledge myself not merely to forget the past, but to aid him as if he were a brother."[30]

When they met, Nicuesa received his late foe with open arms. "It is not," said he, "for Hidalgos, like men of vulgar souls, to remember past differences when they behold one another in distress. Henceforth, let all that has occurred between us be forgotten. Command me as a brother. Myself and my men are at your orders, to follow you wherever you please, until the deaths of Juan de la Cosa and his comrades are revenged."

The spirits of Ojeda were once more lifted up by this gallant and generous offer. The two governors, no longer rivals, landed four hundred of their men and several horses, and set off with all speed for the fatal village. They approached it in the night, and dividing their forces into two parties, gave orders that not an Indian should be taken alive.

The village was buried in deep sleep, but the woods were filled with large parrots, which, being awakened, made a prodigious clamour. The Indians, however, thinking the Spaniards all destroyed, paid no attention to these noises. It was not until their houses were assailed, and wrapped in flames, that they took the alarm. They rushed forth, some with arms, some weaponless, but were received at their doors by the exasperated Spaniards, and either slain on the spot, or driven back into the fire. Women fled wildly forth with children in their arms, but at sight of the Spaniards glittering in steel, and of the horses, which they supposed ravenous monsters, they ran back, shrieking with horror, into their burning habitations. Great was the carnage, for no quarter was shown to age or sex. Many perished by the fire, and many by the sword.

When they had fully glutted their vengeance, the Spaniards ranged about for booty. While thus employed, they found the body of the unfortunate Juan de la Cosa. It was tied to a tree, but swollen and discoloured in a hideous manner by the poison of the arrows with which he had been slain. This dismal spectacle had such an effect upon the common men, that not one would remain in that place during the night. Having sacked the village, therefore, they left it a smoking ruin, and returned in triumph to their ships. The spoil in gold and other articles of value must have been great, for the share of Nicuesa and his men amounted to the value of seven thousand castillanos.[31] The two governors,

now faithful confederates, parted with many expressions of
friendship, and with mutual admiration of each others
prowess, and Nicuesa continued his voyage for the coast
of Veragua.

CHAPTER V

*Ojeda founds the Colony of San Sebastian.—Beleaguered
by the Indians.*

OJEDA now adopted, though tardily, the advice
of his unfortunate lieutenant, Juan de la Cosa,
and, giving up all thoughts of colonising this
disastrous part of the coast, steered his course
for the Gulf of Uraba. He sought for some time the river
Darien, famed among the Indians as abounding in gold, but
not finding it, landed in various places, seeking a favourable
site for his intended colony. His people were disheartened
by the disasters they had already undergone, and the appearance of surrounding objects was not calculated to reassure
them. The country, though fertile and covered with rich and
beautiful vegetation, was in their eyes a land of cannibals
and monsters. They began to dread the strength as well as
fierceness of the savages, who could transfix a man with
their arrows even when covered with armour, and whose
shafts were tipped with deadly poison. They heard the howlings of tigers, panthers, and, as they thought, lions in the
forests, and encountered large and venomous serpents among

the rocks and thickets. As they were passing along the banks of a river one of their horses was seized by the leg by an enormous alligator, and dragged beneath the waves.[32]

At length Ojeda fixed upon a place for his town on a height at the east side of the Gulf. Here, landing all that could be spared from the ships, he began, with all diligence, to erect houses, giving this embryo capital of his province the name of San Sebastian, in honour of that sainted martyr, who was slain by arrows; hoping he might protect the inhabitants from the empoisoned shafts of the savages. As a further protection he erected a large wooden fortress, and surrounded the place with a stockade. Feeling, however, the inadequacy of his handful of men to contend with the hostile tribes around him, he despatched a ship to Hispaniola, with a letter to the Bachelor, Martin Fernandez de Enciso, his Alcalde Mayor, informing him of his having established his seat of government, and urging him to lose no time in joining him with all the recruits, arms and provisions he could command. By the same ship he transmitted to San Domingo all the captives and gold he had collected.

His capital being placed in a posture of defence, Ojeda now thought of making a progress through his wild territory, and set out, accordingly, with an armed band, to pay a friendly visit to a neighbouring cacique, reputed as possessing great treasures of gold. The natives, however, had by this time learnt the nature of these friendly visits and were prepared to resist them. Scarcely had the Spaniards entered into the defiles of the surrounding forest when they were assailed by flights of arrows from the close coverts of the thickets. Some were shot dead on the spot, others, less fortunate, expired raving with the torments of the poison; the survivors, filled with horror at the sight, and, losing all presence of mind, retreated in confusion to the fortress.

It was some time before Ojeda could again persuade his men to take the field, so great was their dread of the poisoned weapons of the Indians. At length their provisions began to fail, and they were compelled to forage among the villages in search, not of gold, but of food.

In one of their expeditions they were surprised by an ambuscade of savages, in a gorge of the mountains, and attacked with such fury and effect, that they were completely routed, and pursued with yells and howlings to the very gates of San Sebastian. Many died in excruciating agony of their wounds, and others recovered with extreme difficulty. Those who were well, no longer dared to venture forth in search of food; for the whole forest teemed with lurking foes. They devoured such herbs and roots as they could find, without regard to their quality. The humours of their bodies became corrupted, and various diseases, combined with the ravages of famine, daily thinned their numbers.

The sentinel who feebly mounted guard at night, was often found dead at his post in the morning. Some stretched themselves on the ground and expired of mere famine and debility; nor was death any longer regarded as an evil, but rather as a welcome relief from a life of horror and despair.

CHAPTER VI

Alonzo de Ojeda supposed by the Savages to have a charmed life.—Their experiment to try the fact.

———————

IN the meantime the Indians continued to harass the garrison, lying in wait to surprise the foraging parties, cutting off all stragglers, and sometimes approaching the walls in open defiance. On such occasions Ojeda sallied forth at the head of his men, and from his great agility was the first to overtake the retreating foe. He slew more of their warriors with his single arm than all his followers together. Though often exposed to showers of arrows none had ever wounded him, and the Indians began to think he had a charmed life. Perhaps they had heard from fugitive prisoners, the idea entertained by himself and his followers of his being under supernatural protection. Determined to ascertain the fact, they placed four of their most dextrous archers in ambush with orders to single him out. A number of them advanced towards the fort sounding their conchs and drums, and uttering yells of defiance. As they expected, the impetuous Ojeda sallied forth immediately at the head of his men. The Indians fled towards the ambuscade, drawing him in furious pursuit. The archers waited until he was full in front and then launched their deadly shafts. Three struck his buckler and glanced harmlessly off, but the fourth pierced his thigh. Satisfied that he was wounded beyond the possibility of cure, the savages retreated with shouts of triumph.

Ojeda was borne back to the fortress in great anguish of body and despondency of spirit. For the first time in his life he had lost blood in battle. The charm in which he had hitherto confided was broken; or rather, the Holy Virgin appeared to have withdrawn her protection. He had the horrible death of his followers before his eyes, who had perished of their wounds in raving frenzy.

One of the symptoms of the poison was to shoot a thrilling chill through the wounded part; from this circumstance, perhaps, a remedy suggested itself to the imagination of Ojeda, which few but himself could have had the courage to undergo. He caused two plates of iron to be made red hot, and ordered a surgeon to apply them to each orifice of the wound. The surgeon shuddered and refused, saying, he would not be the murderer of his general.[33] Upon this Ojeda made a solemn vow that he would hang him unless he obeyed. To avoid the gallows, the surgeon applied the glowing plates. Ojeda refused to be tied down, or that anyone should hold him during this frightful operation. He endured it without shrinking or uttering a murmur, although it so inflamed his whole system, that they had to wrap him in sheets steeped in vinegar, to allay the burning heat which raged throughout his body; and we are assured that a barrel of vinegar was exhausted for the purpose. The desperate remedy succeeded: the cold poison, says Bishop Las Casas, was consumed by the vivid fire.[34] How far the venerable historian is correct in his postulate surgeons may decide; but many incredulous persons will be apt to account for the cure by surmising that the arrow was not envenomed.

CHAPTER VII

Arrival of a strange ship at San Sebastian.

ALONZO DE OJEDA, though pronounced out of danger, was still disabled by his wound, and his helpless situation completed the despair of his companions, for while he was in health and vigour his buoyant and mercurial spirit, his active, restless, and enterprising habits, imparted animation, if not confidence, to everyone around him. The only hope of relief was from the sea, and that was nearly extinct, when one day, to the unspeakable joy of the Spaniards, a sail appeared on the horizon. It made for the port and dropped anchor at the foot of the height of San Sebastian, and there was no longer a doubt that it was the promised succour from San Domingo.

The ship came indeed from the island of Hispaniola, but it had not been fitted out by the Bachelor Enciso. The commander's name was Bernardino de Talavera. This man was one of the loose, heedless adventurers who abounded in San Domingo. His carelessness and extravagance had involved him in debt, and he was threatened with a prison. In the

84

height of his difficulties the ship arrived which Ojeda had sent to San Domingo, freighted with slaves and gold, an earnest of the riches to be found at San Sebastian. Bernardino de Talavera immediately conceived the project of giving his creditors the slip, and escaping to this new settlement. He understood that Ojeda was in need of recruits, and felt assured that from his own reckless conduct in money matters, he would sympathize with anyone harassed by debt. He drew into his schemes a number of desperate debtors like himself, nor was he scrupulous about filling his ranks with recruits whose legal embarrassments arose from more criminal causes. Never did a more vagabond crew engage in a project of colonization.

How to provide themselves with a vessel was now the question. They had neither money nor credit; but then they had cunning and courage, and were troubled by no scruples of conscience; thus qualified, a knave will often succeed better for a time than an honest man; it is in the long run that he fails, as will be illustrated in the case of Talavera and his hopeful associates. While casting about for means to escape to San Sebastian they heard of a vessel belonging to certain Genoese, which was at Cape Tiburon, at the western extremity of the island, taking in a cargo of bacon and cassava bread for San Domingo. Nothing could have happened more opportunely: here was a ship amply stored with provisions, and ready to their hand; they had nothing to do but seize it and embark.

The gang, accordingly, seventy in number, made their way separately and secretly to Cape Tiburon, where, assembling at an appointed time and place, they boarded the vessel, overpowered the crew, weighed anchor and set sail. They were heedless, haphazard mariners, and knew little of the management of a vessel; the historian Charlevoix thinks, therefore, that it was a special providence that guided them to San Sebastian. Whether or not the good father is right in his opinion, it is certain that the arrival of the ship rescued the garrison from the very brink of destruction.[35]

Talavera and his gang, though they had come lightly by their prize, were not disposed to part with it as frankly, but demanded to be paid down in gold for the provisions furnished to the starving colonists. Ojeda agreed to their terms and taking the supplies into his possession, dealt them out sparingly to his companions. Several of his hungry followers were dissatisfied with their portions, and even accused Ojeda of unfairness in reserving an undue share for himself. Perhaps there may have been some ground for this charge, arising, not from any selfishness in the character of Ojeda, but from one of those superstitious fancies with which his mind was tinged; for we are told that, for many years, he

had been haunted by a presentiment that he should eventually die of hunger.[36]

This lurking horror of the mind may have made him depart from his usual free and lavish spirit in doling out these
providential supplies, and may have induced him to set by
an extra portion for himself, as a precaution against his
anticipated fate; certain it is that great clamours rose among
his people, some of whom threatened to return in the pirate
vessel to Hispaniola. He succeeded, however, in pacifying
them for the present, by representing the necessity of hus-
banding their supplies, and by assuring them that the
Bachelor Enciso could not fail soon to arrive, when there
would be provisions in abundance.

CHAPTER VIII

Factions in the Colony.—A Convention made.

DAYS and days elapsed but no relief arrived at San Sebastian. The Spaniards kept a ceaseless watch upon the sea, but the promised ship failed to appear. With all the husbandry of Ojeda the stock of provisions was nearly consumed; famine again prevailed, and several of the garrison perished through their various sufferings and their lack of sufficient nourishment. The survivors now became factious in their misery, and a plot was formed among them to seize upon one of the vessels in the harbour and make sail for Hispaniola.

Ojeda discovered their intentions, and was reduced to great perplexity. He saw that to remain here without relief from abroad was certain destruction, yet he clung to his desperate enterprise. It was his only chance for fortune or command; for should this settlement be broken up he might try in vain, with his exhausted means and broken credit, to obtain another post or to set on foot another expedition. Ruin in fact would overwhelm him, should he return without success.

He exerted himself, therefore, to the utmost to pacify his men; representing the folly of abandoning a place where they had established a foothold, and where they only needed a reinforcement to enable them to control the surrounding country, and to make themselves masters of its riches. Finding they still demurred, he offered, now that he was sufficiently recovered from his wound, to go himself to San Domingo in quest of reinforcements and supplies.

This offer had the desired effect. Such confidence had the people in the energy, ability, and influence of Ojeda, that they felt assured of relief should he seek it in person. They made a kind of convention with him, therefore, in which it was agreed that they should remain quietly at Sebastian's for the space of fifty days. At the end of this time, in case no tidings had been received of Ojeda, they were to be at liberty to abandon the settlement and return in the brigantines to Hispaniola. In the meantime Francisco Pizarro was to command the colony as Lieutenant of Ojeda, until the arrival of his Alcalde Mayor, the Bachelor Enciso. This convention being made, Ojeda embarked in the ship of Bernardino de Talavera. That cut-purse of the ocean and his loose-handed crew were effectually cured of their ambition to colonize. Disappointed in the hope of finding abundant wealth at San Sebastian's, and dismayed at the perils and horrors of the surrounding wilderness, they preferred returning to Hispaniola, even at the risk of chains and dungeons. Doubtless they thought that the influence of Ojeda would be sufficient to obtain their pardon, especially as their timely succour had been the salvation of the colony.

CHAPTER IX

Disastrous Voyage of Ojeda in the Pirate Ship.

O JEDA had scarce put to sea in the ship of these freebooters, when a fierce quarrel arose between him and Talavera. Accustomed to take the lead among his companions, still feeling himself governor, and naturally of a domineering spirit, Ojeda, on coming on board, had assumed the command as a matter of course. Talavera, who claimed dominion over the ship, by the right no doubt of trover and conversion, or, in other words, of downright piracy, resisted this usurpation.

Ojeda, as usual, would speedily have settled the question by the sword, but he had the whole vagabond crew against him, who overpowered him with numbers and threw him in irons. Still his swelling spirit was unsubdued. He reviled Talavera and his gang as recreants, traitors, pirates, and offered to fight the whole of them successively, provided they would give him a clear deck, and come on two at a time. Notwithstanding his diminutive size, they had too high an idea of his prowess, and had heard too much of his exploits, to accept his challenge; so they kept him raging in his chains while they pursued their voyage.

They had not proceeded far, however, when a violent
storm arose. Talavera and his crew knew little of navigation,
and were totally ignorant of those seas. The raging of the
elements, the baffling winds and currents, and the danger of
unknown rocks and shoals filled them with confusion and
alarm. They knew not whither they were driving before the
storm, or where to seek for shelter. In this hour of peril they
called to mind that Ojeda was a sailor as well as soldier,
and that he had repeatedly navigated these seas. Making
a truce, therefore, for the common safety, they took off his
irons, on condition that he would pilot the vessel during the
remainder of her voyage.

Ojeda acquitted himself with his accustomed spirit and
intrepidity; but the vessel had been already swept so far to
the westward that all his skill was ineffectual in endeavouring to work up to Hispaniola against storms and adverse
currents. Borne away by the gulf stream, and tempest-tost
for many days, until the shattered vessel was almost in a
foundering condition, he saw no alternative but to run it on
shore on the southern coast of Cuba.

Here then the crew of free-booters landed from their prize
in more desperate plight than when they first took possession of it. They were on a wild and unfrequented coast, their
vessel lay a wreck upon the sands, and their only chance
was to travel on foot to the eastern extremity of the island,

and seek some means of crossing to Hispaniola, where, after all their toils, they might perhaps only arrive to be thrown into a dungeon. Such, however, is the yearning of civilized men after the haunts of cultivated society, that they set out, at every risk, upon their long and painful journey.

CHAPTER X

*Toilsome March of Ojeda and his Companions through
the morasses of Cuba.*

NOTWITHSTANDING the recent services of
Ojeda, the crew of Talavera still regarded him
with hostility; but, if they had felt the value
of his skill and courage at sea, they were no
less sensible of their importance on shore, and he soon acquired that ascendency over them which belongs to a master-
spirit in time of trouble.

Cuba was as yet uncolonized. It was a place of refuge to
the unhappy natives of Hayti, who fled hither from the
whips and chains of their European task-masters. The forests abounded with these wretched fugitives, who often opposed themselves to the shipwrecked party, supposing them
to be sent by their late masters to drag them back to
captivity.

Ojeda easily repulsed these attacks; but found that these
fugitives had likewise inspired the villagers with hostility to
all European strangers. Seeing that his companions were too
feeble and disheartened to fight their way through the popu-

lous parts of the island, or to climb the rugged mountains of the interior, he avoided all towns and villages, and led them through the close forests and broad green savannahs which extended between the mountains and the sea.

He had only made choice of evils. The forests gradually retired from the coast. The savannahs, where the Spaniards at first had to contend merely with long rank grass and creeping vines, soon ended in salt marshes, where the oozy bottom yielded no firm foot-hold, and the mud and water reached to their knees. Still they pressed forward, continually hoping in a little while to arrive at a firmer soil, and flattering themselves they beheld fresh meadow land before them; but continually deceived. The farther they proceeded, the deeper grew the mire, until, after they had been eight days on this dismal journey, they found themselves in the centre of a vast morass where the water reached to their girdles. Though thus almost drowned, they were tormented with incessant thirst, for all the water around them was as briny as the ocean. They suffered too the cravings of extreme hunger, having but a scanty supply of cassava bread and cheese, and a few potatoes and other roots, which they devoured raw. When they wished to sleep they had to climb among the twisted roots of mangrove trees, which grew in clusters in the waters. Still the dreary marsh widened and deepened. In many places they had to cross rivers and inlets; where some, who could not swim, were drowned, and others were smothered in the mire.

Their situation became wild and desperate. Their cassava bread was spoiled by the water, and their stock of roots nearly exhausted. The interminable morass still extended before them, while, to return, after the distance they had come, was hopeless. Ojeda alone kept up a resolute spirit, and cheered and urged them forward. He had the little Flemish painting of the Madonna, which had been given him by the Bishop Fonseca, carefully stored among the provisions in his knapsack. Whenever he stopped to repose among the roots of the mangrove trees, he took out this picture, placed it among the branches, and kneeling, prayed devoutly to the Virgin for protection. This he did repeatedly in the course of the day, and prevailed upon his companions to follow his example. Nay, more, at a moment of great despondency, he made a solemn vow to his patroness, that if she conducted him alive through this peril, he would erect a chapel in the first Indian village he should arrive at; and leave her picture there, to remain an object of adoration to the Gentiles.[37]

This frightful morass extended for the distance of thirty leagues, and was so deep and difficult, so entangled by roots and creeping vines, so cut up by creeks and rivers, and so beset by quagmires, that they were thirty days in traversing

it. Out of the number of seventy men that set out from the
ship but thirty-five remained. "Certain it is," observes the
venerable Las Casas, "the sufferings of the Spaniards in the
New World, in search of wealth, have been more cruel and
severe than ever nation in the world endured; but those experienced by Ojeda and his men have surpassed all others."

They were at length so overcome by hunger and fatigue,
that some lay down and yielded up the ghost, and others,
seating themselves among the mangrove trees, waited in
despair for death to put an end to their miseries. Ojeda,
with a few of the lightest and most vigorous, continued to
struggle forward, and, to their unutterable joy, at length
arrived to where the land was firm and dry. They soon
descried a foot-path, and, following it, arrived at an Indian
village, commanded by a cacique called Cueybas. No sooner
did they reach the village than they sank to the earth
exhausted.

The Indians gathered round and gazed at them with wonder; but when they learnt their story, they exhibited a
humanity that would have done honour to the most professing Christians. They bore them to their dwellings, set meat
and drink before them, and vied with each other in discharging the offices of the kindest humanity. Finding that
a number of their companions were still in the morass, the
cacique sent a large party of Indians with provisions for their

relief, with orders to bring on their shoulders such as were too feeble to walk. "The Indians," says the Bishop Las Casas, "did more than they were ordered; for so they always do, when they are not exasperated by ill treatment. The Spaniards were brought to the village, succoured, cherished, consoled, and almost worshipped as if they had been angels."

CHAPTER XI

Ojeda performs his Vow to the Virgin.

BEING recovered from his sufferings, Alonzo de Ojeda prepared to perform his vow concerning the picture of the Virgin, though sorely must it have grieved him to part with a relique to which he attributed his deliverance from so many perils. He built a little hermitage or oratory in the village, and furnished it with an altar, above which he placed the picture. He then summoned the benevolent cacique, and explained to him, as well as his limited knowledge of the language, or the aid of interpreters would permit, the main points of the Catholic faith, and especially the history of the Virgin, whom he represented as the mother of the Deity that reigned in the skies, and the great advocate for mortal man.

The worthy cacique listened to him with mute attention, and though he might not clearly comprehend the doctrine, yet he conceived a profound veneration for the picture. The sentiment was shared by his subjects. They kept the little oratory always swept clean, and decorated it with cotton hangings, laboured by their own hands, and with various

votive offerings. They composed couplets or areytos in honour of the Virgin, which they sang to the accompaniment of
rude musical instruments, dancing to the sound under the
groves which surrounded the hermitage.

A further anecdote concerning this relique may not be
unacceptable. The venerable Las Casas, who records these
facts, informs us that he arrived at the village of Cueybás
sometime after the departure of Ojeda. He found the oratory
preserved with the most religious care, as a sacred place,
and the picture of the Virgin regarded with fond adoration.
The poor Indians crowded to attend mass, which he performed at the altar; they listened attentively to his paternal
instructions, and at his request brought their children to be
baptized. The good Las Casas having heard much of this
famous relique of Ojeda, was desirous of obtaining possession of it, and offered to give the cacique in exchange, an
image of the Virgin which he had brought with him. The
chieftain made an evasive answer, and seemed much troubled
in mind. The next morning he did not make his appearance.

Las Casas went to the oratory to perform mass, but found
the altar stripped of its precious relique. On inquiring, he
learnt that in the night the cacique had fled to the woods,
bearing off with him his beloved picture of the Virgin. It
was in vain that Las Casas sent messengers after him,
assuring him that he should not be deprived of the relique,

but, on the contrary, that the image should likewise be presented to him. The cacique refused to venture from the fastnesses of the forest, nor did he return to his village and replace the picture in the oratory until after the departure of the Spaniards.[38]

CHAPTER XII

*Arrival of Ojeda at Jamaica.—His reception by
Juan de Esquibel.*

WHEN the Spaniards were completely restored to health and strength, they resumed their journey. The cacique sent a large body of his subjects to carry their provisions and knapsacks, and to guide them across a desert tract of country to the province of Macaca, where Christopher Columbus had been hospitably entertained on his voyage along this coast. They experienced equal kindness from its cacique and his people, for such seems to have been almost invariably the case with the natives of these islands, before they had held much intercourse with the Europeans.

The province of Macaca was situated at Cape de la Cruz, the nearest point to the island of Jamaica. Here Ojeda learnt that there were Spaniards settled on that island, being in fact the party commanded by the very Juan de Esquibel, whose head he had threatened to strike off, when departing in swelling style from San Domingo. It seemed to be the fortune of Ojeda to have his bravadoes visited on his head in times of trouble and humiliation. He found himself compelled to apply for succour to the very man he had so vaingloriously menaced. This was no time, however, to stand on points of pride; he procured a canoe and Indians from the cacique of Macaca, and one Pedro de Ordas undertook the perilous voyage of twenty leagues in the frail bark, and arrived safe at Jamaica.

No sooner did Esquibel receive the message of Ojeda, than, forgetting past menaces, he instantly despatched a caravel to bring to him the unfortunate discoverer and his companions. He received him with the utmost kindness, lodged him in his own house, and treated him in all things with the most delicate attention. He was a gentleman who had seen prosperous days, but had fallen into adversity and been buffeted about the world, and had learnt how to respect the feelings of a proud spirit in distress. Ojeda had the warm, touchy heart to feel such conduct; he remained several days with Esquibel in frank communion, and when he sailed for San Domingo they parted the best of friends.

And here we cannot but remark, the singular difference in character and conduct of these Spanish adventurers when dealing with each other, or with the unhappy natives. Nothing could be more chivalrous, urbane, and charitable; nothing more pregnant with noble sacrifices of passion and interest, with magnanimous instances of forgiveness of injuries and noble contests of generosity, than the transactions of the discoverers with each other; but the moment they turned to treat with the Indians, even with brave and high-minded caciques, they were vindictive, blood-thirsty, and implacable. The very Juan de Esquibel, who could requite the recent hostility of Ojeda with such humanity and friendship, was the same, who, under the government of Ovando, laid desolate the province of Higuey in Hispaniola, and inflicted atrocious cruelties upon its inhabitants.

When Alonzo de Ojeda set sail for San Domingo, Bernardino de Talavera and his rabble adherents remained at Jamaica. They feared to be brought to account for their piratical exploit in stealing the Genoese vessel, and that in consequence of their recent violence to Ojeda, they would find in him an accuser rather than an advocate. The latter, however, in the opinion of Las Casas, who knew him well, was not a man to make accusations. With all his faults he did not harbour malice. He was quick and fiery, it is true, and his sword was too apt to leap from its scabbard on the least provocation; but after the first flash all was over, and, if he cooled upon an injury, he never sought for vengeance.

CHAPTER XIII

Arrival of Alonzo de Ojeda at San Domingo.—
Conclusion of his Story.

O N arriving at San Domingo the first inquiry of
Alonzo de Ojeda was after the Bachelor Enciso.
He was told that he had departed long before,
with abundant supplies for the colony, and that
nothing had been heard of him since his departure. Ojeda
waited for a time, in hopes of hearing, by some return ship,
of the safe arrival of the Bachelor at San Sebastian. No
tidings, however, arrived, and he began to fear that he had
been lost in those storms which had beset himself on his
return voyage.

Anxious for the relief of his settlement, and fearing that,
by delay, his whole scheme of colonization would be defeated, he now endeavoured to set on foot another armament, and to enlist a new set of adventurers. His efforts,
however, were all ineffectual. The disasters of his colony
were known, and his own circumstances were considered desperate. He was doomed to experience the fate that too often
attends sanguine and brilliant projectors. The world is

dazzled by them for a time, and hails them as heroes while successful; but misfortune dissipates the charm, and they become stigmatized with the appellation of adventurers. When Ojeda figured in San Domingo as the conqueror of Coanabo, as the commander of a squadron, as the governor of a province, his prowess and exploits were the theme of every tongue. When he set sail, in vaunting style, for his seat of government, setting the viceroy at defiance, and threatening the life of Esquibel, everyone thought that fortune was at his beck, and he was about to accomplish wonders. A few months had elapsed, and he walked the streets of San Domingo a needy man, shipwrecked in hope and fortune. His former friends, dreading some new demand upon their purses, looked coldly upon him; his schemes, once so extolled, were now pronounced wild and chimerical, and he was subjected to all kinds of slights and humiliations in the very place which had been the scene of his greatest vain glory.

While Ojeda was thus lingering at San Domingo, the Admiral, Don Diego Columbus, sent a party of soldiers to Jamaica to arrest Talavera and his pirate crew. They were brought in chains to San Domingo, thrown into dungeons, and tried for the robbery of the Genoese vessel. Their crime was too notorious to admit of doubt, and being convicted, Talavera and several of his principal accomplices were hanged. Such was the end of their frightful journey by sea and land. Never had vagabonds travelled farther or toiled harder to arrive at a gallows!

In the course of the trial Ojeda had naturally been summoned as a witness, and his testimony must have tended greatly to the conviction of the culprits. This drew upon him the vengeance of the surviving comrades of Talavera, who still lurked about San Domingo. As he was returning home one night at a late hour he was waylaid and set upon by a number of these miscreants. He displayed his usual spirit. Setting his back against a wall, and drawing his sword, he defended himself admirably against the whole gang; nor was he content with beating them off, but pursued them for some distance through the streets; and having thus put them to utter route, returned tranquil and unharmed to his lodgings.

This is the last achievement recorded of the gallant but reckless Ojeda; for here his bustling career terminated, and he sank into the obscurity that gathers round a ruined man. His health was broken by the various hardships he had sustained, and by the lurking effects of the wound received at San Sebastian, which had been but imperfectly cured. Poverty and neglect, and the corroding sickness of the heart, contributed, no less than the maladies of the body, to quench that sanguine and fiery temper, which had hitherto been the secret of his success, and to render him the mere wreck of his former self; for there is no ruin so hopeless and complete, as that of a towering spirit humiliated and broken down. He appears to have lingered some time at San Domingo. Gomara, in his history of the Indies, affirms that he turned monk, and entered in the convent at San Francisco, where he died. Such a change would not have been surprising in a man, who, in his wildest career, mingled the bigot with the soldier; nor was it unusual with military adventurers in those days, after passing their youth in the bustle and licentiousness of the camp, to end their days in the quiet and mortification of the cloister. Las Casas, however, who was at San Domingo at the time, makes no mention of the fact, as he certainly would have done, had it taken place. He confirms, however, all that has been said of the striking reverse in his character and circumstances; and he adds an affecting picture of his last moments, which may serve as a wholesome comment on his life. He died so poor, that he did not leave money enough to provide for his interment; and so broken in spirit, that, with his last breath, he entreated his body might be buried in the monastery of San Francisco, just at the portal, in humble expiation of his past pride, *"that every one who entered might tread upon his grave."*[39]

Such was the fate of Alonzo de Ojeda,—and who does not forget his errors and his faults at the threshold of his humble and untimely grave! He was one of the most fearless and aspiring of that band of "Ocean chivalry," that followed the footsteps of Columbus. His story presents a lively picture of the daring enterprises, the extravagant exploits, the thousand accidents, by flood and field, that checquered the life of a Spanish cavalier in that roving and romantic age.

"Never," says Charlevoix, "was man more suited for a coup-de-main, or to achieve and suffer great things under the direction of another: none had a heart more lofty, or ambition more aspiring; none ever took less heed of fortune, or showed greater firmness of soul, or found more resources in his own courage; but none was less calculated to be commander in chief of a great enterprize. Good management and good fortune forever failed him."[40]

The Voyage of
DIEGO DE NICUESA

CHAPTER I

*Nicuesa sails to the Westward.—His Shipwreck and
subsequent disasters.*

WE have now to recount the fortunes experienced by the gallant and generous
Diego de Nicuesa, after his parting from
Alonzo de Ojeda at Carthagena. On re-
suming his voyage he embarked in a caravel, that he might
be able to coast the land and reconnoitre; he ordered that
the two brigantines, one of which was commanded by his
lieutenant Lope de Olano, should keep near to him, while
the large vessels, which drew more water, should stand further out to sea. The squadron arrived upon the coast of
Veragua, in stormy weather, and, as Nicuesa could not find
any safe harbour, and was apprehensive of rocks and shoals,
he stood out to sea at the approach of night, supposing that
Lope de Olano would follow him with the brigantines

according to his orders. The night was boisterous, the caravel was much tossed and driven about, and when the morning dawned, not one of the squadron was in sight.

Nicuesa feared some accident had befallen the brigantines; he stood for the land and coasted along it in search of them until he came to a large river, into which he entered and came to anchor. He had not been here long when the stream suddenly subsided, having merely been swollen by the rains. Before he had time to extricate himself the caravel grounded, and at length fell over on one side. The current rushing like a torrent strained the feeble bark to such a degree, that her seams yawned and she appeared ready to go to pieces. In this moment of peril a hardy seaman threw himself into the water to carry the end of a rope on shore as a means of saving the crew. He was swept away by the furious current and perished in sight of his companions. Undismayed by his fate, another brave seaman plunged into the waves and succeeded in reaching the shore. He then fastened one end of a rope firmly to a tree, and the other being secured on board of the caravel, Nicuesa and his crew passed one by one along it, and reached the shore in safety.

Scarcely had they landed when the caravel went to pieces, and with it perished their provisions, clothing and all other necessaries. Nothing remained to them but the boat of the caravel, which was accidentally cast on shore. Here then they were, in helpless plight, on a remote and savage coast, without food, without arms, and almost naked. What had become of the rest of the squadron they knew not. Some feared that the brigantines had been wrecked; others called to mind that Lope de Olano had been one of the loose lawless men confederated with Francisco Roldan in his rebellion against Columbus, and judging him from the school in which he had served, hinted their apprehensions that he had deserted with the brigantines. Nicuesa partook of their suspicions, and was anxious and sad at heart. He concealed his uneasiness, however, and endeavoured to cheer up his companions, proposing that they should proceed westward on foot in search of Veragua, the seat of his intended government, observing, that if the ships had survived the tempest, they would probably repair to that place. They accordingly set off along the sea shore, for the thickness of the forest prevented their traversing the interior. Four of the hardiest sailors put to sea in the boat and kept abreast of them, to help them across the bays and rivers.

Their sufferings were extreme. Most of them were destitute of shoes, and many almost naked. They had to clamber over sharp and rugged rocks, and to struggle through dense forests beset with thorns and brambles. Often they had to wade across rank fens and morasses and drowned lands, or to traverse deep and rapid streams.

Their food consisted of herbs and roots and shell fish gathered along the shore. Had they even met with Indians they would have dreaded, in their unarmed state, to apply to them for provisions, lest they should take revenge for the outrages committed along this coast by other Europeans.

To render their sufferings more intolerable, they were in doubt whether, in the storms which preceded their shipwreck, they had not been driven past Veragua, in which case each step would take them so much the farther from their desired haven.

Still they laboured feebly forward, encouraged by the words and the example of Nicuesa, who cheerfully partook of the toils and hardships of the meanest of his men.

They had slept one night at the foot of impending rocks and were about to resume their weary march in the morning, when they were espied by some Indians from a neighbouring height. Among the followers of Nicuesa was a favourite page, whose tattered finery and white hat caught the quick eyes of the savages. One of them immediately singled him out, and taking a deadly aim, let fly an arrow that laid him expiring at the feet of his master. While the generous cavalier mourned over his slaughtered page, consternation prevailed among his companions, each fearing for his own life. The Indians, however, did not follow up this casual act of hostility, but suffered the Spaniards to pursue their painful journey unmolested.

Arriving one day at the point of a great bay that ran far inland, they were conveyed, a few at a time, in the boat, to what appeared to be the opposite point. Being all landed, and resuming their march, they found to their surprise that they were on an island, separated from the mainland by a great arm of the sea. The sailors who managed the boat were too weary to take them to the opposite shore, they remained therefore all night upon the island.

In the morning they prepared to depart, but, to their consternation, the boat with the four mariners had disappeared. They ran anxiously from point to point, uttering shouts and cries, in hopes the boat might be in some inlet; they clambered the rocks and strained their eyes over the sea. It was all in vain. No boat was to be seen; no voice responded to their call; it was too evident the four mariners had either perished or had deserted them.

CHAPTER II

Nicuesa and his men on a Desolate Island.

THE situation of Nicuesa and his men was dreary and desperate in the extreme. They were on a desolate island, bordering upon a swampy coast, in a remote and lonely sea, where commerce never spread a sail. Their companions in the other ships, if still alive and true to them, had doubtless given them up for lost; and many years might elapse before the casual bark of a discoverer might venture along these shores. Long before that time their fate would be sealed, and their bones, bleaching on the sands, would alone tell their story.

In this hopeless state many abandoned themselves to frantic grief, wandering about the island, wringing their hands and uttering groans and lamentations; others called upon God for succour, and many sat down in silent and sullen despair.

The cravings of hunger and thirst at length roused them to exertion. They found no food but a few shell fish scattered along the shore, and coarse herbs and roots, some of them of an unwholesome quality. The island had neither springs nor streams of fresh water, and they were fain to slake their thirst at the brackish pools of the marshes.

Nicuesa endeavoured to animate his men with new hopes. He employed them in constructing a raft of driftwood and branches of trees, for the purpose of crossing the arm of the sea that separated them from the main land. It was a difficult task, for they were destitute of tools, and when the raft was finished they had no oars with which to manage it. Some of the most expert swimmers undertook to propel it, but they were too much enfeebled by their sufferings. On their first essay, the currents which sweep that coast bore the raft out to sea, and they swam back with difficulty to the island. Having no other chance of escape, and no other means of exercising and keeping up the spirits of his followers, Nicuesa repeatedly ordered new rafts to be constructed, but the result was always the same, and the men at length either grew too feeble to work or renounced the attempt in despair.

Thus day after day, and week after week elapsed, without any mitigation of suffering or any prospect of relief. Every day some one or other sank under his miseries, a victim, not so much to hunger and thirst, as to grief and despondency. His death was envied by his wretched survivers, many of whom were reduced to such debility, that they had to crawl on hands and knees in search of the herbs and shell fish which formed their scanty food.

CHAPTER III

Arrival of a Boat.—Conduct of Lope de Olano.

WHEN the unfortunate Spaniards, without hope of succour, began to consider death as a desirable end to their miseries, they were roused to a new life one day by beholding a sail gleaming on the horizon. Their exultation was checked, however, by the reflection how many chances there were against its approaching this wild and desolate island. Watching it with anxious eyes they put up prayers to God to conduct it to their relief, and at length, to their great joy, they perceived that it was steering directly for the island. On a nearer approach it proved to be one of the brigantines that had been commanded by Lope de Olano. It came to anchor: a boat put off, and among the crew were the four sailors who had disappeared so mysteriously from the island.

These men accounted in a satisfactory manner for their desertion. They had been persuaded that the ships were in some harbour to the eastward, and that they were daily leaving them farther behind. Disheartened at the constant, and, in their opinion, fruitless toil which fell to their share

in the struggle westward, they resolved to take their own
counsel, without risking the opposition of Nicuesa. In the
dead of the night, therefore, when their companions on the
island were asleep, they had silently cast off their boat, and
retraced their course along the coast. After several days' toil
they found the brigantines under the command of Lope de
Olano, in the river of Belen, the scene of the disasters of
Columbus in his fourth voyage.

The conduct of Lope de Olano was regarded with suspicion by his contemporaries, and is still subject to doubt.
He is supposed to have deserted Nicuesa designedly, intending to usurp the command of the expedition. Men, however,
were prone to judge harshly of him from his having been
concerned in the treason and rebellion of Francisco Roldan.
On the stormy night when Nicuesa stood out to sea to avoid
the dangers of the shore, Olano took shelter under the lee
of an island. Seeing nothing of the caravel of his commander
in the morning, he made no effort to seek for it, but proceeded with the brigantines to the river Chagres, where he
found the ships at anchor. They had landed all their cargo,
being almost in a sinking condition from the ravages of the
worms. Olano persuaded the crews that Nicuesa had perished in the late storm, and, being his lieutenant, he assumed
the command. Whether he had been perfidious or not in his
motives, his command was but a succession of disasters. He

sailed from Chagres for the river of Belen, where the ships were found so damaged that they had to be broken to pieces. Most of the people constructed wretched cabins on the shore, where, during a sudden storm, they were almost washed away by the swelling of the river, or swallowed up in the shifting sands. Several of his men were drowned in an expedition in quest of gold, and he himself merely escaped by superior swimming. Their provisions were exhausted, they suffered from hunger and from various maladies, and many perished in extreme misery. All were clamorous to abandon the coast, and Olano set about constructing a caravel, out of the wreck of the ships, for the purpose, as he said, of returning to Hispaniola, though many suspected it was still his intention to persist in the enterprise. Such was the state in which the four seamen had found Olano and his party; most of them living in miserable cabins and destitute of the necessaries of life.

The tidings that Nicuesa was still alive put an end to the sway of Olano. Whether he had acted with truth or perfidy, he now manifested a zeal to relieve his commander, and immediately despatched a brigantine in quest of him, which, guided by the four seamen, arrived at the island in the way that has been mentioned.

CHAPTER IV

Nicuesa rejoins his Crews.

WHEN the crew of the brigantine and the companions of Nicuesa met, they embraced each other with tears, for the hearts, even of the rough mariners, were subdued by the sorrows they had undergone; and men are rendered kind to each other by a community of suffering. The brigantine had brought a quantity of palm nuts, and of such other articles of food as they had been able to procure along the coast. These the famished Spaniards devoured with such voracity that Nicuesa was obliged to interfere, lest they should injure themselves. Nor was the supply of fresh water less grateful to their parched and fevered palates.

When sufficiently revived, they all abandoned the desolate island, and set sail for the river Belen, exulting as joyfully as if their troubles were at an end, and they were bound to a haven of delight, instead of merely changing the scene of suffering and encountering a new variety of horrors.

In the meantime Lope de Olano had been diligently preparing for the approaching interview with his commander, by persuading his fellow-officers to intercede in his behalf, and to place his late conduct in the most favourable light. He had need of their intercessions. Nicuesa arrived, burning with indignation. He ordered him to be instantly seized and punished as a traitor; attributing to his desertion the ruin of the enterprise and the sufferings and death of so many of his brave followers. The fellow-captains of Olano spoke in his favour; but Nicuesa turned indignantly upon them: "You do well," cried he, "to supplicate mercy for him; you, who, yourselves, have need of pardon! You have participated in his crime; why, else, have you suffered so long a time to elapse without compelling him to send one of the vessels in search of me?"

The captains now vindicated themselves by assurances of their belief in his having foundered at sea. They reiterated their supplications for mercy to Olano; drawing the most affecting pictures of their past and present sufferings, and urging the impolicy of increasing the horrors of their situation by acts of severity. Nicuesa at length was prevailed upon to spare his victim; resolving to send him, by the first opportunity, a prisoner to Spain. It appeared, in truth, no time to add to the daily blows of fate that were thinning the number of his followers. Of the gallant armament of seven hundred resolute and effective men that had sailed with him from San Domingo, four hundred had already perished by various miseries; and, of the survivors, many could scarcely be said to live.

CHAPTER V

*Sufferings of Nicuesa and his men on the Coast
of the Isthmus.*

THE first care of Nicuesa, on resuming the general command, was to take measures for the relief of his people, who were perishing with famine and disease. All those who were in health, or who had strength sufficient to bear the least fatigue, were sent on foraging parties, among the fields and villages of the natives. It was a service of extreme peril; for the Indians of this part of the coast were fierce and warlike, and were the same who had proved so formidable to Columbus and his brother, when they attempted to found a settlement in this neighbourhood.

Many of the Spaniards were slain in these expeditions. Even if they succeeded in collecting provisions, the toil of bringing them to the harbour was worse to men in their enfeebled condition, than the task of fighting for them; for they were obliged to transport them on their backs, and, thus heavily laden, to scramble over rugged rocks, through almost impervious forests and across dismal swamps.

Harassed by these perils and fatigues, they broke forth into murmurs against their commander, accusing him, not merely of indifference to their sufferings, but of wantonly imposing severe and unnecessary tasks upon them out of revenge for their having neglected him.

The genial temper of Nicuesa, had in fact, been soured by disappointment; and a series of harassing cares and evils had rendered him irritable and impatient; but he was a cavalier of a generous and honourable nature, and does not appear to have enforced any services that were not indispensable to the common safety. In fact, the famine had increased to such a degree, that, we are told, thirty Spaniards, having on one occasion found the dead body of an Indian in a state of decay, they were driven by hunger to make a meal of it, and were so infected by the horrible repast, that not one of them survived.[41]

Disheartened by these miseries, Nicuesa determined to abandon a place which seemed destined to be the grave of Spaniards. Embarking the greater part of his men in the two brigantines, and the caravel which had been built by Olano, he set sail eastward in search of some more favourable situation for his settlement. A number of the men remained behind, to await the ripening of some maize and vegetables which they had sown. These he left under the command of Alonzo Nuñez, whom he nominated his Alcalde Mayor.

When Nicuesa had coasted about four leagues to the east, a Genoese sailor, who had been with Columbus in his last voyage, informed him that there was a fine harbour somewhere in that neighbourhood, which had pleased the old admiral so highly, that he had given it the name of Puerto Bello. He added, that they might know the harbour by an anchor, half buried in the sand, which Columbus had left there; near to which was a fountain of remarkably cool and sweet water, springing up at the foot of a large tree. Nicuesa ordered search to be made along the coast, and at length they found the anchor, the fountain, and the tree. It was the same harbour which bears the name of Portobello at the present day. A number of the crew were sent on shore in search of provisions, but were assailed by the Indians: and, being too weak to wield their weapons with their usual prowess, were driven back to the vessels with the loss of several slain or wounded.

Dejected at these continual misfortunes, Nicuesa continued his voyage seven leagues farther, until he came to the harbour to which Columbus had given the name of Puerto de Bastimientos, or, Port of Provisions. It presented an advantageous situation for a fortress, and was surrounded by a fruitful country. Nicuesa resolved to make it his abiding place. "Here," said he, "let us stop, *en el nombre de Dios!*" (in the name of God). His followers, with the superstitious feeling with which men in adversity are prone to interpret everything into omens, persuaded themselves that there was favourable augury in his words, and called the harbour "Nombre de Dios," which name it afterwards retained.

Nicuesa now landed, and drawing his sword, took solemn possession in the name of the Catholic sovereigns. He immediately began to erect a fortress to protect his people against the attacks of the savages. As this was a case of exigency, he exacted the labour of everyone capable of exertion. The Spaniards, thus equally distressed by famine and toil, forgot their favourable omen, cursed the place as fated to be their grave, and called down imprecations on the head of their commander, who compelled them to labour when ready to sink with hunger and debility. Those murmured no less who were sent in quest of food, which was only to be gained by fatigue and bloodshed; for whatever they collected they had to transport from great distances, and they were frequently waylaid and assaulted by the Indians.

When he could spare men for the purpose, Nicuesa despatched the caravel for those whom he had left at the river Belen. Many of them had perished, and the survivers had been reduced to such famine at times, as to eat all kinds of reptiles until a part of an alligator was a banquet to them. On mustering all his forces when thus united, Nicuesa found that but one hundred emaciated and dejected wretches remained.

He despatched the caravel to Hispaniola, to bring a quantity of bacon which he had ordered to have prepared there, but it never returned. He ordered Gonzalo de Badajos, at the head of twenty men, to scour the country for provisions; but the Indians had ceased to cultivate: they could do with little food, and could subsist on the roots and wild fruits of the forest. The Spaniards, therefore, found deserted villages and barren fields, but lurking enemies at every defile. So deplorably were they reduced by their sufferings, that at length there were not left a sufficient number in health and strength to mount guard at night; and the fortress remained without sentinels. Such was the desperate situation of this once gay and gallant cavalier, and of his brilliant armament, which but a few months before had sallied from San Domingo, flushed with the consciousness of power, and the assurance that they had the means of compelling the favours of fortune.

It is necessary to leave them for a while, and turn our attention to other events which will ultimately be found to bear upon their destinies.

CHAPTER VI

Expedition of the Bachelor Enciso in search of the Seat of Government of Ojeda.—(1510.]

IN calling to mind the narrative of the last expedition of Alonzo de Ojeda, the reader will doubtless remember the Bachelor Martin Fernandez de Enciso, who was inspired by that adventurous cavalier with an ill-starred passion for colonizing, and freighted a vessel at San Domingo with reinforcements and supplies for the settlement at San Sebastian.

When the Bachelor was on the eve of sailing, a number of the loose hangers-on of the colony, and men encumbered with debt, concerted to join his ship from the coast and the outports. Their creditors, however, getting notice of their intention, kept a close watch upon everyone that went on board while in the harbour, and obtained an armed vessel from the Admiral Don Diego Columbus, to escort the enterprising Bachelor clear of the island. One man, however, contrived to elude these precautions, and, as he afterwards rose to great importance, it is proper to notice him particularly. His name was Vasco Nuñez de Balboa. He was a native of

Xeres de los Caballeros, and of a noble though impoverished family. He had been brought up in the service of Don Pedro Puerto Carrero, Lord of Moguer, and he afterwards enlisted among the adventurers who accompanied Rodrigo de Bastides in his voyage of discovery. Peter Martyr, in his Latin decades, speaks of him by the appellation of "egregius digladiator," which has been interpreted by some as a skilful swordsman, by others, as an adroit fencing master. He intimates, also, that he was a mere soldier of fortune, of loose prodigal habits, and the circumstances under which he is first introduced to us justify this character. He had fixed himself for a time in Hispaniola, and undertaken to cultivate a farm at the town of Salvatierra, on the sea coast, but in a little time had completely involved himself in debt. The expedition of Enciso presented him with an opportunity of escaping from his embarrassments, and of indulging his adventurous habits. To elude the vigilance of his creditors and of the armed escort, he concealed himself in a cask, which was conveyed from his farm on the sea coast on board of the vessel, as if containing provisions for the voyage. When the vessel was fairly out to sea, and abandoned by the escort, Vasco Nuñez emerged like an apparition from his cask, to the great surprise of Enciso, who had been totally ignorant of the stratagem. The Bachelor was indignant at being thus outwitted, even though he gained a recruit by

the deception; and, in the first ebullition of his wrath, gave
the fugitive debtor a very rough reception, threatening to
put him on shore on the first uninhabited island they should
encounter. Vasco Nuñez, however, succeeded in pacifying
him, "for God," says the venerable Las Casas, "reserved
him for greater things." It is probable the Bachelor beheld
in him a man well fitted for his expedition, for Vasco Nuñez
was in the prime and vigour of his days, tall and muscular,
seasoned to hardships, and of intrepid spirit.

Arriving at the mainland, they touched at the fatal harbour of Carthagena, the scene of the sanguinary conflicts
of Ojeda and Nicuesa with the natives, and of the death of
the brave Juan de la Cosa. Enciso was ignorant of those
events, having had no tidings from those adventurers since
their departure from San Domingo; without any hestitation,
therefore, he landed a number of his men to repair his boat,
which was damaged, and to procure water. While the men
were working upon the boat, a multitude of Indians gathered at a distance, well armed, and with menacing aspect,
sounding their shells and brandishing their weapons. The
experience they had had of the tremendous powers of the
strangers, however, rendered them cautious of attacking,
and for three days they hovered in this manner about the
Spaniards, the latter being obliged to keep continually on
the alert. At length two of the Spaniards ventured one day

from the main body to fill a water cask from the adjacent
river. Scarcely had they reached the margin of the stream,
when eleven savages sprang from the thickets and surrounded them, bending their bows and pointing their arrows.
In this way they stood for a moment or two in fearful suspense, the Indians refraining from discharging their shafts,
but keeping them constantly pointed at their breasts. One
of the Spaniards attempted to escape to his comrades who
were repairing the boat, but the other called him back, and,
understanding something of the Indian tongue, addressed a
few amicable words to the savages. The latter, astonished at
being spoken to in their own language, now relaxed a little
from their fierceness, and demanded of the strangers who
they were, who were their leaders, and what they sought
upon their shores. The Spaniard replied that they were
harmless people, who came from other lands and merely
touched there through necessity, and he wondered that they
should meet them with such hostility; he at the same time
warned them to beware, as there would come many of his
countrymen well armed, and would wreak terrible vengeance
upon them for any mischief they might do. While they were
thus parleying, the Bachelor Enciso, hearing that two of his
men were surrounded by the savages, sallied instantly from
his ship, and hastened with an armed force to their rescue.
As he approached, however, the Spaniard who had held the

parley, made him a signal that the natives were pacific. In fact the latter had supposed that this was a new invasion of Ojeda and Nicuesa, and had thus arrayed themselves, if not to take vengeance for past outrages, at least to defend their houses from a second desolation. When they were convinced, however, that these were a totally different band of strangers and without hostile intentions, their animosity was at an end, they threw by their weapons, and came forward with the most confiding frankness. During the whole time that the Spaniards remained there, they treated them with the greatest friendship, supplying them with bread made from maize, with salted fish, and with the fermented and spiritous beverages common along that coast. Such was the magnanimous conduct of men who were considered among the most ferocious and warlike of these savage nations; and who, but recently, had beheld their shores invaded, their villages ravaged and burnt, and their friends and relations butchered, without regard to age or sex by the countrymen of these very strangers. When we recall the bloody and indiscriminate vengeance wreaked upon this people by Ojeda and his followers for their justifiable resistance of invasion, and compare it with their placable and considerate spirit when an opportunity for revenge presented itself, we confess we feel a momentary doubt whether the arbitrary appellation of savage is always applied to the right party.

CHAPTER VII

The Bachelor hears unwelcome tidings of his destined Jurisdiction.

NOT long after the arrival of Enciso at this eventful harbour he was surprised by the circumstance of a brigantine entering and coming to anchor. To encounter an European sail in these almost unknown seas, was always a singular and striking occurrence, but the astonishment of the Bachelor was mingled with alarm when, on boarding the brigantine, he found that it was manned by a number of the men who had embarked with Ojeda. His first idea was, that they had mutinied against their commander, and deserted with the vessel. The feelings of the magistrate were aroused within him by the suspicion, and he determined to take his first step as Alcalde Mayor, by seizing them and inflicting on them the severity of the law. He altered his tone, however, on conversing with their resolute commander. This was no other than Francisco Pizarro, whom Ojeda had left as his locum tenens at San Sebastian, and who showed the Bachelor his letter patent, signed by that unfortunate governor.

In fact, the little brigantine contained the sad remnant of the once vaunted colony. After the departure of Ojeda in the pirate ship, his followers, whom he had left behind under the command of Pizarro, continued in the fortress until the stipulated term of fifty days had expired. Receiving no succour, and hearing no tidings of Ojeda, they then determined to embark and sail for Hispaniola; but here an unthought of difficulty presented itself, they were seventy in number, and the two brigantines which had been left with them were incapable of taking so many. They came to the forlorn agreement, therefore, to remain until famine, sickness, and the poisoned arrows of the Indians should reduce their number to the capacity of the brigantines. A brief space of time was sufficient for the purpose. They then prepared for the voyage. Four mares, which had been kept alive as terrors to the Indians, were killed and salted for sea-stores. Then taking whatever other articles of provision remained, they embarked and made sail. One brigantine was commanded by Pizarro, the other by one Valenzuela.

They had not proceeded far when, in a storm, a sea struck the crazy vessel of Valenzuela with such violence as to cause it to founder with all its crew. The other brigantine was so near that the mariners witnessed the struggles of their drowning companions and heard their cries. Some of the sailors, with the common disposition to the marvellous, declared that they had beheld a great whale, or some other monster of the deep, strike the vessel with its tail, and either stave in its sides or shatter the rudder, so as to cause the shipwreck.[42] The surviving brigantine then made the best of its way to the harbour of Carthagena, to seek provisions.

Such was the disastrous account rendered to the Bachelor by Pizarro, of his destined jurisdiction. Enciso, however, was of a confident mind and sanguine temperament, and trusted to restore all things to order and prosperity on his arrival.

CHAPTER VIII

Crusade of the Bachelor Enciso against the Sepulchres of Zenu.

THE Bachelor Enciso, as has been shown, was a man of the sword as well as of the robe; having doubtless imbibed a passion for military exploit from his intimacy with the discoverers. Accordingly, while at Carthagena, he was visited by an impulse of the kind, and undertook an enterprise that would have been worthy of his friend Ojeda. He had been told by the Indians that about twenty-five leagues to the west lay a province called Zenu, the mountains of which abounded with the finest gold. This was washed down by torrents during the rainy season, in such quantities that the natives stretched nets across the rivers to catch the largest particles; some of which were said to be as large as eggs.

The idea of taking gold in nets captivated the imagination of the Bachelor, and his cupidity was still more excited by further accounts of this wealthy province. He was told that Zenu was the general place of sepulture of the Indian tribes throughout the country, whither they brought their dead, and buried them, according to their custom, decorated with their most precious ornaments.

It appeared to him a matter of course, therefore, that there must be an immense accumulation of riches in the Indian tombs, from the golden ornaments that had been buried with the dead through a long series of generations. Fired with the thought, he determined to make a foray into this province, and to sack the sepulchres! Neither did he feel any compunction at the idea of plundering the dead, considering the deceased as pagans and infidels, who had forfeited even the sanctuary of the grave, by having been buried according to the rites and ceremonies of their idolatrous religion.

Enciso, accordingly, made sail from Carthagena and landed with his forces on the coast of Zenu. Here he was promptly opposed by two caciques, at the head of a large band of warriors. The Bachelor, though he had thus put on the soldier, retained sufficient of the spirit of his former calling not to enter into quarrel without taking care to have the law on his side; he proceeded regularly, therefore, according to the legal form recently enjoined by the crown. He caused to be read and interpreted to the caciques, the same formula used by Ojeda, expounding the nature of the Deity, the supremacy of the pope, and the right of the Catholic sovereigns to all these lands, by virtue of a grant from his holiness. The caciques listened to the whole very attentively and without interruption, according to the laws of Indian courtesy. They then replied that, as to the assertion that there was but one God, the sovereign of heaven and earth, it seemed to them good, and that such must be the case; but as to the doctrine that the pope was regent of the world in place of God, and that he had made a grant of their country to the Spanish king, they observed that the pope must have been drunk to give away what was not his, and the king must have been somewhat mad to ask at his hands what belonged to others. They added, that they were lords of those lands and needed no other sovereign, and if this king should come to take possession, they would cut off his head and put it on a pole; that being their mode of dealing with their enemies.—As an illustration of this custom they pointed out to Enciso the very uncomfortable spectacle of a row of grisly heads impaled in the neighbourhood.

Nothing daunted either by the reply or the illustration, the Bachelor menaced them with war and slavery as the consequences of their refusal to believe and submit. They replied by threatening to put his head upon a pole as a representative of his sovereign. The Bachelor having furnished them with the law now proceeded to the commentary. He attacked the Indians, routed them, and took one of the caciques prisoner, but in the skirmish two of his men were slightly wounded with poisoned arrows, and died raving with torment.[43]

It does not appear, however, that his crusade against the sepulchres was attended with any lucrative advantage. Perhaps the experience he had received of the hostility of the natives, and of the fatal effects of their poisoned arrows, prevented his penetrating into the land, with his scanty force. Certain it is, the reputed wealth of Zenu, and the tale of its fishery for gold with nets, remained unascertained and uncontradicted, and were the cause of subsequent and disastrous enterprises. The Bachelor contented himself with his victory, and returning to his ships, prepared to continue his voyage for the seat of government established by Ojeda in the Gulf of Uraba.

CHAPTER IX

The Bachelor arrives at San Sebastian.—His disasters there, and subsequent Exploits at Darien.

IT was not without extreme difficulty, and the peremptory exercise of his authority as Alcalde Mayor, that Enciso prevailed upon the crew of Pizarro to return with him to the fated shores of San Sebastian. He at length arrived in sight of the long wished-for seat of his anticipated power and authority; but here he was doomed like his principal, Ojeda, to meet with nothing but misfortune. On entering the harbour his vessel struck on a rock on the eastern point. The rapid currents and tumultuous waves rent it to pieces; the crew escaped with great difficulty to the brigantine of Pizarro; a little flour, cheese and biscuit, and a small part of the arms were saved, but the horses, mares, swine and all other colonial supplies were swept away, and the unfortunate Bachelor beheld the proceeds of several years of prosperous litigation swallowed up in an instant.

His dream of place and dignity seemed equally on the point of vanishing, for, on landing, he found the fortress and its adjacent houses mere heaps of ruins, having been destroyed with fire by the Indians.

For a few days the Spaniards maintained themselves with palm nuts, and with the flesh of a kind of wild swine, of which they met with several herds. These supplies failing, the Bachelor sallied forth with a hundred men to forage the country. They were waylaid by three Indians, who discharged all the arrows in their quivers with incredible rapidity, wounded several Spaniards, and then fled with a swiftness that defied pursuit. The Spaniards returned to the harbour in dismay. All their dread of the lurking savages and their poisoned weapons revived, and they insisted upon abandoning a place marked out for disaster.

The Bachelor Enciso was himself disheartened at the situation of this boasted capital of San Sebastian;—but whither could he go where the same misfortunes might not attend him? In this moment of doubt and despondency, Vasco Nuñez, the same absconding debtor who had been smuggled on board in the cask, stepped forward to give counsel. He informed the Bachelor that several years previously he had sailed along that coast with Rodrigo de Bastides. They had explored the whole gulf of Uraba; and he well remembered an Indian village situated on the western side, on the banks of a river which the natives called Darien. The country around was fertile and abundant, and was said to possess mines of gold; and the natives, though a warlike race, never made use of poisoned weapons. He offered to guide the Bachelor to this place, where they might get a supply of provisions, and even found their colony.

The Spaniards hailed the words of Vasco Nuñez as if revealing a land of promise. The Bachelor adopted his advice, and, guided by him, set sail for the village, determined to eject the inhabitants and take possession of it as the seat of government. Arrived at the river, he landed, put his men in martial array, and marched along the banks. The place was governed by a brave cacique named Zemaco. When he heard of the approach of the Spaniards, he sent off the women and children to a place of safety, and posting himself with five hundred of his warriors on a height, prepared to give the intruders a warm reception. The Bachelor was a discoverer at all points, pious, daring, and rapacious. On beholding this martial array he recommended himself and his followers to God, making a vow in their name to "Our Lady of Antigua," whose image is adored with great devotion in Seville, that the first church and town which they built should be dedicated to her, and that they would make a pilgrimage to Seville to offer the spoils of the heathen at her shrine. Having thus endeavoured to propitiate the favour of heaven, and to retain the Holy Virgin in his cause, he next proceeded to secure the fidelity of his followers. Doubting that they might have some lurking dread of poisoned arrows, he exacted from them all an oath that they would not turn their backs upon the foe, whatever might happen. Never did warrior enter into battle with more preliminary forms and covenants than the Bachelor Enciso. All these points being arranged, he assumed the soldier, and attacked the enemy with such valour, that though they made at first a show of fierce resistance, they were soon put to flight, and many of them slain. The Bachelor entered the village in triumph, took possession of it by unquestionable right of conquest, and plundered all the hamlets and houses of the surrounding country; collecting great quantities of food and cotton, with bracelets, anklets, plates and other ornaments of gold, to the value of ten thousand castellanos.[44] His heart was wonderfully elated by his victory and his booty; his followers, also, after so many hardships and disasters, gave themselves up to joy at this turn of good fortune, and it was unanimously agreed that the seat of government should be established in this village; to which, in fulfilment of his vow, Enciso gave the name of Santa Maria de la Antigua del Darien.

CHAPTER X

*The Bachelor Enciso undertakes the command.—His
Downfall.*

THE Bachelor Enciso now entered upon the exercise of his civil functions as Alcalde Mayor, and Lieutenant of the absent governor, Ojeda. His first edict was stern and peremptory; he forbade all trafficking with the natives for gold, on private account, under pain of death. This was in conformity to royal command; but it was little palatable to men who had engaged in the enterprise in the hopes of enjoying free trade, lawless liberty, and golden gains. They murmured among themselves, and insinuated that Enciso intended to reserve all the profit to himself.

Vasco Nuñez was the first to take advantage of the general discontent. He had risen to consequence among his fellow-adventurers, from having guided them to this place, and from his own intrinsic qualities, being hardy, bold, and intelligent, and possessing the random spirit and open-handed generosity common to a soldier of fortune, and calculated to dazzle and delight the multitude.

He bore no good will to the Bachelor, recollecting his
threat of landing him on an uninhabited island, when he
escaped in a cask from San Domingo. He sought, therefore,
to make a party against him, and to unseat him from his
command. He attacked him in his own way, with legal
weapons, questioning the legitimacy of his pretensions. The
boundary line, he observed, which separated the jurisdictions of Ojeda and Nicuesa, ran through the centre of the
gulf of Uraba. The village of Darien lay on the western side,
which had been allotted to Nicuesa. Enciso, therefore, as
Alcalde Mayor and Lieutenant of Ojeda, could have no
jurisdiction here, and his assumed authority was a sheer
usurpation.

The Spaniards, already incensed at the fiscal regulations
of Enciso, were easily convinced; so with one accord they refused allegiance to him; and the unfortunate Bachelor found
the chair of authority to which he had so fondly and anxiously aspired, suddenly wrested from under him, before he
had well time to take his seat.

CHAPTER XI

Perplexities at the Colony.—Arrival of Colmenares.

TO depose the Bachelor had been an easy matter, for most men are ready to assist in pulling down; but to choose a successor was a task of far more difficulty. The people at first agreed to elect mere civil magistrates, and accordingly appointed Vasco Nuñez and one Zemudio as alcaldes, together with a cavalier of some merit of the name of Valdivia, as regidor. They soon, however, became dissatisfied with this arrangement, and it was generally considered advisable to vest the authority in one person. Who this person should be, was now the question. Some proposed Nicuesa, as they were within his province; others were strenuous for Vasco Nuñez. A violent dispute ensued, which was carried on with such heat and obstinacy, that many, anxious for a quiet life, declared it would be better to reinstate Enciso until the pleasure of the king should be known.

In the height of these factious altercations the Spaniards were aroused one day by the thundering of cannon from the opposite side of the gulf, and beheld columns of smoke rising from the hills. Astonished at these signals of civilized man on these wild shores, they replied in the same manner, and in a short time two ships were seen standing across the gulf. They proved to be an armament commanded by one Roderigo de Colmenares, and were in search of Nicuesa with supplies. They had met with the usual luck of adventurers on this disastrous coast, storms at sea and savage foes on shore, and many of their number had fallen by poisoned arrows. Colmenares had touched at San Sebastian to learn tidings of Nicuesa; but, finding the fortress in ruins, had made signals, in hopes of being heard by the Spaniards, should they be yet lingering in the neighbourhood.

The arrival of Colmenares caused a temporary suspension of the feuds of the colonists. He distributed provisions among them and gained their hearts. Then, representing the legitimate right of Nicuesa to the command of all that part of the coast as a governor appointed by the king, he persuaded the greater part of the people to acknowledge his authority. It was generally agreed, therefore, that he should cruise along the coast in search of Nicuesa, and that Diego de Albitez, and an active member of the law, called the Bachelor Corral, should accompany him as ambassadors, to invite that cavalier to come and assume the government of Darien.

CHAPTER XII

Colmenares goes in quest of Nicuesa.

RODERIGO DE COLMENARES proceeded along the coast to the westward, looking into every bay and harbour, but for a long time without success. At length one day he discovered a brigantine at a small island in the sea. On making up to it, he found that it was part of the armament of Nicuesa, and had been sent out by him to forage for provisions. By this vessel he was piloted to the port of Nombre de Dios, the nominal capital of the unfortunate governor, but which was so surrounded and over-shadowed by forests, that he might have passed by without noticing it.

The arrival of Colmenares was welcomed with transports and tears of joy. It was scarcely possible for him to recognise the once buoyant and brilliant Nicuesa in the squalid and dejected man before him. He was living in the most abject misery. Of all his once gallant and powerful band of followers, but sixty men remained, and those so feeble, yellow, emaciated, and woe-begone, that it was piteous to behold them.[45]

147

Colmenares distributed food among them, and told them that he had come to convey them to a plenteous country, and one rich in gold. When Nicuesa heard of the settlement at Darien, and that the inhabitants had sent for him to come and govern them, he was as a man suddenly revived from death. All the spirit and munificence of the cavalier again awakened in him. He gave a kind of banquet that very day to Colmenares and the ambassadors, from the provisions brought in the ship. He presided at his table with his former hilarity, and displayed a feat of his ancient office as royal carver, by holding up a fowl in the air and dissecting it with wonderful adroitness.

Well would it have been for Nicuesa had the sudden buoyancy of his feelings carried him no further, but adversity had not taught him prudence. In conversing with the envoys about the colony of Darien, he already assumed the tone of governor, and began to disclose the kind of policy with which he intended to rule. When he heard that great quantities of gold had been collected and retained by private individuals, his ire was kindled. He vowed to make them refund it, and even talked of punishing them for trespassing upon the privileges and monopolies of the crown. This was the very error that had unseated the Bachelor Enciso from his government, and it was a strong measure for one to threaten who as yet was governor but in expectation. The

menace was not lost upon the watchful ambassadors Diego
de Albitez and the Bachelor Corral. They were put still more
on the alert by a conversation which they held that very
evening with Lope de Olano, who was still detained a prisoner
for his desertion, but who found means to commune with
the envoys, and to prejudice them against his unsuspecting
commander. "Take warning," said he, "by my treatment. I
sent relief to Nicuesa and rescued him from death when
starving on a desert island. Behold my recompense. He re-
pays me with imprisonment and chains. Such is the gratitude
the people of Darien may look for at his hands!"

The subtle Bachelor Corral and his fellow envoy laid these
matters to heart, and took their measures accordingly. They
hurried their departure before Nicuesa, and setting all sail on
their caravel, hastened back to Darien. The moment they
arrived they summoned a meeting of the principal inhabitants. "A blessed change we have made," said they, "in summoning this Diego de Nicuesa to the command! We have
called in the stork to take the rule, who will not rest satisfied
until he has devoured us." They then related, with the usual
exaggeration, the unguarded threats that had fallen from
Nicuesa, and instanced his treatment of Olano as a proof of a
tyrannous and ungrateful disposition.

The words of the subtle Bachelor Corral and his associate
produced a violent agitation among the people, especially

among those who had amassed treasures which would have to be refunded. Nicuesa, too, by a transaction which almost destroys sympathy in his favour, gave time for their passions to ferment. On his way to Darien he stopped for several days among a group of small islands, for the purpose of capturing Indians to be sold as slaves. While committing these outrages against humanity, he sent forward Juan de Cayzedo in a boat to announce his coming. His messenger had a private pique against him, and played him false. He assured the people of Darien that all they had been told by their envoys concerning the tyranny and ingratitude of Nicuesa was true. That he treated his followers with wanton severity; that he took from them all they won in battle, saying, that the spoils were his rightful property; and that it was his intention to treat the people of Darien in the same manner. "What folly is it in you," added he, "being your own masters, and in such free condition, to send for a tyrant to rule over you!"

The people of Darien were convinced by this concurring testimony, and confounded by the overwhelming evil they had thus invoked upon their heads. They had deposed Enciso for his severity, and they had thrown themselves into the power of one who threatened to be ten times more severe! Vasco Nuñez de Balboa observed their perplexity and consternation. He drew them one by one apart, and conversed with them in private. "You are cast down in heart," said he, "and so you might well be, were the evil beyond all cure. But do not despair; there is an effectual relief, and you hold it in your hands. If you have committed an error in inviting Nicuesa to Darien, it is easily remedied by not receiving him when he comes!" The obviousness and simplicity of the remedy struck every mind, and it was unanimously adopted.

CHAPTER XIII

Catastrophe of the unfortunate Nicuesa.

WHILE this hostile plot was maturing at Darien, the unsuspecting Nicuesa pursued his voyage leisurely and serenely, and arrived in safety at the mouth of the river. On approaching the shore he beheld a multitude, headed by Vasco Nuñez, waiting, as he supposed, to receive him with all due honour. He was about to land when the public procurator, or attorney, called to him with a loud voice, warning him not to disembark, but advising him to return with all speed to his government at Nombre de Dios.

Nicuesa remained for a moment as if thunderstruck by so unlooked-for a salutation. When he recovered his self-possession he reminded them that he had come at their own request; he entreated, therefore, that he might be allowed to land and have an explanation, after which he would be ready to act as they thought proper. His entreaties were vain; they only provoked insolent replies, and threats of violence should he venture to put foot on shore. Night coming on, therefore, he was obliged to stand out to sea, but returned the next morning, hoping to find this capricious people in a different mood.

There did, indeed appear to be a favourable change, for he was now invited to land. It was a mere stratagem to get him in their power, for no sooner did he set foot on shore than the multitude rushed forward to seize him. Among his many bodily endowments, Nicuesa was noted for swiftness of foot. He now trusted to it for safety, and, throwing off the dignity of governor, fled for his life along the shore, pursued by the rabble. He soon distanced his pursuers and took refuge in the woods.

Vasco Nuñez de Balboa, who was himself a man of birth, seeing this high-bred cavalier reduced to such extremity, and at the mercy of a violent rabble, repented of what he had done. He had not anticipated such popular fury, and endeavoured, though too late, to allay the tempest he had raised. He succeeded in preventing the people from pursuing Nicuesa into the forest, and then endeavoured to mollify the vindictive rage of his fellow Alcalde, Zamudio, whose hostility was quickened by the dread of losing his office, should the new governor be received; and who was supported in his boisterous conduct by the natural love of the multitude for what are called "strong measures." Nicuesa now held a parley with the populace, through the mediation of Vasco Nuñez. He begged that, if they would not acknowledge him as governor, they would at least admit him as a companion. This they refused, saying, that if they admitted him in one capacity, he would end by attaining to the other. He then implored, that if he could be admitted on no other terms, they would treat him as a prisoner, and put him in irons, for he would rather die among them than return to Nombre de Dios, to perish of famine, or by the arrows of the Indians.

It was in vain that Vasco Nuñez exerted his eloquence to obtain some grace for this unhappy cavalier. His voice was drowned by the vociferations of the multitude. Among these was a noisy swaggering fellow named Francisco Benitez, a great talker and jester, who took a vulgar triumph in the distresses of a cavalier, and answered every plea in his behalf with scoffs and jeers. He was an adherent of the Alcalde Zamudio, and under his patronage felt emboldened to bluster. His voice was even uppermost in the general clamour, until, to the expostulations of Vasco Nuñez, he replied by merely bawling with great vociferation, "No, no, no!—we will receive no such a fellow among us as Nicuesa!" The patience of Vasco Nuñez was exhausted; he availed himself of his authority as Alcalde, and suddenly, before his fellow magistrate could interfere, ordered the brawling ruffian to be rewarded with a hundred lashes, which were taled out roundly to him upon the shoulders.[46]

Seeing that the fury of the populace was not to be pacified,

he sent word to Nicuesa to retire to his brigantine, and not
to venture on shore until advised by him to do so. The counsel was fruitless. Nicuesa, above deceit himself, suspected it
not in others. He retired to his brigantine, it is true, but
suffered himself to be enveigled on shore by a deputation
professing to come on the part of the public, with offers to
reinstate him as governor. He had scarcely landed when he
was set upon by an armed band, headed by the base minded
Zamudio, who seized him and compelled him, by menaces of
death, to swear that he would immediately depart, and make
no delay in any place until he had presented himself before
the king and council in Castile.

It was in vain that Nicuesa reminded them that he was
governor of that territory and representative of the king,
and that they were guilty of treason in thus opposing him; it
was in vain that he appealed to their humanity, or protested
before God against their cruelty and persecution. The people
were in that state of tumult when they are apt to add cruelty
to injustice. Not content with expelling the discarded governor from their shores, they allotted him the worst vessel in
the harbour; an old crazy brigantine totally unfit to encounter the perils and labours of the sea.

Seventeen followers embarked with him; some being of his
household and attached to his person; the rest were volunteers who accompanied him out of respect and sympathy.

The frail bark set sail on the first of March, 1511, and steered across the Caribbean sea for the island of Hispaniola, but was never seen or heard of more!

Various attempts have been made to penetrate the mystery that covers the fate of the brigantine and its crew. A rumour prevailed some years afterwards that several Spaniards, wandering along the shore of Cuba, found the following inscription carved on a tree;—

Aqui fenecio el desdicado Nicuesa.
(Here perished the unfortunate Nicuesa.)

Hence it was inferred that he and his followers had landed there, and been massacred by the Indians. Las Casas, however, discredits this story. He accompanied the first Spaniards who took possession of Cuba, and heard nothing of the fact, as he most probably would have done had it really occurred. He imagines, rather, that the crazy bark was swallowed up by the storms and currents of the Caribbean sea, or that the crew perished with hunger and thirst, having been but scantily supplied with provisions. The good old bishop adds with the superstitious feeling prevalent in that age, that a short time before Nicuesa sailed from Spain on his expedition, an astrologer warned him not to depart on the day he had appointed, or under a certain sign; the cavalier replied, however, that he had less confidence in the stars than in God who made them. "I recollect, moreover," adds Las Casas, "that about this time a comet was seen over this island of Hispaniola, which, if I do not forget, was in the shape of a sword; and it was said that a monk warned several of those about to embark with Nicuesa, to avoid that captain, for the heavens foretold he was destined to be lost. The same, however," he concludes, "might be said of Alonzo de Ojeda, who sailed at the same time, yet returned to San Domingo and died in his bed."[47]

VASCO NUÑEZ DE BALBOA

DISCOVERER OF THE PACIFIC OCEAN

CHAPTER I

Factions at Darien.—Vasco Nuñez elevated to the Command.

WE have traced the disastrous fortunes of Alonzo de Ojeda and Diego de Nicuesa, we have now to record the story of Vasco Nuñez de Balboa, an adventurer equally daring, far more renowned, and not less unfortunate, who, in a manner, rose upon their ruins.

When the bark disappeared from view which bore the ill-starred Nicuesa from the shores of Darien, the community relapsed into factions, as to who should have the rule. The Bachelor Enciso insisted upon his claims as paramount, but he met with a powerful opponent in Vasco Nuñez, who had become a great favourite with the people, from his frank and fearless character, and his winning affability. In fact, he was peculiarly calculated to manage the fiery and factious, yet generous and susceptible, nature of his countrymen; for the Spaniards, though proud and resentful, and impatient of indignity or restraint, are easily dazzled by valour, and won by courtesy and kindness. Vasco Nuñez had the external requisites also to captivate the multitude. He was now about thirty-five years of age; tall, well formed, and vigorous, with reddish hair, and an open prepossessing countenance. His office of Alcalde, while it clothed him with influence and importance, tempered those irregular and dissolute habits he might have indulged while a mere soldier of fortune; and his superior talent soon gave him a complete ascendancy over his official colleague Zamudio. He was thus enabled to set on foot a vigorous opposition to Enciso. Still he proceeded according to the forms of law, and summoned the Bachelor to trial, on the charge of usurping the powers of Alcalde Mayor, on the mere appointment of Alonzo de Ojeda, whose jurisdiction did not extend to this province.

Enciso was an able lawyer, and pleaded his cause skilfully; but his claims were, in fact, fallacious, and, had they not been so, he had to deal with men who cared little for law, who had been irritated by his legal exactions, and who were disposed to be governed by a man of the sword rather than of the robe. He was readily found guilty therefore, and thrown into prison, and all his property was confiscated. This was a violent verdict, and rashly executed; but justice seemed to grow fierce and wild when transplanted to the wilderness of the new world. Still there is no place where

wrong can be committed with impunity; the oppression of
the Bachelor Enciso, though exercised under the forms of
law, and in a region remote from the pale of civilized life,
redounded to the eventual injury of Vasco Nuñez, and contributed to blast the fruits of that ambition it was intended
to promote.

The fortunes of the enterprising Bachelor had indeed run
strangely counter to the prospects with which he had embarked at San Domingo; he had become a culprit at the bar
instead of a judge upon the bench; and now was left to
ruminate in a prison on the failure of his late attempt at
general command. His friends, however, interceded warmly
in his behalf, and at length obtained his release from confine-
ment, and permission for him to return to Spain. Vasco Nuñez foresaw that the lawyer would be apt to plead his cause
more effectually at the court of Castile than he had done
before the partial and prejudiced tribunal of Darien. He prevailed upon his fellow Alcalde Zamudio, therefore, who was
implicated with him in the late transactions, to return to
Spain in the same vessel with the Bachelor, so as to be on the
spot to answer his charges, and to give a favourable report of
the case. He was also instructed to set forth the services of
Vasco Nuñez, both in guiding the colonists to this place, and
in managing the affairs of the settlement; and to dwell with
emphasis on the symptoms of great riches in the surrounding
country.

The Bachelor and the Alcalde embarked in a small caravel; and, as it was to touch at Hispaniola, Vasco Nuñez sent his confidential friend, the Regidor Valdivia, to that island to obtain provisions and recruits. He secretly put into his hands a round sum of gold as a present to Miguel de Pasamonte, the royal treasurer of Hispaniola, whom he knew to have great credit with the king, and to be invested with extensive powers, craving at the same time his protection in the new world and his influence at court.

Having taken these shrewd precautions, Vasco Nuñez saw the caravel depart without dismay, though bearing to Spain his most dangerous enemy; he consoled himself, moreover, with the reflection that it likewise bore off his fellow Alcalde Zamudio, and thus left him in sole command of the colony.

CHAPTER II

Expedition to Coyba.—Vasco Nuñez receives the daughter of a Cacique as hostage.

VASCO NUÑEZ now exerted himself to prove his capacity for the government to which he had aspired; and as he knew that no proof was more convincing to King Ferdinand than ample remittances, and that gold covered all sins in the new world, his first object was to discover those parts of the country which most abounded in the precious metals. Hearing exaggerated reports of the riches of a province about thirty leagues distant, called Coyba, he sent Francisco Pizarro with six men to explore it.

The cacique Zemaco, the native lord of Darien, who cherished a bitter hostility against the European intruders, and hovered with his warriors about the settlement, received notice of this detachment from his spies, and planted himself in ambush to waylay and destroy it. The Spaniards had scarcely proceeded three leagues along the course of the river when a host of savages burst upon them from the surrounding thickets, uttering frightful yells, and discharging showers

of stones and arrows. Pizarro and his men, though sorely
bruised and wounded, rushed into the thickest of the foe,
slew many, wounded more, and put the rest to flight; but,
fearing another assault, they made a precipitate retreat,
leaving one of their companions, Francisco Hernan, disabled
on the field. They arrived at the settlement crippled and
bleeding; but when Vasco Nuñez heard the particulars of the
action, his anger was roused against Pizarro, and he ordered
him, though wounded, to return immediately and recover
the disabled man. "Let it not be said, for shame," said he,
"that Spaniards fled before savages, and left a comrade in
their hands!" Pizarro felt the rebuke, returned to the scene
of combat, and brought off Francisco Hernan in safety.

Nothing having been heard of Nicuesa since his departure,
Vasco Nuñez despatched two brigantines for those followers
of that unfortunate adventurer who had remained at Nombre de Dios. They were overjoyed at being rescued from
their forlorn situation, and conveyed to a settlement where
there was some prospect of comfortable subsistence. The
brigantines, in coasting the shores of the Isthmus, picked up
two Spaniards, clad in painted skins, and looking as wild as
the native Indians. These men, to escape some punishment,
had fled from the ship of Nicuesa about a year and a half
before, and had taken refuge with Careta, the cacique of
Coyba. The savage chieftain had treated them with hospitable

kindness; their first return for which, now that they found themselves safe among their countrymen, was to advise the latter to invade the cacique in his dwelling, where they assured them they would find immense booty. Finding their suggestion listened to, one of them proceeded to Darien to serve as a guide to any expedition that might be set on foot; the other returned to the cacique, to assist in betraying him.

Vasco Nuñez was elated by the intelligence received through these vagabonds of the wilderness. He chose a hundred and thirty well armed and resolute men, and set off for Coyba, the dominions of Careta. The cacique received the Spaniards in his mansion with the accustomed hospitality of a savage, setting before them meat and drink, and whatever his house afforded; but when Vasco Nuñez asked for a large supply of provisions for the colony, he declared that he had none to spare, his people having been prevented from cultivating the soil by a war which he was waging with the neighbouring cacique of Ponca. The Spanish traitor, who had remained to betray his benefactor, now took Vasco Nuñez aside, and assured him that the cacique had an abundant hoard of provisions in secret; he advised him, however, to seem to believe his words, and to make a pretended departure for Darien with his troops, but to return in the night and take the village by surprise. Vasco Nuñez adopted the advice of the traitor. He took a cordial leave of Careta and set off for the settlement. In the dead of the night, however, when the savages were buried in deep sleep, Vasco Nuñez led his men into the midst of the village, and, before the inhabitants could rouse themselves to resistance, made captives of Careta, his wives, and children, and many of his people. He discovered also the hoard of provisions, with which he loaded two brigantines, and returned with his booty and his captives to Darien.

When the unfortunate cacique beheld his family in chains, and in the hands of strangers, his heart was wrung with despair; "What have I done to thee," said he to Vasco Nuñez, "that thou shouldst treat me thus cruelly? none of thy people ever came to my land that were not fed, and sheltered, and treated with loving kindness. When thou camest to my dwelling, did I meet thee with a javelin in my hand? Did I not set meat and drink before thee, and welcome thee as a brother? Set me free therefore, with my family and people, and we will remain thy friends. We will supply thee with provisions, and reveal to thee the riches of the land. Dost thou doubt my faith? Behold my daughter, I give her to thee as a pledge of friendship. Take her for thy wife, and be assured of the fidelity of her family and her people!"

Vasco Nuñez felt the force of these words and knew the importance of forming a strong alliance among the natives. The captive maid, also, as she stood trembling and dejected before him, found great favour in his eyes, for she was young and beautiful. He granted, therefore, the prayer of the cacique, and accepted his daughter, engaging moreover, to aid the father against his enemies, on condition of his furnishing provisions to the colony.

Careta remained three days at Darien, during which time, he was treated with the utmost kindness. Vasco Nuñez took him on board of his ships and showed him every part of them. He displayed before him also the war horses, with their armour and rich caparisons, and astonished him with the thunder of artillery. Lest he should be too much daunted by these warlike spectacles, he caused the musicians to perform a harmonious concert on their instruments, at which the cacique was lost in admiration. Thus having impressed him with a wonderful idea of the power and endowments of his new allies, he loaded him with presents and permitted him to depart.[48]

Careta returned joyfully to his territories, and his daughter remained with Vasco Nuñez, willingly for his sake giving up her family and native home. They were never married, but she considered herself his wife, as she really was, according to the usages of her own country, and he treated her with fondness, allowing her gradually to acquire great influence over him. To his affection for this damsel, his ultimate ruin is, in some measure, to be ascribed.

CHAPTER III

Vasco Nuñez hears of a Sea beyond the Mountains.

VASCO NUÑEZ kept his word with the father of his Indian beauty. Taking with him eighty men, and his companion in arms Rodrigo Enriquez de Colmenares, he repaired by sea to Coyba, the province of the cacique. Here landing, he invaded the territories of Ponca, the great adversary of Careta, and obliged him to take refuge in the mountains. He then ravaged his lands, and sacked his villages, in which he found considerable booty. Returning to Coyba, where he was joyfully entertained by Careta, he next made a friendly visit to the adjacent province of Comagre, which was under the sway of a cacique, of the same name, who had 3000 fighting men at his command.

This province was situated at the foot of a lofty mountain in a beautiful plain, twelve leagues in extent. On the approach of Vasco Nuñez, the cacique came forth to meet him, attended by seven sons, all fine young men, the offspring of his various wives. He was followed by his principal chiefs and warriors, and by a multitude of his people. The

Spaniards were conducted with great ceremony to the village, where quarters were assigned them, and they were furnished with abundance of provisions, and men and women were appointed to attend upon them.

The dwelling of the cacique surpassed any they had yet seen for magnitude, and for the skill and solidity of the architecture. It was one hundred and fifty paces in length, and eighty in breadth, founded upon great logs, surrounded with a stone wall; while the upper part was of wood work, curiously interwoven, and wrought with such beauty as to fill the Spaniards with surprise and admiration. It contained many commodious apartments. There were store rooms also; one filled with bread, with venison, and other provisions; another with various spirituous beverages, which the Indians made from maize, from a species of the palm, and from roots of different kinds. There was also a great hall in a retired and secret part of the building, wherein Comagre preserved the bodies of his ancestors and relatives. These had been dried by the fire, so as to free them from corruption, and afterwards wrapped in mantles of cotton, richly wrought and interwoven with pearls and jewels of gold, and with certain stones held precious by the natives. They were then hung about the hall with cords of cotton, and regarded with great reverence, if not a species of religious devotion.

Among the sons of the cacique, the eldest was of a lofty

and generous spirit, and distinguished above the rest by his superior intelligence and sagacity. Perceiving, says old Peter Martyr, that the Spaniards were a "wandering kind of men, living only by shifts and spoil," he sought to gain favour for himself and family by gratifying their avarice. He gave Vasco Nuñez and Colmenares, therefore, 4000 ounces of gold, wrought into various ornaments, together with sixty slaves, being captives that he had taken in the wars. Vasco Nuñez ordered one fifth of the gold to be weighed out and set apart for the crown, and the rest to be shared among his followers.

The division of the gold took place in the porch of the dwelling of Comagre, in the presence of the youthful cacique who had made the gift. As the Spaniards were weighing it out, a violent quarrel arose among them as to the size and value of the pieces which fell to their respective shares. The high minded savage was disgusted at this sordid brawl among beings whom he had regarded with such reverence. In the first impulse of his disdain he struck the scales with his fist, and scattered the glittering gold about the porch. Before the Spaniards could recover from their astonishment at this sudden act, he thus addressed them, "Why should you quarrel for such a trifle? If this gold is indeed so precious in your eyes, that for it alone you abandon your homes, invade the peaceful lands of others, and expose yourselves to such sufferings and perils, I will tell you of a region where you may gratify your wishes to the utmost. Behold these lofty mountains," continued he, pointing to the south. "Beyond these lies a mighty sea, which may be discerned from their summit. It is navigated by people who have vessels almost as large as yours, and furnished, like them, with sails and oars. All the streams which flow down the southern side of those mountains into that sea abound in gold; and the kings who reign upon its borders eat and drink out of golden vessels. Gold, in fact, is as plentiful and common among those people of the south as iron is among you Spaniards."

Struck with this intelligence, Vasco Nuñez inquired eagerly as to the means of penetrating to this sea and to the opulent regions on its shores. "The task," replied the prince, "is difficult and dangerous. You must pass through the territories of many powerful caciques, who will oppose you with hosts of warriors. Some parts of the mountain are infested by fierce and cruel cannibals, a wandering lawless race: but, above all, you will have to encounter the great cacique Tubanamá, whose territories are at the distance of six days journey, and more rich in gold than any other province; this cacique will be sure to come forth against you with a mighty force. To accomplish your enterprise, therefore, will require at least a thousand men armed like those who follow you."

The youthful cacique gave him further information on the

subject, collected from various captives whom he had taken in battle, and from one of his own nation, who had been for a long time in captivity to Tubanamá, the powerful cacique of the golden realm. The prince, moreover, offered to prove the sincerity of his words by accompanying Vasco Nuñez in any expedition to those parts at the head of his father's warriors.

Such was the first intimation received by Vasco Nuñez of the Pacific Ocean and its golden realms, and it had an immediate effect upon his whole character and conduct. This hitherto wandering and desperate man had now an enterprise opened to his ambition, which, if accomplished, would elevate him to fame and fortune, and entitle him to rank among the great captains and discoverers of the earth. Henceforth the discovery of the sea beyond the mountains was the great object of his thoughts, and his whole spirit seemed roused and ennobled by the idea.

He hastened his return to Darien, to make the necessary preparations for this splendid enterprise. Before departing from the province of Comagre he baptized that cacique by the name of Don Carlos, and performed the same ceremony upon his sons and several of his subjects;—thus singularly did avarice and religion go hand in hand in the conduct of the Spanish discoverers.

Scarcely had Vasco Nuñez returned to Darien when the

Regidor Valdivia arrived there from Hispaniola, but with no more provisions than could be brought in his small caravel. These were soon consumed, and the general scarcity continued. It was heightened also by a violent tempest of thunder, lightning, and rain, which brought such torrents from the mountains that the river swelled and overflowed its banks, laying waste all the adjacent fields that had been cultivated. In this extremity Vasco Nuñez despatched Valdivia a second time to Hispaniola for provisions. Animated also by the loftier views of his present ambition, he wrote to Don Diego Columbus, who governed at San Domingo, informing him of the intelligence he had received of a great sea and opulent realms beyond the mountains, and entreating him to use his influence with the king that one thousand men might be immediately furnished him for the prosecution of so grand a discovery. He sent him also the amount of fifteen thousand crowns in gold, to be remitted to the king as the royal fifths of what had already been collected under his jurisdiction. Many of his followers, also, forwarded sums of gold to be remitted to their creditors in Spain. In the meantime, Vasco Nuñez prayed the admiral to yield him prompt succour to enable him to keep his footing in the land, representing the difficulty he had in maintaining, with a mere handful of men, so vast a country in a state of subjection.

CHAPTER IV

Expedition of Vasco Nuñez in quest of the Golden Temple of Dobayba.—[1512.]

WHILE Vasco Nuñez awaited the result of this mission of Valdivia, his active disposition prompted him to undertake foraging excursions into the surrounding country. Among various rumours of golden realms in the interior of this unknown land, was one concerning a province called Dobayba, situated about forty leagues distant, on the banks of a great river which emptied itself, by several mouths, into a corner of the Gulf of Uraba.

This province derived its name, according to Indian tradition, from a mighty female of the olden time, the mother of the god who created the sun and moon and all good things. She had power over the elements, sending thunder and lightning to lay waste the lands of those who displeased her, but showering down fertility and abundance upon the lands of her faithful worshippers. Others described her as having been an Indian princess who once reigned amongst the mountains of Dobayba, and was renowned throughout the land for her supernatural power and wisdom. After her death, divine honours were paid her, and a great temple was erected for her worship. Hither the natives repaired from far and near, on a kind of pilgrimage, bearing offerings of their most valuable effects. The caciques who ruled over distant territories, also sent golden tributes, at certain times of the year, to be deposited in this temple, and slaves to be sacrificed at its shrine. At one time, it was added, this worship fell into disuse, the pilgrimages were discontinued, and the caciques neglected to send their tributes; whereupon the deity, as a punishment, inflicted a drought upon the country. The springs and fountains failed, the rivers were dried up; the inhabitants of the mountains were obliged to descend into the plains, where they digged pits and wells, but these likewise failing, a great part of the nations perished with thirst. The remainder hastened to propitiate the deity by tributes and sacrifices, and thus succeeded in averting her displeasure. In consequence of offerings of the kind, made for generations from all parts of the country, the temple was said to be filled with treasure, and its walls to be covered with golden gifts.[49] In addition to the tale of this temple, the Indians gave marvellous accounts of the general wealth of this province, declaring that it abounded with mines of gold, the veins of which reached from the dwelling of the cacique to the borders of his dominions.

To penetrate to this territory, and above all to secure the treasures of the golden temple, was an enterprise suited to the adventurous spirit of the Spaniards. Vasco Nuñez chose one hundred and seventy of his hardiest men for the purpose. Embarking them in two brigantines and a number of canoes, he set sail from Darien, and, after standing about nine leagues to the east, came to the mouth of the Rio Grande de San Juan, or the Great River of St. John, also called the Atrato, which is since ascertained to be one of the branches of the river Darien. Here he detached Rodrigo Enriquez de Colmenares with one third of his forces to explore the stream, while he himself proceeded with the residue to another branch of the river, which he was told flowed from the province of Dobayba, and which he ascended, flushed with sanguine expectations.[50]

His old enemy Zemaco, the cacique of Darien, however, had discovered the object of his expedition, and had taken measures to disappoint it: repairing to the province of Dobayba, he had prevailed upon its cacique to retire at the approach of the Spaniards, leaving his country deserted.

Vasco Nuñez found a village situated in a marshy neighbourhood, on the banks of the river, and mistook it for the residence of the cacique: it was silent and abandoned. There was not an Indian to be met with, from whom he could obtain any information about the country, or who could guide him to the golden temple. He was disappointed, also, in his hopes of obtaining a supply of provisions, but he found weapons of various kinds hanging in the deserted houses, and gathered jewels and pieces of gold to the value of seven thousand castellanos. Discouraged by the savage look of the surrounding wilderness, which was perplexed by deep morasses, and having no guides to aid him in exploring it, he put all the booty he had collected into two large canoes, and made his way back to the Gulf of Uraba. Here he was assailed by a violent tempest which nearly wrecked his two brigantines, and obliged him to throw a great part of their cargoes overboard. The two canoes containing the booty were swallowed up by the raging sea, and all their crews perished.

Thus baffled and tempest-tost, Vasco Nuñez at length succeeded in getting into what was termed the Grand River, which he ascended, and rejoined Colmenares and his detachment. They now extended their excursions up a stream which emptied into the Grand River, and which, from the dark hue of its waters, they called Rio Negro, or the Black River. They also explored certain other tributary streams, branching from it, though not without occasional skirmishes with the natives.

Ascending one of these minor rivers with a part of his men, Vasco Nuñez came to the territories of a cacique named Abibeyba, who reigned over a region of marshes and shallow lakes. The habitations of the natives were built amidst the branches of immense and lofty trees. They were large enough to contain whole family connexions, and were constructed partly of wood, partly of a kind of wicker work, combining strength and pliability, and yielding uninjured to the motion of the branches when agitated by the wind. The inhabitants ascended to them, with great agility, by light ladders, formed of great reeds split through the middle, for the reeds on this coast grow to the thickness of a man's body. These ladders they drew up after them at night, or in case of attack. These habitations were well stocked with provisions; but the fermented beverages, of which these people had always a supply, were buried in vessels in the earth, at the foot of the tree, lest they should be rendered turbid by the rocking of the houses. Close by, also, were the canoes with which they navigated the rivers and ponds of their marshy country, and followed their main occupation of fishing.

On the approach of the Spaniards, the Indians took refuge in their tree-built castles, and drew up the ladders. The former called upon them to descend and to fear nothing. Upon this the cacique replied, entreating that he might not be molested, seeing he had done them no injury. They threatened, unless he came down, to fell the trees, or to set fire to them and burn him and his wives and children. The cacique was disposed to consent, but was prevented by the entreaties of his people. Upon this the Spaniards prepared to hew down the trees, but were assailed by showers of stones. They covered themselves however with their bucklers, assailed the trees vigorously with their hatchets, and soon compelled the inhabitants to capitulate. The cacique descended with his wife and two of his children. The first demand of the Spaniards was for gold. He assured them he had none; for, having no need of it, he had never made it an object of his search. Being importuned, however, he assured them that if he were permitted to repair to certain mountains at a distance, he would in a few days return, and bring them what they desired. They permitted him to depart, retaining his wife and children as hostages, but they saw no more of the cacique. After remaining here a few days, and regaling on the provisions which they found in abundance, they continued their foraging expeditions, often opposed by the bold and warlike natives, and suffering occasional loss, but inflicting great havoc on their opposers.

Having thus overrun a considerable extent of country, and no grand object presenting to lure him on to further enterprise, Vasco Nuñez at length returned to Darien with the spoils and captives he had taken, leaving Bartolome Hurtado with thirty men in an Indian village on the Rio Negro, or Black River, to hold the country in subjection. Thus terminated the first expedition in quest of the golden temple Dobayba, which, for some time, continued to be a favourite object of enterprise among the adventurers of Darien.

CHAPTER V

Disaster on the Black River.—Indian plot against Darien.

BARTOLOME HURTADO, being left to his own
discretion on the banks of the Black River, occupied himself occasionally in hunting the scattered natives who straggled about the surrounding forests. Having in this way picked up twenty-four captives, he put them on board of a large canoe, like so much
live stock, to be transported to Darien and sold as slaves.
Twenty of his followers, who were infirm either from wounds
or the diseases of the climate, embarked also in the canoe, so
that only ten men remained with Hurtado.

The great canoe, thus heavily freighted, descended the
Black River slowly, between banks overhung with forests.
Zemaco, the indefatigable cacique of Darien, was on the
watch, and waylaid the ark with four canoes filled with
warriors, armed with war clubs, and lances hardened in the
fire. The Spaniards being sick, could make but feeble resistance; some were massacred, others leaped into the river
and were drowned. Two only escaped, by clinging to two
trunks of trees that were floating down the river, and covering themselves with the branches. Reaching the shore in

safety, they returned to Bartolome Hurtado with the tragical tidings of the death of his followers. Hurtado was so disheartened by the news, and so dismayed at his own helpless situation, in the midst of a hostile country, that he resolved to abandon the fatal shores of the Black River and return to Darien. He was quickened in this resolution by receiving intimation of a conspiracy forming among the natives. The implacable Zemaco had drawn four other caciques into a secret plan to assemble their vassals and make a sudden attack upon Darien. Hurtado hastened with the remnant of his followers to carry tidings to the settlement of this conspiracy. Many of the inhabitants were alarmed at his intelligence; others treated it as a false rumour of the Indians, and no preparations were made against what might be a mere imaginary danger.

Fortunately for the Spaniards, among the female captives owned by Vasco Nuñez was an Indian damsel named Fulvia; to whom, in consequence of her beauty, he had shown great favour, and who had become strongly attached to him. She had a brother among the warriors of Zemaco, who often visited her in secret. In one of his visits, he informed her that on a certain night the settlement would be attacked and every Spaniard destroyed. He charged her, therefore, to hide herself that night in a certain place until he should come to her aid, lest she should be slain in the confusion of the massacre.

When her brother was gone, a violent struggle took place in the bosom of the Indian girl between her feeling for her family and her people, and her affection for Vasco Nuñez. The latter at length prevailed, and she revealed all that had been told to her. Vasco Nuñez prevailed upon her to send for her brother under pretence of aiding her to escape. Having him in his power, he extorted from him all that he knew of the designs of the enemy. His confessions showed what imminent danger had been lurking round Vasco Nuñez in his most unsuspecting moments. The prisoner informed him that he had been one of forty Indians sent some time before by the cacique Zemaco to Vasco Nuñez, in seeming friendship, to be employed by him in cultivating the fields adjacent to the settlement. They had secret orders, however, to take an opportunity when Vasco Nuñez should come forth to inspect their work, to set upon him in an unguarded moment, and destroy him. Fortunately, Vasco Nuñez always visited the fields mounted on his war horse, and armed with lance and target. The Indians were therefore so awed by his martial appearance, and by the terrible animal he bestrode, that they dared not attack him.

Foiled in this and other attempts of the kind, Zemaco resorted to the conspiracy with the neighbouring caciques with which the settlement was menaced.

Five caciques had joined in the confederacy: they had

prepared a hundred canoes; had amassed provisions for an army, and had concerted to assemble five thousand picked warriors at a certain time and place; with these they were to make an attack on the settlement by land and water, in the middle of the night, and to slaughter every Spaniard.

Having learnt where the confederate chiefs were to be found, and where they had deposited their provisions, Vasco Nuñez chose seventy of his best men well armed, and made a circuit by land, while Colmenares, with sixty men, sallied forth secretly in four canoes, guided by the Indian prisoner. In this way they surprised the general of the Indian army and several of the principal confederates, and got possession of all their provisions, though they failed to capture the formidable Zemaco. The Indian general was shot to death with arrows, and the leaders of the conspiracy were hanged in the presence of their captive followers. The defeat of this deep laid plan, and the punishment of its devisers, spread terror throughout the neighbouring provinces, and prevented any further attempt at hostilities. Vasco Nuñez, however, caused a strong fortress of wood to be immediately erected, to guard against any future assaults of the savages.

CHAPTER VI

*Further Factions in the Colony.—Arrogance of Alonzo Perez
and the Bachelor Corral.—[1512.]*

A CONSIDERABLE time had now elapsed since the departure of Valdivia for Hispaniola, yet no tidings had been received from him. Many began to fear that some disaster had befallen him; while others insinuated that it was possible both he and Zamudio might have neglected the objects of their mission, and, having appropriated to their own use the gold with which they had been entrusted, might have abandoned the colony to its fate.

Vasco Nuñez himself was harassed by these surmises; and by the dread lest the Bachelor Enciso should succeed in prejudicing the mind of his sovereign against him. Impatient of this state of anxious suspense, he determined to repair to Spain, to communicate in person all that he had heard concerning the Southern Sea, and to ask for the troops necessary for its discovery.

Everyone, however, both friend and foe, exclaimed against such a measure, representing his presence as indispensable to the safety of the colony, from his great talents as a commander, and the fear entertained of him by the Indians.

After much debate and contention, it was at length agreed that Juan de Cayzedo and Rodrigo Enriquez de Colmenares should go in his place, instructed to make all necessary representations to the king. Letters were written also, containing the most extravagant accounts of the riches of the country, partly dictated by the sanguine hopes of the writers, and partly by the fables of the natives. The rumoured wealth of the province of Dobayba, and the treasures of its golden temple were not forgotten; and an Indian was taken to Spain by the commissioners, a native of the province of Zenu, where gold was said to be gathered in nets stretched across the mountain streams. To give more weight to all these stories, every one contributed some portion of gold from his private hoard, to be presented to the king in addition to the amount arising from his fifths.

But little time elapsed after the departure of the commissioners when new dissensions broke out in the colony. It was hardly to be expected that a fortuitous assemblage of adventurers could remain long tranquil during a time of suffering, under rulers of questionable authority. Vasco Nuñez, it is true, had risen by his courage and abilities: but he had risen from among their ranks; he was in a manner of their own creation; and they had not become sufficiently accustomed to him as a governor, to forget that he was recently but a mere soldier of fortune, and an absconding debtor.

Their factious discontent, however, was directed at first against a favourite of Vasco Nuñez, rather than against himself. He had invested Bartolome Hurtado, the commander of the Black River, with considerable authority in the colony, and the latter gave great offence by his oppressive conduct. Hurtado had particularly aggrieved by his arrogance one Alonzo Perez de la Rua, a touchy cavalier, jealous of his honour, who seems to have peculiarly possessed the sensitive punctilio of a Spaniard. Firing at some indignity, whether real or fancied, Alonzo Perez threw himself into the ranks of the disaffected, and was immediately chosen as their leader. Thus backed by a faction, he clamoured loudly for the punishment of Hurtado; and, finding his demands unattended to, threw out threats of deposing Vasco Nuñez. The latter no sooner heard of these menaces, than with his usual spirit and promptness, he seized upon the testy Alonzo Perez, and threw him in prison, to digest his indignities and cool his passions at leisure.

The conspirators flew to arms to liberate their leader. The friends of Vasco Nuñez were equally on the alert. The two parties drew out in battle array in the public square, and a sanguinary conflict was on the point of taking place. Fortunately there were some cool heads left in the colony. These interfered at the critical moment, representing to the angry adversaries that, if they fought among themselves, and diminished their already scanty numbers, even the conquerors must eventually fall a prey to the Indians.

Their remonstrances had effect. A parley ensued, and, after much noisy debate, a kind of compromise was made. Alonzo Perez was liberated, and the mutineers dispersed quietly to their homes. The next day, however, they were again in arms, and seized upon Bartolome Hurtado; but after a little while were prevailed upon to set him free. Their factious views seemed turned to a higher object. They broke forth into loud murmurs against Vasco Nuñez, complaining that he had not made a fair division of the gold and slaves taken in the late expeditions, and threatening to arrest him and bring him to account. Above all, they clamoured for an immediate distribution of ten thousand castellanos in gold, which yet remained unshared.

Vasco Nuñez understood too well the riotous nature of the people under him, and his own precarious hold on their obedience, to attempt to cope with them in this moment of turbulence. He shrewdly determined, therefore, to withdraw from the sight of the multitude, and to leave them to divide the spoil among themselves, trusting to their own strife for his security. That very night he sallied forth into the country, under pretence of going on a hunting expedition.

The next morning the mutineers found themselves in possession of the field. Alonzo Perez, the pragmatical ringleader, immediately assumed the command, seconded by the Bachelor Corral. Their first measure was to seize upon the ten thousand castellanos, and to divide them among the multitude, by way of securing their own popularity. The event proved the sagacity and forethought of Vasco Nuñez. Scarcely had these hot-headed inter-meddlers entered upon the partition of the gold, than a furious strife arose. Everyone was dissatisfied with his share, considering his merits entitled to peculiar recompense. Every attempt to appease the rabble only augmented their violence, and in their rage they swore that Vasco Nuñez had always shown more judgment and discrimination in his distributions to men of merit.

The adherents of the latter now ventured to lift up their voices; "Vasco Nuñez," said they, "won the gold by his enterprise and valour, and would have shared it with the brave and deserving; but these men have seized upon it by factious means, and would squander it upon their minions." The multitude, who in fact, admired the soldier-like qualities of Vasco Nuñez, displayed one of the customary reverses of popular feeling. The touchy Alonzo Perez, his coadjutor the Bachelor Corral, and several other of the ringleaders were seized, thrown in irons, and confined in the fortress; and Vasco Nuñez was recalled with loud acclamations to the settlement.

How long this pseudo commander might have been able to manage the unsteady populace it is impossible to say, but just at this juncture two ships arrived from Hispaniola, freighted with supplies, and bringing a reinforcement of one hundred and fifty men. They brought also a commission to Vasco Nuñez, signed by Miguel de Pasamonte, the royal treasurer of Hispaniola, to whom he had sent a private present of gold, constituting him captain-general of the colony. It is doubtful whether Pasamonte possessed the power to confer such a commission, though it is affirmed that the king had clothed him with it, as a kind of check upon the authority of the admiral Don Diego Columbus, then Governor of Hispaniola, of whose extensive sway in the new world the monarch was secretly jealous. At any rate, the treasurer appears to have acted in full confidence of the ultimate approbation of his sovereign.

Vasco Nuñez was rejoiced at receiving a commission which clothed him with at least the semblance of royal sanction. Feeling more assured in his situation, and being naturally of a generous and forgiving temper, he was easily prevailed upon, in his moment of exultation, to release and pardon Alonzo Perez, the Bachelor Corral, and the other ringleaders of the late commotions, and for a time the feuds and factions of this petty community were lulled to repose.

CHAPTER VII

Vasco Nuñez determines to seek the Sea beyond the Mountains.—[1513.]

THE temporary triumph of Vasco Nuñez was soon overcast by tidings received from Spain. His late colleague, the Alcalde Zamudio wrote him word that the Bachelor Enciso had carried his complaints to the foot of the throne, and succeeded in rousing the indignation of the king, and had obtained a sentence in his favour, condemning Vasco Nuñez in costs and damages. Zamudio informed him in addition, that he would be immediately summoned to repair to Spain, and answer in person the criminal charges advanced against him on account of the harsh treatment and probable death of the unfortunate Nicuesa.

Vasco Nuñez was at first stunned by this intelligence, which seemed at one blow to annihilate all his hopes and fortunes. He was a man, however, of prompt decision and intrepid spirit. The information received from Spain was private and informal, no order had yet arrived from the king, he was still master of his actions, and had control over the colony. One brilliant achievement might atone for all the past, and fix him in the favour of the monarch. Such an achievement was within his reach—the discovery of the southern sea. It is true, a thousand soldiers had been required for the expedition, but were he to wait for their arrival from Spain, his day of grace would be past. It was a desperate thing to undertake the task with the handful of men at his command, but the circumstances of the case were desperate. Fame, fortune, life itself, depended upon the successful and the prompt execution of the enterprise. To linger was to be lost.

Vasco Nuñez looked round upon the crew of daring and reckless adventurers that formed the colony, and chose one hundred and ninety of the most resolute and vigorous, and of those most devoted to his person. These he armed with swords, targets, cross bows, and arquebusses. He did not conceal from them the peril of the enterprise into which he was about to lead them; but the spirit of these Spanish adventurers was always roused by the idea of perilous and extravagant exploit. To aid his slender forces, he took with him a number of bloodhounds, which had been found to be terrific allies in Indian warfare.

The Spanish writers make particular mention of one of those animals, named Leoncico, which was a constant companion, and as it were body guard of Vasco Nuñez, and describe him as minutely as they would a favourite warrior. He was of a middle size, but immensely strong: of a dull yellow or reddish colour, with a black muzzle, and his body was scarred all over with wounds received in innumerable battles with the Indians. Vasco Nuñez always took him on his expeditions, and sometimes lent him to others, receiving for his services the same share of booty allotted to an armed man. In this way he gained by him, in the course of his campaigns, upwards of a thousand crowns. The Indians, it is said, had conceived such terror of this animal, that the very sight of him was sufficient to put a host of them to flight.[51]

In addition to these forces, Vasco Nuñez took with him a number of the Indians of Darien, whom he had won to him by kindness, and whose services were important, from their knowledge of the wilderness, and of the habits and resources of savage life. Such was the motley armament that set forth from the little colony of Darien, under the guidance of a daring, if not desperate commander, in quest of the great Pacific Ocean.

CHAPTER VIII

Expedition in quest of the Southern Sea.

IT was on the first of September that Vasco Nuñez embarked with his followers in a brigantine and nine large canoes or pirogues, followed by the cheers and good wishes of those who remained at the settlement. Standing to the northwestward, he arrived without accident at Coyba, the dominions of the cacique Careta, whose daughter he had received as a pledge of amity. That Indian beauty had acquired a great influence over Vasco Nuñez, and appears to have cemented his friendship with her father and her people. He was received by the cacique with open arms, and furnished with guides and warriors to aid him in his enterprise.

Vasco Nuñez left about half of his men at Coyba to guard the brigantine and canoes, while he should penetrate the wilderness with the residue. The importance of his present expedition, not merely as affecting his own fortunes, but as it were unfolding a mighty secret of nature, seems to have impressed itself upon his spirit, and to have given correspondent solemnity to his conduct. Before setting out upon his

march, he caused mass to be performed, and offered up prayers to God for the success of his perilous undertaking.

It was on the sixth of September, that he struck off for the
mountains. The march was difficult and toilsome in the extreme. The Spaniards, encumbered with the weight of their
armour and weapons, and oppressed by the heat of a tropical
climate, were obliged to climb rocky precipices, and to struggle through close and tangled forests. Their Indian allies
aided them by carrying their ammunition and provisions,
and by guiding them to the most practicable paths.

On the eighth of September they arrived at the village of
Ponca, the ancient enemy of Careta. The village was lifeless
and abandoned; the cacique and his people had fled to the
fastnesses of the mountains. The Spaniards remained here
several days to recruit the health of some of their number
who had fallen ill. It was necessary also to procure guides acquainted with the mountain wilderness they were approaching. The retreat of Ponca was at length discovered, and he
was prevailed upon, though reluctantly, to come to Vasco
Nuñez. The latter had a peculiar facility in winning the confidence and friendship of the natives. The cacique was soon
so captivated by his kindness, that he revealed to him in
secret all he knew of the natural riches of the country. He
assured him of the truth of what had been told him about a
great pechry or sea beyond the mountains, and gave him

several ornaments ingeniously wrought of fine gold, which had been brought from the countries upon its borders. He told him, moreover, that when he had attained the summit of a lofty ridge, to which he pointed, and which seemed to rise up to the skies, he would behold that sea spread out far below him.

Animated by the accounts, Vasco Nuñez procured fresh guides from the cacique, and prepared to ascend the mountains. Numbers of his men having fallen ill from fatigue and the heat of the climate, he ordered them to return slowly to Coyba, taking with him none but such as were in robust and vigorous health.

On the 20th of September, he again set forward through a broken rocky country, covered with a matted forest and intersected by deep and turbulent streams, many of which it was necessary to cross upon rafts.

So toilsome was the journey, that in four days they did not advance above ten leagues, and in the meantime they suffered excessively from hunger. At the end of this time they arrived at the province of a warlike cacique, named Quaraqua, who was at war with Ponca.

Hearing that a band of strangers were entering his territories, guided by the subjects of his inveterate foe, the cacique took the field with a large number of warriors, some armed with bows and arrows, others with long spears, or with double handed maces of palm wood, almost as heavy and hard as iron. Seeing the inconsiderable number of the Spaniards, they set upon them with furious yells, thinking to overcome them in an instant. The first discharge of fire-arms, however, struck them with dismay. They thought they were contending with demons who vomited forth thunder and lightning, especially when they saw their companions fall bleeding and dead beside them, without receiving any apparent blow. They took to headlong flight, and were hotly pursued by the Spaniards and their bloodhounds. Some were transfixed with lances, others hewn down with swords, and many were torn to pieces by the dogs, so that Quaraqua and six hundred of his warriors were left dead upon the field.

A brother of the cacique and several chiefs were taken prisoners. They were clad in robes of white cotton. Either from their effeminate dress, or from the accusations of their enemies, the Spaniards were induced to consider them guilty of unnatural crimes, and, in their abhorrence and disgust, gave them to be torn to pieces by the bloodhounds.[52]

It is also affirmed, that among the prisoners were several negroes, who had been slaves to the cacique. The Spaniards, we are told, were informed by the other captives, that these black men came from a region at no great distance, where there was a people of that colour with whom they were fre-quently at war. "These," adds the Spanish writer, "were the first negroes ever found in the New World, and I believe no others have since been discovered."[53]

After this sanguinary triumph, the Spaniards marched to the village of Quaraqua, where they found considerable booty in gold and jewels. Of this Vasco Nuñez reserved one-fifth for the crown, and shared the rest liberally among his followers. The village was at the foot of the last mountain that remained for them to climb: several of the Spaniards, however, were so disabled by the wounds they had received in battle, or so exhausted by the fatigue and hunger they had endured, that they were unable to proceed. They were obliged, therefore, reluctantly to remain in the village, within sight of the mountain-top that commanded the long-sought prospect. Vasco Nuñez selected fresh guides from among his prisoners, who were natives of the province, and sent back the subjects of Ponca. Of the band of Spaniards who had set out with him in this enterprise, sixty-seven alone remained in sufficient health and spirits for this last effort. These he ordered to retire early to repose, that they might be ready to set off at the cool and fresh hour of day-break, so as to reach the summit of the mountain before the noon-tide heat.

CHAPTER IX

Discovery of the Pacific Ocean.

THE day had scarcely dawned, when Vasco Nuñez and his followers set forth from the Indian village and began to climb the height. It was a severe and rugged toil for men so wayworn, but they were filled with new ardour at the idea of the triumphant scene that was so soon to repay them for all their hardships.

About ten o'clock in the morning they emerged from the thick forests through which they had hitherto struggled, and arrived at a lofty and airy region of the mountain. The bald summit alone remained to be ascended, and their guides pointed to a moderate eminence from which they said the southern sea was visible.

Upon this Vasco Nuñez commanded his followers to halt, and that no man should stir from his place. Then, with a palpitating heart, he ascended alone the bare mountain-top. On reaching the summit the long-desired prospect burst upon his view. It was as if a new world were unfolded to him, separated from all hitherto known by this mighty barrier of mountains. Below him extended a vast chaos of rock and forest, and green savannahs and wandering streams, while at a distance the waters of the promised ocean glittered in the morning sun.

At this glorious prospect Vasco Nuñez sank upon his knees, and poured out thanks to God for being the first European to whom it was given to make that great discovery. He then called his people to ascend: "Behold, my friends," said he, "that glorious sight which we have so much desired. Let us give thanks to God that he has granted us this great honour and advantage. Let us pray to him that he will guide and aid us to conquer the sea and land which we have discovered, and in which Christian has never entered to preach the holy doctrine of the Evangelists. As to yourselves, be as you have hitherto been, faithful and true to me, and by the favour of Christ you will become the richest Spaniards that have ever come to the Indies; you will render the greatest services to your king that ever vassal rendered to his lord; and you will have the eternal glory and advantage of all that is here discovered, conquered, and converted to our holy Catholic faith."

The Spaniards answered this speech by embracing Vasco Nuñez and promising to follow him to death. Among them was a priest, named Andres de Vara, who lifted up his voice and chanted *Te Deum laudamus*—the usual anthem of Spanish discoverers. The people, kneeling down, joined in the

strain with pious enthusiasm and tears of joy; and never did a
more sincere oblation rise to the Deity from a sanctified altar
than from that wild mountain summit. It was indeed one of
the most sublime discoveries that had yet been made in the
New World, and must have opened a boundless field of con-
jecture to the wondering Spaniards. The imagination delights
to picture forth the splendid confusion of their thoughts.
Was this the great Indian Ocean, studded with precious
islands, abounding in gold, in gems, and spices, and bordered
by the gorgeous cities and wealthy marts of the East? Or
was it some lonely sea locked up in the embraces of savage
uncultivated continents, and never traversed by a bark,
excepting the light pirogue of the Indian? The latter could
hardly be the case, for the natives had told the Spaniards of
golden realms, and populous and powerful and luxurious
nations upon its shores. Perhaps it might be bordered by
various people, civilized in fact, but differing from Europe in
their civilization; who might have peculiar laws and customs
and arts and sciences; who might form, as it were, a world of
their own, intercommuning by this mighty sea, and carrying
on commerce between their own islands and continents; but
who might exist in total ignorance and independence of the
other hemisphere.

Such may naturally have been the ideas suggested by the
sight of this unknown ocean. It was the prevalent belief of

the Spaniards, however, that they were the first Christians who had made the discovery. Vasco Nuñez, therefore, called upon all present to witness that he took possession of that sea, its islands, and surrounding lands, in the name of the sovereigns of Castile, and the notary of the expedition made a testimonial of the same, to which all present, to the number of sixty-seven men, signed their names. He then caused a fair and tall tree to be cut down and wrought into a cross, which was elevated on the spot from whence he had at first beheld the sea. A mound of stones was likewise piled up to serve as a monument, and the names of the Castilian sovereigns were carved on the neighbouring trees. The Indians beheld all these ceremonials and rejoicings in silent wonder, and, while they aided to erect the cross and pile up the mound of stones, marvelled exceedingly at the meaning of these monuments, little thinking that they marked the subjugation of their land.

The memorable event here recorded took place on the 26th of September, 1513; so that the Spaniards had been twenty days performing the journey from the province of Careta to the summit of the mountain, a distance which at present, it is said, does not require more than six days' travel. Indeed the isthmus in this neighbourhood is not more than eighteen leagues in breadth in its widest part, and in some places merely seven; but it consists of a ridge of extremely high and rugged mountains. When the discoverers traversed it, they had no route but the Indian paths, and often had to force their way amidst all kinds of obstacles, both from the savage country and its savage inhabitants. In fact, the details of this narrative sufficiently account for the slowness of their progress, and present an array of difficulties and perils, which, as has been well observed, none but those "men of iron" could have subdued and overcome.[54]

CHAPTER X

Vasco Nuñez marches to the shores of the South Sea.

HAVING taken possession of the Pacific Ocean and all its realms from the summit of the mountain, Vasco Nuñez now descended with his little band, to seek the regions of reputed wealth upon its shores. He had not proceeded far when he came to the province of a warlike cacique, named Cheapes, who, issuing forth at the head of his warriors, looked with scorn upon the scanty number of straggling Spaniards, and forbade them to set foot within his territories. Vasco Nuñez depended for safety upon his power of striking terror into the ignorant savages. Ordering his arquebusiers to the front, he poured a volley into the enemy, and then let loose the bloodhounds. The flash and noise of the firearms, and the sulphureous smoke which was carried by the wind among the Indians, overwhelmed them with dismay. Some fell down in a panic as though they had been struck by thunderbolts, the rest betook themselves to headlong flight.

Vasco Nuñez commanded his men to refrain from needless slaughter. He made many prisoners, and on arriving at the village, sent some of them in search of their cacique accompanied by several of his Indian guides. The latter informed Cheapes of the supernatural power of the Spaniards, assuring him that they exterminated with thunder and lightning all who dared to oppose them, but loaded all such as submitted to them with benefits. They advised him therefore, to throw himself upon their mercy and seek their friendship.

The cacique listened to their advice, and came trembling to the Spaniards, bringing with him five hundred pounds weight of wrought gold as a peace offering, for he had already learnt the value they set upon that metal. Vasco Nuñez received him with great kindness, and graciously accepted his gold, for which he gave him beads, hawks' bells, and looking glasses, making him, in his own conceit, the richest potentate on that side of the mountains.

Friendship being thus established between them, Vasco Nuñez remained at the village for a few days, sending back the guides who had accompanied him from Quaraqua, and ordering his people whom he had left at that place to rejoin him. In the meantime he sent out three scouting parties of twelve men each, under Francisco Pizarro, Juan de Escary and Alonzo Martin de Don Benito, to explore the surrounding country and discover the best route to the sea. Alonzo Martin was the most successful. After two days journey, he came to a beach, where he found two large canoes lying high

and dry, without any water being in sight. While the Spaniards were regarding these canoes, and wondering why they
should be so far on land, the tide, which rises to a great
height on that coast, came rapidly in and set them afloat;
upon this, Alonzo Martin stepped into one of them, and
called his companions to bear witness that he was the first
European that embarked upon that sea; his example was
followed by one Blas de Etienza, who called them likewise to
testify that he was the second.[55]

We mention minute particulars of the kind, as being characteristic of these extraordinary enterprises, and of the extraordinary people who undertook them. The humblest of
these Spanish adventurers seemed actuated by a swelling
and ambitious spirit, that rose superior at times to mere
sordid considerations, and aspired to share the glory of these
great discoveries. The scouting party having thus explored a
direct route to the sea coast, returned to report their success
to their commander.

Vasco Nuñez being rejoined by his men from Quaraqua
now left the greater part of his followers to repose and
recover from their sickness and fatigues in the village of
Cheapes, and, taking with him twenty-six Spaniards, well
armed, he set out on the twenty-ninth of September, for the
sea coast, accompanied by the cacique and a number of his
warriors. The thick forest which covered the mountains,

descended to the very margin of the sea, surrounding and
overshadowing the wide and beautiful bays that penetrated
far into the land. The whole coast, as far as the eye could
reach, was perfectly wild, the sea without a sail, and both
seemed never to have been under the dominion of civilized
man.

Vasco Nuñez arrived on the borders of one of those vast
bays, to which he gave the name of Saint Michael, it being
discovered on that saint's day. The tide was out, the water
was above half a league distant, and the intervening beach
was covered with mud; he seated himself, therefore, under
the shade of the forest trees until the tide should rise. After
awhile, the water came rushing in with great impetuosity,
and soon reached nearly to the place where the Spaniards
were reposing. Upon this Vasco Nuñez rose and took a banner, on which were painted the Virgin and child, and under
them the arms of Castile and Leon; then drawing his sword
and throwing his buckler on his shoulder, he marched into
the sea until the water reached above his knees, and waving
his banner, exclaimed with a loud voice; "Long live the high
and mighty monarchs Don Ferdinand and Donna Juanna,
sovereigns of Castile, of Leon, and of Arragon, in whose
name, and for the royal crown of Castile I take real, and
corporal, and actual possession of these seas, and lands, and
coasts, and ports, and islands of the South, and all thereunto

annexed; and of the kingdoms and provinces which do or may appertain to them in whatever manner, or by whatever right or title, ancient or modern, in times past, present, or to come, without any contradiction; and if other prince or captain, christian or infidel, or of any law, sect or condition whatsoever, shall pretend any right to these lands and seas, I am ready and prepared to maintain and defend them in the name of the Castilian sovereigns, present and future, whose is the empire and dominion over these Indias, islands, and terra firma, northern and southern, with all their seas both at the arctic and antarctic poles, on either side of the equinoxial line, whether within or without the tropics of Cancer and Capricorn, both now and in all times, as long as the world endures, and until the final day of judgment of all mankind."

This swelling declaration and defiance being uttered with a loud voice, and no one appearing to dispute his pretensions, Vasco Nuñez called upon his companions to bear witness of the fact of his having duly taken possession. They all declared themselves ready to defend his claim to the uttermost, as became true and loyal vassals to the Castilian sovereigns; and the notary having drawn up a document for the occasion, they all subscribed it with their names.

This done, they advanced to the margin of the sea, and stooping down tasted its waters. When they found, that, though severed by intervening mountains and continents, they were salt like the seas of the north, they felt assured that they had indeed discovered an ocean, and again returned thanks to God.

Having concluded all these ceremonies, Vasco Nuñez drew a dagger from his girdle and cut a cross on a tree which grew within the water, and made two other crosses on two adjacent trees in honour of the Three Persons of the Trinity, and in token of possession. His followers likewise cut crosses on many of the trees of the adjacent forest, and lopped off branches with their swords to bear away as trophies.[56]

Such was the singular medley of chivalrous and religious ceremonial, with which these Spanish adventurers took possession of the vast Pacific Ocean, and all its lands—a scene strongly characteristic of the nation and the age.

CHAPTER XI

Adventures of Vasco Nuñez on the borders of the Pacific Ocean.

WHILE he made the village of Cheapes his headquarters, Vasco Nuñez foraged the adjacent country and obtained considerable quantity of gold from the natives. Encouraged by his success, he undertook to explore by sea the borders of a neighbouring gulf of great extent, which penetrated far into the land. The cacique Cheapes warned him of the danger of venturing to sea in the stormy season, which comprises the months of October, November, and December, assuring him that he had beheld many canoes swallowed up in the mighty waves and whirlpools, which at such times render the gulf almost unnavigable.

These remonstrances were unavailing: Vasco Nuñez expressed a confident belief that God would protect him, seeing that his voyage was to redound to the propagation of the faith, and the augmentation of the power of the Castilian monarchs over the infidels; and in truth this bigoted reliance on the immediate protection of heaven seems to have been in a great measure the cause of the extravagant daring of

the Spaniards in their expeditions in those days, whether
against Moors or Indians.

Seeing his representations of no effect, Cheapes volunteered to take part in this perilous cruise, lest he should
appear wanting in courage, or in good will to his guest.
Accompanied by the cacique, therefore, Vasco Nuñez embarked on the 17th of October with sixty of his men in nine
canoes, managed by Indians, leaving the residue of his followers to recruit their health and strength in the village
of Cheapes.

Scarcely however had they put forth on the broad bosom
of the gulf when the wisdom of the cacique's advice was
made apparent. The wind began to blow freshly, raising a
heavy and tumultuous sea, which broke in roaring and
foaming surges on the rocks and reefs, and among the numerous islets with which the gulf was studded. The light
canoes were deeply laden with men unskilled in their management. It was frightful to those in one canoe to behold
their companions, one instant tossed on high on the breaking
crest of a wave, the next plunging out of sight, as if swallowed in a watery abyss. The Indians themselves, though
almost amphibious in their habits, showed signs of consternation; for amidst these rocks and breakers even the skill of
the expert swimmer would be of little avail. At length the
Indians succeeded in tying the canoes in pairs, side by side,

to prevent their being overturned, and in this way they kept afloat, until towards evening they were enabled to reach a small island. Here they landed, and fastening the canoes to the rocks, or to small trees that grew upon the shore, they sought an elevated dry place, and stretched themselves to take repose. They had but escaped from one danger to encounter another. Having been for a long time accustomed to the sea on the northern side of the isthmus, where there is little, if any, rise or fall of the tide, they had neglected to take any precaution against such an occurrence. In a little while they were awakened from their sleep by the rapid rising of the water. They shifted their situation to a higher ground, but the waters continued to gain upon them, the breakers rushing and roaring and foaming upon the beach like so many monsters of the deep seeking for their prey. Nothing, it is said, can be more dismal and appalling than the sullen bellowing of the sea among the islands of that gulf at the rising and falling of the tide. By degrees, rock after rock, and one sand bank after another disappeared, until the sea covered the whole island, and rose almost to the girdles of the Spaniards. Their situation was now agonizing. A little more and the waters would overwhelm them: or, even as it was, the least surge might break over them and sweep them from their unsteady footing. Fortunately the wind had lulled, and the sea, having risen above the rocks which had fretted

it, was calm. The tide had reached its height and began to
subside, and after a time they heard the retiring waves
beating against the rocks below them.

When the day dawned they sought their canoes; but here
a sad spectacle met their eyes. Some were broken to pieces,
others yawning open in many parts. The clothing and food
left in them had been washed away, and replaced by sand
and water. The Spaniards gazed on the scene in mute despair; they were faint and weary, and needed food and repose, but famine and labour awaited them, even if they
should escape with their lives. Vasco Nuñez, however, rallied
their spirits, and set them an example by his own cheerful
exertions. Obeying his directions, they set to work to repair,
in the best manner they were able, the damages of the
canoes. Such as were not too much shattered they bound and
braced up with their girdles, with slips of the bark of trees,
or with the tough long stalks of certain sea weeds. They then
peeled off the bark from the small sea plants, pounded it
between stones, and mixed it with grass, and with this endeavoured to caulk the seams and stop the leaks that remained. When they re-embarked, their numbers weighed
down the canoes almost to the water's edge, and as they
rose and sank with the swelling waves there was danger of
their being swallowed up. All day they laboured with the
sea, suffering excessively from the pangs of hunger and

thirst, and at nightfall they landed in a corner of the gulf, near the abode of a cacique named Túmaco. Leaving a part of his men to guard the canoes, Vasco Nuñez set out with the residue for the Indian town. He arrived there about midnight, but the inhabitants were on the alert to defend their habitations. The fire-arms and dogs soon put them to flight, and the Spaniards pursuing them with their swords, drove them howling into the woods. In the village were found provisions in abundance, beside a considerable amount of gold and a great quantity of pearls, many of them of a large size. In the house of the cacique were several huge shells of mother of pearl, and four pearl oysters quite fresh, which showed that there was a pearl fishery in the neighbourhood. Eager to learn the sources of this wealth, Vasco Nuñez sent several of the Indians of Cheapes in search of the cacique, who traced him to a wild retreat among the rocks. By their persuasions Túmaco sent his son, a fine young savage, as a mediator. The latter returned to his father loaded with presents, and extolling the benignity of these superhuman beings, who had shown themselves so terrible in battle. By these means, and by a mutual exchange of presents, a friendly intercourse was soon established. Among other things the cacique gave Vasco Nuñez jewels of gold weighing six hundred and fourteen crowns, and two hundred pearls of great size and beauty, excepting that they were somewhat discoloured in consequence of the oysters having been opened by fire.

The cacique seeing the value which the Spaniards set upon the pearls, sent a number of his men to fish for them at a place about ten miles distant. Certain of the Indians were trained from their youth to this purpose, so as to become expert divers, and to acquire the power of remaining a long time beneath the water. The largest pearls are generally found in the deepest water, sometimes in three and four fathoms, and are only sought in calm weather; the smaller sort are found at the depth of two and three feet, and the oysters containing them are often driven in quantities on the beach during violent storms.

The party of pearl divers sent by the cacique consisted of thirty Indians, with whom Vasco Nuñez sent six Spaniards as eye-witnesses. The sea, however, was so furious at that stormy season that the divers dared not venture into the deep water. Such a number of the shell-fish, however, had been driven on shore, that they collected enough to yield pearls to the value of twelve marks of gold. They were small, but exceedingly beautiful, being newly taken and uninjured by fire. A number of these shell-fish and their pearls were selected to be sent to Spain as specimens.

In reply to the inquiries of Vasco Nuñez, the cacique informed him that the coast which he saw stretching to the west continued onwards without end, and that far to the south there was a country abounding in gold, where the inhabitants made use of certain quadrupeds to carry burthens. He moulded a figure of clay to represent these animals, which some of the Spaniards supposed to be a deer, others a camel, others a tapir, for as yet they knew nothing of the llama, the native beast of burthen of South America. This was the second intimation received by Vasco Nuñez of the great empire of Peru; and, while it confirmed all that had been told him by the son of Comagre, it filled him with glowing anticipations of the glorious triumphs that awaited him.

CHAPTER XII

Further adventures and exploits of Vasco Nuñez on the borders of the Pacific Ocean.

L EST any ceremonial should be wanting to secure this grand discovery to the crown of Spain, Vasco Nuñez determined to sally from the gulf and take possession of the mainland beyond. The cacique Túmaco furnished him with a canoe of state, formed from the trunk of an enormous tree, and managed by a great number of Indians. The handles of the paddles were inlaid with small pearls, a circumstance which Vasco Nuñez caused his companions to testify before the notary, that it might be reported to the sovereigns as a proof of the wealth of this newly discovered sea.[57]

Departing in the canoe on the 29th of October, he was piloted cautiously by the Indians along the borders of the gulf, over drowned lands where the sea was fringed by inundated forests, and as still as a pool. Arrived at the point of the gulf, Vasco Nuñez landed on a smooth sandy beach, laved by the waters of the broad ocean, and, with buckler on arm, sword in hand, and banner displayed, again marched into the sea and took possession of it, with like ceremonials to those observed in the Gulf of St. Michael's.

The Indians now pointed to a line of land rising above the horizon about four or five leagues distant, which they described as being a great island, the principal one of an archipelago. The whole group abounded with pearls, but those taken on the coasts of this island were represented as being of immense size, many of them as large as a man's eye, and found in shell-fish as big as bucklers. This island and the surrounding cluster of small ones, they added, were under the dominion of a tyrannical and puissant cacique, who often, during the calm seasons, made descents upon the mainland with fleets of canoes, plundering and desolating the coasts, and carrying the people into captivity.

Vasco Nuñez gazed with an eager and wistful eye at this land of riches, and would have immediately undertaken an expedition to it, had not the Indians represented the danger of venturing on such a voyage in that tempestuous season in their frail canoes. His own recent experience convinced him of the wisdom of their remonstrances. He postponed his visit, therefore, to a future occasion, when, he assured his allies, he would avenge them upon this tyrant invader, and deliver their coasts from his maraudings. In the meantime he gave to this island the name of Isla Rica, and the little archipelago surrounding it the general appellation of the Pearl Islands.

On the third of November Vasco Nuñez departed from the province of Túmaco, to visit other parts of the coast. He embarked with his men in the canoes, accompanied by Cheapes and his Indians, and guided by the son of Túmaco, who had become strongly attached to the Spaniards. The young man piloted them along an arm of the sea, wide in some places, but in others obstructed by groves of mangrove trees, which grew within the water and interlaced their branches from shore to shore, so that at times the Spaniards were obliged to cut a passage with their swords.

At length they entered a great and turbulent river, which they ascended with difficulty, and, early the next morning surprised a village on its banks, making the cacique Teaochan, prisoner; who purchased their favour and kind treatment by a quantity of gold and pearls, and an abundant supply of provisions. As it was the intention of Vasco Nuñez to abandon the shores of the Southern Ocean at this place, and to strike across the mountains for Darien, he took leave of Cheapes and of the youthful son of Túmaco, who were to return to their houses in the canoes. He sent at the same time, a message to his men, whom he had left in the village of Cheapes, appointing a place in the mountains where they were to rejoin him on his way back to Darien.

The talent of Vasco Nuñez for conciliating and winning the good will of the savages is often mentioned, and to such a degree had he exerted it in the present instance, that the two chieftains shed tears at parting. Their conduct had a favourable effect upon the cacique Teaochan; he entertained Vasco Nuñez with the most devoted hospitality during three days that he remained in his village; when about to depart he furnished him with a stock of provisions sufficient for several days, as his route would lay over rocky and sterile mountains. He sent also a numerous band of his subjects to carry the burthens of the Spaniards. These he placed under the command of his son, whom he ordered never to separate from the strangers, nor to permit any of his men to return without the consent of Vasco Nuñez.

CHAPTER XIII

Vasco Nuñez sets out on his return across the mountains.—
His contests with the Savages.

URNING their backs upon the Southern Sea, the
Spaniards now began painfully to clamber the
rugged mountains on their return to Darien.

In the early part of their route an unlooked-
for suffering awaited them: there was neither brook nor
fountain nor standing pool. The burning heat, which produced intolerable thirst, had dried up all the mountain torrents, and they were tantalized by the sight of naked and
dusty channels where water had once flowed in abundance.
Their sufferings at length increased to such a height that
many threw themselves fevered and panting upon the earth,
and were ready to give up the ghost. The Indians, however,
encouraged them to proceed, by hopes of speedy relief, and
after awhile, turning aside from the direct course, led them
into a deep and narrow glen, refreshed and cooled by a
fountain which bubbled out of a cleft of the rocks.

While refreshing themselves at the fountain, and reposing
in the little valley, they learnt from their guides that they

were in the territories of a powerful chief named Poncra, famous for his riches. The Spaniards had already heard of the golden stores of this Crœsus of the mountains, and being now refreshed and invigorated, pressed forward with eagerness for his village.

The cacique and most of his people fled at their approach, but they found an earnest of his wealth in the deserted houses, amounting to the value of three thousand crowns in gold. Their avarice thus whetted, they despatched Indians in search of Poncra, who found him trembling in his secret retreat, and partly by threats, partly by promises, prevailed upon him and three of his principal subjects to come to Vasco Nuñez. He was a savage, it is said, so hateful of aspect, so misshapen in body and deformed in all his members, that he was hideous to behold. The Spaniards endeavoured by gentle means to draw from him information of the places from whence he had procured his gold. He professed utter ignorance in the matter, declaring that the gold found in his village had been gathered by his predecessors in times long past, and that as he himself set no value on the metal, he had never troubled himself to seek it. The Spaniards resorted to menaces, and even, it is said, to tortures, to compel him to betray his reputed treasures, but with no better success. Disappointed in their expectations, and enraged at his supposed obstinacy, they listened too readily to charges

advanced against him by certain caciques of the neighbourhood, who represented him as a monster of cruelty, and as
guilty of crimes repugnant to nature;[58] whereupon, in the
heat of the moment, they gave him and his three companions, who were said to be equally guilty, to be torn in pieces
by the dogs.—A rash and cruel sentence, given on the evidence of avowed enemies; and which, however it may be
palliated by the alleged horror and disgust of the Spaniards
at the imputed crimes of the cacique, bears too much the
stamp of haste and passion, and remains a foul blot on the
character of Vasco Nuñez.

The Spaniards remained for thirty days reposing in the
village of the unfortunate Poncra, during which time they
were rejoined by their companions, who had been left behind
at the village of Cheapes. They were accompanied by a
cacique of the mountains, who had lodged and fed them,
and made them presents of the value of two thousand crowns
in gold. This hospitable savage approached Vasco Nuñez with
a serene countenance, and taking him by the hand, "Behold,"
said he, "most valiant and powerful chief, I bring thee thy
companions safe and well, as they entered under my roof.
May he who made the thunder and lightning, and who gives
us the fruits of the earth, preserve thee and thine in safety!"
So saying, he raised his eyes to the sun, as if he worshipped
that as his deity and the dispenser of all temporal blessings.[59]

Departing from this village, and being still accompanied by the Indians of Teaochan, the Spaniards now bent their course along the banks of the river Comagre, which descends the northern side of the Isthmus, and flows through the territories of the cacique of the same name. This wild stream, which in the course of ages had worn a channel through the deep clefts and ravines of the mountains, was bordered by precipices, or overhung by shagged forests: they soon abandoned it, therefore, and wandered on without any path, but guided by the Indians. They had to climb terrible precipices, and to descend into deep valleys, darkened by thick forests and beset by treacherous morasses, where, but for their guides, they might have been smothered in the mire.

In the course of this rugged journey they suffered excessively in consequence of their own avarice. They had been warned of the sterility of the country they were about to traverse, and of the necessity of providing amply for the journey. When they came to lade the Indians, however, who bore their burdens, their only thought was how to convey the most treasure; and they grudged even a slender supply of provisions, as taking up the place of an equal weight of gold. The consequences were soon felt. The Indians could carry but small burdens, and at the same time assisted to consume the scanty stock of food which formed part of their

load. Scarcity and famine ensued, and relief was rarely to be
procured, for the villages on this elevated part of the mountains were scattered and poor, and nearly destitute of provisions. They held no communication with each other; each
contenting itself with the scanty produce of its own fields
and forest. Some were entirely deserted; at other places, the
inhabitants, forced from their retreats, implored pardon, and
declared they had hidden themselves through shame, not
having the means of properly entertaining such celestial
visitors. They brought peace-offerings of gold, but no provisions. For once the Spaniards found that even their darling
gold could fail to cheer their drooping spirits. Their sufferings from hunger became intense, and many of their Indian
companions sank down and perished by the way. At length
they reached a village where they were enabled to obtain
supplies, and where they remained thirty days, to recruit
their wasted strength.

CHAPTER XIV

*Enterprise against Tubanama, the warlike Cacique of
the Mountains.—Return to Darien.*

THE Spaniards had now to pass through the territories of Tubanama, the most potent and warlike cacique of the mountains. This was the same chieftain of whom a formidable character had been given by the young Indian prince, who first informed Vasco Nuñez of the southern sea. He had erroneously represented the dominions of Tubanama as lying beyond the mountains: and when he dwelt upon the quantities of gold to be found in them, had magnified the dangers that would attend any attempt to pass their borders. The name of this redoubtable cacique was in fact a terror throughout the country; and when Vasco Nuñez looked round upon his handful of pale and emaciated followers, he doubted whether even the superiority of their weapons, and their military skill, would enable them to cope with Tubanama and his armies in open contest. He resolved, therefore, to venture upon a perilous stratagem. When he made it known to his men, everyone pressed forward to engage in it. Choosing seventy of the most vigorous, he ordered the rest to maintain their post in the village.

As soon as night had fallen he departed silently and secretly with his chosen band, and made his way with such rapidity through the labyrinths of the forests and the defiles of the mountains, that he arrived in the neighbourhood of the residence of Tubanama by the following evening, though at the distance of two regular days' journey.

There waiting until midnight he assailed the village suddenly, and with success, so as to surprise and capture the cacique and his whole family, in which were eighty females. When Tubanama found himself a prisoner in the hands of the Spaniards, he lost all presence of mind, and wept bitterly. The Indian allies of Vasco Nuñez beholding their once dreaded enemy thus fallen and captive, now urged that he should be put to death, accusing him of various crimes and cruelties. Vasco Nuñez pretended to listen to their prayers, and gave orders that his captive should be tied hand and foot, and given to the dogs. The cacique approached him trembling, and laid his hand upon the pommel of his sword. "Who can pretend, "said he, "to strive with one who bears this weapon, which can cleave a man asunder with a blow? Ever since thy fame has reached among these mountains have I reverenced thy valour. Spare my life, and thou shalt have all the gold I can procure."

Vasco Nuñez, whose anger was assumed, was readily pacified. As soon as the day dawned, the cacique gave him
armlets and other jewels of gold to the value of three thousand crowns, and sent messengers throughout his dominions
ordering his subjects to aid in paying his ransom. The poor
Indians, with their accustomed loyalty hastened in crowds,
bringing their golden ornaments, until in the course of three
days they had produced an amount equal to six thousand
crowns. This done, Vasco Nuñez set the cacique at liberty,
bestowing on him several European trinkets, with which he
considered himself richer than he had been with all his gold.
Nothing would draw from him, however, the disclosure of
the mines from whence this treasure was procured. He declared that it came from the territories of his neighbours,
where gold and pearls were to be found in abundance; but
that his lands produced nothing of the kind. Vasco Nuñez
doubted his sincerity, and secretly caused the brooks and
rivers in his dominions to be searched, where gold was found
in such quantities that he determined, at a future time, to
found two settlements in the neighbourhood.

On parting with Tubanama, the cacique sent his son with
the Spaniards to learn their language and religion. It is said
also, that the Spaniards carried off his eighty women; but
of this particular fact Oviedo, who writes with the papers
of Vasco Nuñez before him, says nothing. He affirms, gen-

erally, however, that the Spaniards, throughout this expedition, were not scrupulous in their dealings with the wives and daughters of the Indians; and adds, that in this their commander set them the example.[60]

Having returned to the village where he had left the greater part of his men, Vasco Nuñez resumed his homeward march. His people were feeble and exhausted, and several of them sick; so that some had to be carried and others led by the arms. He himself was part of the time afflicted by a fever, and had to be borne in a hammock on the shoulders of the Indians.

Proceeding thus slowly and toilfully, they at length arrived on the northern seacoast, at the territories of their ally, Comagre. The old cacique was dead, and had been succeeded by his son, the same intelligent youth who had first given information of the southern sea and the kingdom of Peru. The young chief, who had embraced Christianity, received them with great hospitality, making them presents of gold. Vasco Nuñez gave him trinkets in return, and a shirt and a soldier's cloak; with which, says Peter Martyr, he thought himself half a god among his naked countrymen. After having reposed for a few days, Vasco Nuñez proceeded to Ponca, where he heard that a ship and caravel had arrived at Darien from Hispaniola, with reinforcements and supplies. Hastening, therefore, to Coyba, the territories of his ally, Careta, he embarked on the 18th of January, 1514, with twenty of his men, in the brigantine which he had left there, and arrived at Santa Maria de la Antigua, in the river of Darien, on the following day. All the inhabitants came forth to receive him; and when they heard the news of the great southern sea, and of his returning from its shores laden with pearls and gold, there were no bounds to their joy. He immediately despatched the ship and caravel to Coyba for the companions he had left behind, who brought with them the remaining booty, consisting of gold and pearls, mantles, hammocks, and other articles of cotton, and a great number of captives of both sexes. A fifth of the spoil was set apart for the crown; the rest was shared, in just proportions, among those who had been in the expedition, and those who had remained at Darien. All were contented with their allotment, and elated with the prospects of still greater gain from future enterprises.

Thus ended one of the most remarkable expeditions of the early discoverers. The intrepidity of Vasco Nuñez in penetrating, with a handful of men, far into the interior of a wild and mountainous country, peopled by warlike tribes: his skill in managing his band of rough adventurers, stimulating their valour, enforcing their obedience, and attaching their affections, shows him to have possessed great qualities as a general. We are told that he was always foremost in peril, and the last to quit the field. He shared the toils and dangers of the meanest of his followers, treating them with frank affability; watching, fighting, fasting, and labouring with them; visiting and consoling such as were sick or infirm, and dividing all his gains with fairness and liberality. He was chargeable at times with acts of bloodshed and injustice, but it is probable that these were often called for as measures of safety and precaution; he certainly offended less against humanity than most of the early discoverers; and the unbounded amity and confidence reposed in him by the natives, when they became intimately acquainted with his character, speak strongly in favour of his kind treatment of them.

The character of Vasco Nuñez had, in fact, risen with his circumstances, and now assumed a nobleness and grandeur from the discovery he had made, and the important charge it had devolved upon him. He no longer felt himself a mere soldier of fortune, at the head of a band of adventurers, but a great commander conducting an immortal enterprise. "Behold," says old Peter Martyr, "Vasco Nuñez de Balboa, at once transformed from a rash roister to a politic and discreet captain:" and thus it is that men are often made by their fortunes; that is to say, their latent qualities are brought out, and shaped and strengthened by events, and by the necessity of every exertion to cope with the greatness of their destiny.

CHAPTER XV

Transactions in Spain.—Pedrarias Davila appointed to the
command of Darien.—Tidings received in Spain
of the discovery of the Pacific Ocean.

ASCO NUÑEZ DE BALBOA now flattered himself that he had made a discovery calculated to silence all his enemies at court, and to elevate him to the highest favour with his sovereign. He wrote letters to the king, giving a detail of his expedition, and setting forth all that he had seen or heard of this Southern Sea, and of the rich countries upon its borders. Beside the royal fifths of the profits of the expedition, he prepared a present for the sovereign, in the name of himself and his companions, consisting of the largest and most precious pearls they had collected. As a trusty and intelligent envoy to bear these tidings, he chose Pedro de Arbolancha, an old and tried friend, who had accompanied him in his toils and dangers, and was well acquainted with all his transactions.

The fate of Vasco Nuñez furnishes a striking instance how prosperity and adversity, how even life and death hang bal-

anced upon a point of time, and are affected by the improve-
ment or neglect of moments. Unfortunately, the ship which
was to convey the messenger to Spain lingered in port until
the beginning of March; a delay which had a fatal influence
on the fortunes of Vasco Nuñez. It is necessary here to cast
an eye back upon the events which had taken place in Spain
while he was employed in his conquests and discoveries.

The Bachelor Enciso had arrived in Castile full of his
wrongs and indignities. He had friends at court, who aided
him in gaining a ready hearing, and he lost not a moment
in availing himself of it. He declaimed eloquently upon the
alleged usurpation of Vasco Nuñez, and represented him as
governing the colony by force and fraud. It was in vain that
the Alcalde Zamudio, the ancient colleague and the envoy
of Vasco Nuñez, attempted to speak in his defence; he was
unable to cope with the facts and arguments of the Bachelor,
who was a pleader by profession, and now pleaded his own
cause. The king determined to send a new governor to
Darien, with power to inquire into and remedy all abuses.
For this office he chose Don Pedro Arias Davila, commonly
called Pedrarias.[61] He was a native of Segovia, who had been
brought up in the royal household, and had distinguished
himself as a brave soldier, both in the war in Granada
and at the taking of Oran and Bugia in Africa. He possessed those personal accomplishments which captivate the

soldiery, and was called *el Galan*, for his gallant array and courtly demeanour, and *el Justador*, or *the Tilter*, for his dexterity in jousts and tournaments. These, it must be admitted, were not the qualifications most adapted for the government of rude and factious colonies in a wilderness; but he had an all-powerful friend in the Bishop Fonseca. The Bishop was as thoroughgoing in patronage as in persecution. He assured the king that Pedrarias had understanding equal to his valour; that he was as capable of managing the affairs of peace as of war, and that, having been brought up in the royal household, his loyalty might be implicitly relied on.

Scarcely had Don Pedrarias been appointed, when Cayzedo and Colmenares arrived on their mission from Darien, to communicate the intelligence received from the son of the cacique Comagre, of the Southern Sea beyond the mountains, and to ask one thousand men to enable Vasco Nuñez to make the discovery.

The avarice and ambition of Ferdinand were inflamed by the tidings. He rewarded the bearers of the intelligence, and, after consulting with Bishop Fonseca, resolved to despatch immediately a powerful armada, with twelve hundred men, under the command of Pedrarias, to accomplish the enterprise.

Just about this time the famous Gonsalvo Hernandez de

Cordova, commonly called the Great Captain, was preparing
to return to Naples, where the allies of Spain had experienced a signal defeat, and had craved the assistance of this
renowned general to retrieve their fortunes. The chivalry of
Spain thronged to enlist under the banner of Gonsalvo. The
Spanish nobles, with their accustomed prodigality, sold or
mortgaged their estates to buy gorgeous armour, silks, bro-
cades, and other articles of martial pomp and luxury, that
they might figure, with becoming magnificence, in the campaigns of Italy. The armament was on the point of sailing
for Naples with this host of proud and gallant spirits, when
the jealous mind of Ferdinand took offence at the enthusiasm
thus shown towards his general, and he abruptly counter-
manded the expedition. The Spanish cavaliers were overwhelmed with disappointment at having their dreams of
glory thus suddenly dispelled; when, as if to console them,
the enterprise of Pedrarias was set on foot, and opened a
different career of adventure. The very idea of an unknown
sea and splendid empire, where never European ship had
sailed or foot had trodden, broke upon the imagination with
the vague wonders of an Arabian tale. Even the countries
already known, in the vicinity of the settlement of Darien,
were described in the usual terms of exaggeration. Gold was
said to lie on the surface of the ground, or to be gathered
with nets out of the brooks and rivers; insomuch that the

region hitherto called Terra Firma, now received the pompous and delusive appellation of Castilla del Oro, or Golden Castile.

Excited by these reports, many of the youthful cavaliers, who had prepared for the Italian campaign, now offered themselves as volunteers to Don Pedrarias. He accepted their services, and appointed Seville as the place of assemblage. The streets of that ancient city soon swarmed with young and noble cavaliers splendidly arrayed, full of spirits, and eager for the sailing of the Indian armada. Pedrarias, on his arrival at Seville, made a general review of his forces, and was embarrassed to find that the number amounted to three thousand. He had been limited in his first armament to twelve hundred; on representing the nature of the case, however, the number was extended to fifteen hundred; but through influence, entreaty and stratagem, upwards of two thousand eventually embarked.[62] Happy did he think himself who could in any manner, and by any means, get admitted on board of the squadron. Nor was this eagerness for the enterprise confined merely to young and buoyant and ambitious adventurers; we are told that there were many covetous old men, who offered to go at their own expense, without seeking any pay from the king. Thus every eye was turned with desire to this squadron of modern Argonauts, as it lay anchored on the bosom of the Guadalquiver.

The pay and appointments of Don Pedrarias Davila were on the most liberal scale, and no expense was spared in fitting out the armament; for the objects of the expedition were both colonization and conquest. Artillery and powder were procured from Malaga. Beside the usual weapons, such as muskets, crossbows, swords, pikes, lances and Neapolitan targets, there was armour devised of quilted cotton, as being light and better adapted to the climate, and sufficiently proof against the weapons of the Indians; and wooden bucklers from the Canary islands, to ward off the poisoned arrows of the Caribs.

Santa Maria de la Antigua was, by royal ordinance, elevated into the metropolitan city of Golden Castile, and a Franciscan friar, named Juan de Quevedo was appointed as bishop, with powers to decide in all cases of conscience. A number of friars were nominated to accompany him, and he was provided with the necessary furniture and vessels for a chapel.

Among the various regulations made for the good of the infant colony, it was ordained that no lawyers should be admitted there, it having been found at Hispaniola and elsewhere, that they were detrimental to the welfare of the settlements, by fomenting disputes and litigations. The judicial affairs were to be entirely confided to the Licentiate Gaspar de Espinosa, who was to officiate as Alcalde Mayor or chief judge.

Don Pedrarias had intended to leave his wife in Spain. Her name was Doña Isabella de Bobadilla; she was niece to the Marchioness de Moya, a great favourite of the late Queen Isabella, who had been instrumental in persuading her royal mistress to patronize Columbus.[63] Her niece partook of her high and generous nature. She refused to remain behind in selfish security, but declared that she would accompany her husband in every peril, whether by sea or land. This self-devotion is the more remarkable when it is considered that she was past the romantic period of youth; and that she had a family of four sons and four daughters, whom she left behind her in Spain.

Don Pedrarias was instructed to use great indulgence towards the people of Darien, who had been the followers of Nicuesa, and to remit the royal tithe of all the gold they might have collected previous to his arrival. Towards Vasco Nuñez de Balboa alone the royal countenance was stern and severe. Pedrarias was to depose him from his assumed authority, and to call him to strict account before the Alcalde Mayor, Gaspar de Espinosa, for his treatment of the Bachelor Enciso.

The splendid fleet, consisting of fifteen sail, weighed anchor at St. Lucar on the 12th of April, 1514, and swept proudly out of the Guadalquiver, thronged with the chivalrous adventurers for Golden Castile. But a short time had

elapsed after its departure, when Pedro Arbolancho arrived
with the tardy missions of Vasco Nuñez. Had he arrived
a few days sooner, how different might have been the
fortunes of his friend!

He was immediately admitted to the royal presence, where
he announced the adventurous and successful expedition of
Vasco Nuñez, and laid before the king the pearls and golden
ornaments which he had brought as the first fruits of the
discovery. King Ferdinand listened with charmed attention
to this tale of unknown seas and wealthy realms added to
his empire. It filled, in fact, the imaginations of the most
sage and learned with golden dreams, and anticipations of
unbounded riches. Old Peter Martyr, who received letters
from his friends in Darien, and communicated by word of
mouth with those who came from thence, writes to Leo the
Tenth in exulting terms of this event. "Spain," says he, "will
hereafter be able to satisfy with pearls the greedy appetite
of such as in wanton pleasures are like unto Cleopatra and
Æsopus; so that henceforth we shall neither envy nor reverence the nice fruitfulness of Trapoban or the Red Sea.
The Spaniards will not need hereafter to mine and dig far
into the earth, nor to cut asunder mountains in quest of
gold, but will find it plentifully, in a manner, on the upper
crust of the earth, or in the sands of rivers dried up by the
heats of summer. Certainly the reverend antiquity obtained

not so great a benefit of nature, nor even aspired to the knowledge thereof, since never man before, from the known world, penetrated to these unknown regions."[64]

The tidings of this discovery at once made all Spain resound with the praises of Vasco Nuñez; and, from being considered a lawless and desperate adventurer, he was lauded to the skies as a worthy successor to Columbus. The king repented of the harshness of his late measures towards him, and ordered the Bishop Fonseca to devise some mode of rewarding his transcendent services.

CHAPTER XVI

*Arrival and grand Entry of Don Pedrarias Davila
into Darien.*

WHILE honours and rewards were preparing in Europe for Vasco Nuñez, that indefatigable commander, inspired by his fortunes with redoubled zeal and loftier ambition, was exercising the paternal forethought and discretion of a patriotic governor over the country subjected to his rule. His most strenuous exertions were directed to bring the neighbourhood of Darien into such a state of cultivation as might render the settlement independent of Europe for supplies. The town was situated on the banks of a river, and contained upwards of two hundred houses and cabins. Its population amounted to five hundred and fifteen Europeans, all men, and fifteen hundred Indians, male and female. Orchards and gardens had been laid out, where European as well as native fruits and vegetables were cultivated, and already gave promise of future abundance. Vasco Nuñez devised all kinds of means to keep up the spirits of his people. On holidays they had their favourite national sports

and games, and particularly tilting matches, of which chivalrous amusements the Spaniards in those days were extrava-
gantly fond. Sometimes he gratified their restless and roving
habits by sending them in expeditions to various parts of
the country, to acquire a knowledge of its resources, and to
strengthen his sway over the natives. He was so successful
in securing the amity or exciting the awe of the Indian
tribes, that a Spaniard might go singly about the land in
perfect safety; while his own followers were zealous in their
devotion to him, both from admiration of his past exploits
and from hopes of soon being led by him to new discoveries
and conquests. Peter Martyr, in his letter to Leo the Tenth,
speaks in high terms of these "old soldiers of Darien," the
remnants of those well-tried adventurers who had followed
the fortunes of Ojeda, Nicuesa, and Vasco Nuñez. "They
were hardened," says he, "to abide all sorrows, and were
exceedingly tolerant of labour, heat, hunger, and watching,
insomuch that they merrily make their boast that they have
observed a longer and sharper Lent than ever your Holiness
enjoined, since, for the space of four years, their food has
been herbs and fruits, with now and then fish, and very
seldom flesh."[65]

Such were the hardy and well seasoned veterans that were
under the sway of Vasco Nuñez; and the colony gave signs of
rising in prosperity under his active and fostering manage-

ment, when in the month of June, the fleet of Don Pedrarias Davila arrived in the Gulf of Uraba.

The Spanish cavaliers who accompanied the new governor were eager to get on shore, and to behold the anticipated wonders of the land; but Pedrarias, knowing the resolute character of Vasco Nuñez, and the devotion of his followers, apprehended some difficulty in getting possession of the colony. Anchoring, therefore, about a league and a half from the settlement, he sent a messenger on shore to announce his arrival. The envoy, having heard so much in Spain of the prowess and exploits of Vasco Nuñez and the riches of Golden Castile, expected, no doubt, to find a blustering warrior, maintaining barbaric state in the government which he had usurped. Great was his astonishment therefore to find this redoubtable hero a plain unassuming man, clad in a cotton frock and drawers, and hempen sandals, directing and aiding the labour of several Indians who were thatching a cottage in which he resided.

The messenger approached him respectfully, and announced the arrival of Don Pedrarias Davila as governor of the country.

Whatever Vasco Nuñez may have felt at this intelligence, he suppressed his emotions, and answered the messenger with great discretion; "Tell Don Pedrarias Davilla," said he, "that he is welcome, that I congratulate him on his safe arrival, and am ready, with all who are here, to obey his orders."

The little community of rough and daring adventurers was immediately in an uproar when they found a new governor had arrived. Some of the most zealous adherents of Vasco Nuñez were disposed to sally forth, sword in hand, and repel the intruder; but they were restrained by their more considerate chieftain, who prepared to receive the new governor with all due submission.

Pedrarias disembarked on the thirtieth of June, accompanied by his heroic wife, Doña Isabella; who, according to old Peter Martyr, had sustained the roarings and rages of the ocean with no less stout courage than either her husband or even the mariners who had been brought up among the surges of the sea.

Pedrarias set out for the embryo city at the head of two thousand men, all well armed. He led his wife by the hand, and on the other side of him was the bishop of Darien in his robes; while a brilliant train of youthful cavaliers, in glittering armour and brocade, formed a kind of body-guard.

All this pomp and splendour formed a striking contrast with the humble state of Vasco Nuñez, who came forth unarmed, in simple attire, accompanied by his councillors and a handful of the "old soldiers of Darien," scarred and battered, and grown half wild in Indian warfare, but without weapons, and in garments much the worse for wear.

Vasco Nuñez saluted Don Pedrarias Davila with profound reverence, and promised him implicit obedience, both in his own name and in the name of the community. Having entered the town, he conducted his distinguished guests to his straw-thatched habitation, where he had caused a repast to be prepared of such cheer as his means afforded, consisting of roots and fruits, maize and casava bread, with no other beverage than water from the river; a sorry palace and a meagre banquet in the eyes of the gay cavaliers, who had anticipated far other things from the usurper of Golden Castile. Vasco Nuñez, however, acquitted himself in his humble wigwam with the courtesy and hospitality of a prince, and showed that the dignity of an entertainment depends more upon the giver than the feast. In the meantime a plentiful supply of European provisions was landed from the fleet, and a temporary abundance was diffused through the colony.

CHAPTER XVII

Perfidious conduct of Don Pedrarias towards Vasco Nuñez.

O N THE day after his entrance into Darien, Don Pedrarias held a private conference with Vasco Nuñez in presence of the historian Oviedo, who had come out from Spain as the public notary of the colony. The governor commenced by assuring him that he was instructed by the king to treat him with great favour and distinction, to consult him about the affairs of the colony, and to apply to him for information relative to the surrounding country. At the same time he professed the most amicable feelings on his own part, and an intention to be guided by his counsels in all public measures.

Vasco Nuñez was of a frank confiding nature, and was so captivated by this unexpected courtesy and kindness, that he threw off all caution and reserve, and opened his whole soul to the politic courtier. Pedrarias availed himself of this communicative mood to draw from him a minute and able statement in writing, detailing the circumstances of the colony, and the information collected respecting various parts of the country; the route by which he had traversed

the mountains; his discovery of the South Sea; the situation
and reputed wealth of the Pearl Islands; the rivers and ravines
most productive of gold; together with the names and territories of the various caciques with whom he had made treaties.

When Pedrarias had thus beguiled the unsuspecting
soldier of all the information necessary for his purposes, he
dropped the mask, and within a few days proclaimed a
judicial scrutiny into the conduct of Vasco Nuñez and his
officers. It was to be conducted by the Licentiate Gaspar de
Espinosa, who had come out as Alcalde Mayor, or chief
judge. The Licentiate was an inexperienced lawyer, having
but recently left the university of Salamanca. He appears to
have been somewhat flexible in his opinions, and prone to be
guided or governed by others. At the outset of his career he
was much under the influence of Quevedo, the Bishop of
Darien. Now, as Vasco Nuñez knew the importance of this
prelate in the colony, he had taken care to secure him to his
interests by paying him the most profound deference and
respect, and by giving him a share in his agricultural enterprises and his schemes of traffic. In fact, the good bishop
looked upon him as one eminently calculated to promote his
temporal prosperity, to which he was by no means insensi-
ble. Under the influence of the prelate, therefore, the Alcalde
commenced his investigation in the most favourable manner.
He went largely into an examination of the discoveries of

Vasco Nuñez, and of the nature and extent of his various services. The governor was alarmed at the course which the inquiry was taking. If thus conducted, it would but serve to illustrate the merits and elevate the reputation of the man whom it was his interest and intent to ruin. To counteract it he immediately set on foot a secret and invidious course of interrogatories of the followers of Nicuesa and Ojeda, to draw from them testimony which might support the charge against Vasco Nuñez of usurpation and tyrannical abuse of power. The bishop and the Alcalde received information of this inquisition, carried on thus secretly, and without their sanction. They remonstrated warmly against it, as an infringement of their rights, being coadjutors in the government; and they spurned the testimony of the followers of Ojeda and Nicuesa, as being dictated and discoloured by ancient enmity. Vasco Nuñez was therefore acquitted by them of the criminal charges made against him, though he remained involved in difficulties from the suits brought against him by individuals, for losses and damages occasioned by his measures.

Pedrarias was incensed at this acquittal, and insisted upon the guilt of Vasco Nuñez, which he pretended to have established to his conviction by his secret investigations; and he even determined to send him in chains to Spain, to be tried for the death of Nicuesa, and for other imputed offences.

It was not the inclination or the interest of the bishop that
Vasco Nuñez should leave the colony; he therefore managed
to awaken the jealous apprehensions of the governor as to
the effect of his proposed measure. He intimated that the
arrival of Vasco Nuñez in Spain would be signalized by
triumph rather than disgrace. By that time his grand discoveries would be blazoned to the world, and would atone
for all his faults. He would be received with enthusiasm by
the nation, with favour by the king, and would probably be
sent back to the colony clothed with new dignity and power.

Pedrarias was placed in a perplexing dilemma by these
suggestions; his violent proceedings against Vasco Nuñez
were also in some measure restrained by the influence of his
wife, Doña Isabel de Bobadilla, who felt a great respect and
sympathy for the discoverer. In his perplexity, the wily
governor adopted a middle course. He resolved to detain
Vasco Nuñez at Darien under a cloud of imputation, which
would gradually impair his popularity; while his patience
and means would be silently consumed by protracted and ex-
pensive litigation. In the meantime, however, the property
which had been sequestrated was restored to him.

While Pedrarias treated Vasco Nuñez with this severity,
he failed not to avail himself of the plans of that able commander. The first of these was to establish a line of posts
across the mountains between Darien and the South Sea. It

was his eager desire to execute this before any order should arrive from the king in favour of his predecessor, in order that he might have the credit of having colonized the coast, and Vasco Nuñez, merely that of having discovered and visited it.[66] Before he could complete these arrangements, however, unlooked-for calamities fell upon the settlement, that for a time interrupted every project, and made every one turn his thoughts merely to his own security.

CHAPTER XVIII

Calamities of the Spanish Cavaliers at Darien.

THE town of Darien was situated in a deep valley surrounded by lofty hills, which, while they kept off the breezes so grateful in a sultry climate, reflected and concentrated the rays of the sun, insomuch, that at noontide the heat was insupportable; the river which passed it was shallow, with a muddy channel and bordered by marshes; overhanging forests added to the general humidity, and the very soil on which the town was built was of such a nature, that on digging to the depth of a foot there would ooze forth brackish water.[67]

It is not a matter of surprise that a situation of this kind, in a tropical climate, should be fatal to the health of Europeans. Many of those who had recently arrived were swept off speedily; Pedrarias himself fell sick and was removed, with most of his people, to a healthier spot on the river Corobari; the malady, however, continued to increase. The provisions which had been brought out in the ships had been partly damaged by the sea, the residue grew scanty, and the people were put upon short allowance; the debility thus produced increased the ravages of disease; at length the provisions were exhausted and the horrors of absolute famine ensued.

Every one was more or less affected by these calamities; even the veterans of the colony quailed beneath them; but to none were they more fatal than to the crowd of youthful cavaliers who had once glittered so gaily about the streets of Seville, and had come out to the new world elated with the most sanguine expectations. From the very moment of their landing they had been disheartened at the savage scenes around them, and disgusted with the squalid life they were doomed to lead. They shrunk with disdain from the labours with which alone wealth was to be procured in this land of gold and pearls, and were impatient of the humble exertions necessary for the maintenance of existence. As the famine increased, their case became desperate; for they were unable to help themselves, and their rank and dignity commanded neither deference nor aid at a time when common misery made every one selfish. Many of them, who had mortgaged estates in Spain to fit themselves out sumptuously for their Italian campaign, now perished for lack of food. Some would be seen bartering a robe of crimson silk, or some garment of rich brocade, for a pound of Indian bread or European biscuit; others sought to satisfy the cravings of hunger with the herbs and roots of the field, and one of the principal cavaliers absolutely expired of hunger in the public streets.

In this wretched way, and in the short space of one month, perished seven hundred of the little army of youthful and buoyant spirits who had embarked with Pedrarias. The bodies of some remained for a day or two without sepulture, their friends not having sufficient strength to bury them. Unable to remedy the evil, Pedrarias gave permission for his men to flee from it. A ship-load of starving adventurers departed for Cuba, where some of them joined the standard of Diego Velasquez, who was colonizing that island; others made their way back to Spain, where they arrived broken in health, in spirits and in fortune.

CHAPTER XIX

Fruitless expedition of Pedrarias.

———

THE departure of so many hungry mouths was some temporary relief to the colony; and Pedrarias, having recovered from his malady, bestirred himself to send expeditions in various directions for the purpose of foraging the country and collecting the treasure.

These expeditions, however, were entrusted to his own favourites, and partisans; while Vasco Nuñez, the man most competent to carry them into effect, remained idle and neglected. A judicial inquiry, tardily carried on, overshadowed him, and though it substantiated nothing, served to embarrass his actions, to cool his friends, and to give him the air of a public delinquent. Indeed, to the other evils of the colony was now added that of excessive litigation, arising out of the disputes concerning the government of Vasco Nuñez, and which increased to such a degree, that according to the report of the Alcalde Espinosa, if the law-suits should be divided among the people, at least forty would fall to each man's share.[68] This too was in a colony into which the government had commanded that no lawyer should be admitted.

Wearied and irritated by the check which had been given to his favourite enterprises, and confident of the ultimate approbation of the king, Vasco Nuñez now determined to take his fortunes in his own hands, and to prosecute in secret his grand project of exploring the regions beyond the mountains. For this purpose he privately despatched one Andres Garabito to Cuba to enlist men, and to make the requisite provisions for an expedition across the isthmus, from Nombre de Dios, and for the founding a colony on the shores of the Southern Ocean, from whence he proposed to extend his discoveries by sea and land.

While Vasco Nuñez awaited the return of Garabito, he had the mortification of beholding various of his colonising plans pursued and marred by Pedrarias. Among other enterprises, the governor despatched his lieutenant-general Juan de Ayora, at the head of four hundred men, to visit the provinces of those caciques with whom Vasco Nuñez had sojourned and made treaties on his expedition to the Southern Sea. Ayora partook of the rash and domineering spirit of Pedrarias, and harassed and devastated the countries which he pretended to explore. He was received with amity and confidence by various caciques who had formed treaties with Vasco Nuñez; but he repaid their hospitality with the basest ingratitude, seizing upon their property, taking from them their wives and daughters, and often torturing them to make them reveal their hidden or supposed treasures. Among those treated with this perfidy, we grieve to enumerate the youthful cacique who first gave Vasco Nuñez information of the sea beyond the mountains.

The enormities of Ayora and of other captains of Pedrarias produced the usual effect; the natives were roused to desperate resistance; caciques, who had been faithful friends, were converted into furious enemies, and the expedition ended in disappointment and disaster.

The adherents of Vasco Nuñez did not fail to contrast these disastrous enterprises with those which had been conducted with so much glory and advantage by their favourite commander; and their sneers and reproaches had such an effect upon the jealous and irritable disposition of Pedrarias, that he determined to employ their idol in a service that would be likely to be attended with defeat, and to impair his popularity. None seemed more fitting for the purpose than an expedition to Dobayba, where he had once already attempted in vain to penetrate, and where so many of his followers had fallen victims to the stratagems and assaults of the natives.

CHAPTER XX

*Second Expedition of Vasco Nuñez in quest of the
Golden Temple of Dobayba.*

———————

THE rich mines of Dobayba, and the treasures of its golden temple, had continued to form a favourite theme with the Spanish adventurers. It was ascertained that Vasco Nuñez had stopped short of the wealthy region on his former expedition, and had mistaken a frontier village for the residence of the cacique. The enterprise of the temple was, therefore, still to be achieved; and it was solicited by several of the cavaliers in the train of Pedrarias, with all the chivalrous ardour of that romantic age. Indeed common report had invested the enterprise with difficulties and danger sufficient to stimulate the ambition of the keenest seeker of adventure. The savages who inhabited that part of the country, were courageous and adroit. They fought by water as well as by land, forming ambuscades with their canoes in the bays and rivers. The country was intersected by dreary fens and morasses, infested by all kinds of reptiles. Clouds of gnats and mosquitoes filled the air; there were large bats also, supposed to have the baneful properties

255

of the vampire; alligators lurked in the waters, and the gloomy recesses of the fens were said to be the dens of dragons![69]

Besides these objects of terror, both true and fabulous, the old historian, Peter Martyr, makes mention of another monstrous animal, said to infest this golden region, and which deserves to be cited, as showing the imaginary dangers with which the active minds of the discoverers peopled the unexplored wilderness around them.

According to the tales of the Indians, there had occurred, shortly before the arrival of the Spaniards, a violent tempest, or rather hurricane, in the neighbourhood of Dobayba, which demolished houses, tore up trees by the roots, and laid waste whole forests. When the tempest had subsided and the affrighted inhabitants ventured to look abroad, they found that two monstrous animals had been brought into the country by the hurricane. According to their accounts they were not unlike the ancient harpies, and one being smaller than the other, was supposed to be its young. They had the faces of women, with the claws and wings of eagles, and were of such prodigious size that the very boughs of the trees on which they alighted broke beneath them. They would swoop down and carry off a man as a hawk would bear off a chicken, flying with him to the tops of the mountains, where they would tear him in pieces and devour him. For some time they were the scourge and terror of the land, until the Indians succeeded in killing the old one by stratagem, and hanging her on their long spears, bore her through all the towns to assuage the alarm of the inhabitants. The younger harpy, says the Indian tradition, was never seen afterwards.[70]

Such were some of the perils, true and fabulous, with which the land of Dobayba was said to abound; and, in fact, the very Indians had such a dread of its dark and dismal morasses, that, in their journeyings, they carefully avoided them, preferring the circuitous and rugged paths of the mountains.

Several of the youthful cavaliers, as has been observed, were stimulated rather than deterred by these dangers, and contended for the honour of the expedition; but Pedrarias selected his rival for the task, hoping, as has been hinted, that it would involve him in disgrace. Vasco Nuñez promptly accepted the enterprise, for his pride was concerned in its success. Two hundred resolute men were given to him for the purpose; but his satisfaction was diminished when he found that Luis Carrillo, an officer of Pedrarias, who had failed in a perilous enterprise, was associated with him in the command.

Few particulars remain to us of the events of this affair. They embarked in a fleet of canoes, and, traversing the gulf, arrived at the river which flowed down from the region of

Dobayba. They were not destined, however, to achieve the enterprise of the golden temple. As they were proceeding rather confidently and unguardedly up the river, they were suddenly surprised and surrounded by an immense swarm of canoes, filled with armed savages, which darted out from lurking places along the shores. Some of the Indians assailed them with lances, others with clouds of arrows, while some plunging into the water, endeavoured to overturn their canoes. In this way one half of the Spaniards were killed or drowned. Among the number fell Luis Carrillo, pierced through the breast by an Indian lance. Vasco Nuñez himself was wounded, and had great difficulty in escaping to the shore with the residue of his forces.

The Indians pursued him and kept up a skirmishing attack, but he beat them off until the night, when he silently abandoned the shore of the river, and directed his retreat towards Darien. It is easier to imagine than to describe the toils and dangers and horrors which beset him and the remnant of his men as they traversed rugged mountains, or struggled through these fearful morasses of which they had heard such terrific tales. At length they succeeded in reaching the settlement of Darien.

The partizans of Pedrarias exulted in seeing Vasco Nuñez return thus foiled and wounded, and taunted his adherents with their previous boastings. The latter, however, laid all the blame upon the unfortunate Carrillo. "Vasco Nuñez," said they, "had always absolute command in his former enterprises, but in this he has been embarrassed by an associate. Had the expedition been confided to him alone, the event had been far different."

CHAPTER XXI

Letters from the King in favour of Vasco Nuñez.—Arrival
of Garabito.—Arrest of Vasco Nuñez.—[1515.]

ABOUT this time despatches arrived from Spain that promised to give a new turn to the fortunes of Vasco Nuñez and to the general affairs of the colony. They were written after the tidings of the discovery of the South Sea, and the subjugation of so many important provinces of the Isthmus. In a letter addressed to Vasco Nuñez, the king expressed his high sense of his merits and services, and constituted him Adelantado of the South Sea, and Governor of the provinces of Panama and Coyba, though subordinate to the general command of Pedrarias. A letter was likewise written by the king to Pedrarias, informing him of this appointment, and ordering him to consult Vasco Nuñez on all public affairs of importance. This was a humiliating blow to the pride and consequence of Pedrarias, but he hoped to parry it. In the meantime, as all letters from Spain were first delivered into his hands, he withheld that intended for Vasco Nuñez, until he should determine what course of conduct to adopt. The latter, how-

ever, heard of the circumstance, as did his friend the Bishop
of Darien. The prelate made loud complaints of this interruption of the royal correspondence, which he denounced,
even from the pulpit, as an outrage upon the rights of the
subject, and an act of disobedience to the sovereign.

Upon this the governor called a council of his public officers; and, after imparting the contents of his letter, requested
their opinion as to the propriety of investing Vasco Nuñez
with the dignities thus granted to him. The Alcalde Mayor,
Espinosa, had left the party of the bishop, and was now devoted to the governor. He insisted, vehemently, that the
offices ought in no wise to be given to Vasco Nuñez, until the
king should be informed of the result of the inquest which
was still going on against him. In this he was warmly supported by the treasurer and the accountant. The bishop replied, indignantly, that it was presumptuous and disloyal in
them to dispute the commands of the king, and to interfere
with the rewards conscientiously given by him to a meri-
torious subject. In this way, he added, they were defeating,
by their passions, the grateful intentions of their sovereign.
The governor was overawed by the honest warmth of the
bishop, and professed to accord with him in opinion. The
council lasted until midnight; and it was finally agreed that
the titles and dignities should be conferred on Vasco Nuñez
on the following day.[71]

Pedrarias and his officers reflected, however, that if the jurisdiction implied by these titles were absolutely vested in Vasco Nuñez, the government of Darien and Castilla del Oro would virtually be reduced to a trifling matter; they resolved, therefore, to adopt a middle course; to grant him the empty titles, but to make him give security not to enter upon the actual government of the territories in question, until Pedrarias should give him permission. The bishop and Vasco Nuñez assented to this arrangement; satisfied, for the present, with securing the titles, and trusting to the course of events to get dominion over the territories.[72]

The new honours of Vasco Nuñez were now promulgated to the world, and he was everywhere addressed by the title of Adelantado. His old friends lifted up their heads with exultation, and new adherents flocked to his standard. Parties began to form for him and for Pedrarias, for it was deemed impossible they could continue long in harmony.

The jealousy of the governor was excited by these circumstances; and he regarded the newly created Adelantado as a dangerous rival and an insidious foe. Just at this critical juncture, Andres Garabito, the agent of Vasco Nuñez, arrived on the coast in a vessel which he had procured at Cuba, and had freighted with arms and ammunition, and seventy resolute men, for the secret expedition to the shores of the

Pacific Ocean. He anchored six leagues from the harbour, and sent word privately to Vasco Nuñez of his arrival.

Information was immediately carried to Pedrarias, that a mysterious vessel, full of armed men, was hovering on the coast, and holding secret communication with his rival. The suspicious temper of the governor immediately took the alarm. He fancied some treasonable plot against his authority; his passions mingled with his fears; and, in the first burst of his fury, he ordered that Vasco Nuñez should be seized and confined in a wooden cage. The Bishop of Darien interposed in time to prevent an indignity which it might have been impossible to expiate. He prevailed upon the passionate governor, not merely to retract the order respecting the cage, but to examine the whole matter with coolness and deliberation. The result proved that his suspicions had been erroneous; and that the armament had been set on foot without any treasonable intent. Vasco Nuñez was therefore set at liberty, after having agreed to certain precautionary conditions; but he remained cast down in spirit and impoverished in fortune, by the harassing measures of Pedrarias.

CHAPTER XXII

Expedition of Morales and Pizarro to the shores of the Pacific Ocean.—Their visit to the Pearl Islands.— Their disastrous return across the mountains.

THE Bishop of Darien, encouraged by the success of his intercession, endeavoured to persuade the governor to go still further, and to permit the departure of Vasco Nuñez on his expedition to the South Sea. The jealousy of Pedrarias, however, was too strong to permit him to listen to such counsel. He was aware of the importance of the expedition, and was anxious that the Pearl Islands should be explored, which promised such abundant treasures; but he feared to increase the popularity of Vasco Nuñez, by adding such an enterprise to the number of his achievements. Pedrarias, therefore, set on foot an expedition, consisting of sixty men, but gave the command to one of his own relations, named Gaspar Morales. The latter was accompanied by Francisco Pizarro, who had already been to those parts in the train of Vasco Nuñez, and who soon rose to importance in the present enterprise by his fierce courage and domineering genius.

264

A brief notice of the principal incidents of this expedition
is all that is necessary for the present narration.

Morales and Pizarro traversed the mountains of the isthmus by a shorter and more expeditious route than that which
had been taken by Vasco Nuñez, and arrived on the shores
of the South Sea at the territories of a cacique named Tutibra, by whom they were amicably entertained. Their great
object was to visit the Pearl Islands: the cacique, however,
had but four canoes, which were insufficient to contain their
whole party. One half of their number, therefore, remained
at the village of Tutibra, under the command of a captain
named Peñalosa; the residue embarked in the canoes with
Morales and Pizarro. After a stormy and perilous voyage,
they landed on one of the smaller islands, where they had
some skirmishing with the natives, and thence made their
way to the principal island of the Archipelago, to which,
from the report of its great pearl fishery, Vasco Nuñez had
given the name of Isla Rica.

The cacique of this island had long been the terror of the
neighbouring coasts, invading the mainland with fleets of
canoes, and carrying off the inhabitants into captivity. His
reception of the Spaniards was worthy of his fame. Four
times did he sally forth to defend his territory, and as often
was he repulsed with great slaughter. His warriors were overwhelmed with terror at the firearms of the Spaniards, and at

their ferocious blood-hounds. Finding all resistance unavailing, the cacique was at length compelled to sue for peace. His prayers being granted, he received the conquerors into his habitation, which was well built, and of immense size. Here he brought them, as a peace-offering, a basket curiously wrought, and filled with pearls of great beauty. Among these were two of extraordinary size and value. One weighed twenty-five carats; the other was of the size of a Muscadine pear, weighing upwards of three drachms, and of oriental colour and lustre. The cacique considered himself more than repaid by a present of hatchets, beads, and hawks-bells: and, on the Spaniards smiling at his joy, observed, "These things I can turn to useful purpose, but of what value are those pearls to me?"

Finding, however, that these baubles were precious in the eyes of the Spaniards, he took Morales and Pizarro to the summit of a wooden tower, commanding an unbounded prospect. "Behold, before you," said he, "the infinite sea, which extends even beyond the sun-beams. As to these islands which lie to the right and left, they are all subject to my sway. They possess but little gold, but the deep places of the sea around them are full of pearls. Continue to be my friends, and you shall have as many as you desire; for I value your friendship more than pearls, and, as far as in me lies, will never forfeit it."

He then pointed to the mainland, where it stretched away towards the east, mountain beyond mountain, until the summit of the last faded in the distance, and was scarcely seen above the watery horizon. In that direction, he said, there lay a vast country of inexhaustible riches, inhabited by a mighty nation. He went on to repeat the vague but wonderful rumours which the Spaniards had frequently heard about the great kingdom of Peru. Pizarro listened greedily to his words, and while his eye followed the finger of the cacique, as it ranged along the line of shadowy coast, his daring mind kindled with the thought of seeking this golden empire beyond the waters.[73]

Before leaving the island, the two captains impressed the cacique with so great an idea of the power of the king of Castile, that he agreed to become his vassal, and to render him an annual tribute of one hundred pounds weight of pearls.

The party having returned in safety to the mainland, though to a different place from that where they had embarked, Gaspar Morales sent his relation, Bernardo Morales, with ten men in quest of Peñalosa and his companions, who had remained in the village of Tutibra.

Unfortunately for the Spaniards, during the absence of the commanders, this Peñalosa had so exasperated the natives by his misconduct, that a conspiracy had been formed by the caciques along the coast to massacre the whole of the strangers, when the party should return from the islands.

Bernardo Morales and his companions, on their way in quest of Peñalosa, put up for the night in the village of a cacique named Chuchama, who was one of the conspirators. They were entertained with pretended hospitality. In the dead of the night, however, the house in which they were sleeping was wrapped in flames, and most of them were destroyed. Chuchama then prepared with his confederates to attack the main body of the Spaniards who remained with Morales and Pizarro.

Fortunately for the latter, there was among the Indians who had accompanied them to the islands a cacique named Chiruca, who was in secret correspondence with the conspirators. Some circumstances in his conduct excited their suspicions; they put him to the torture and drew from him a relation of the massacre of their companions, and of the attack with which they were menaced.

Morales and Pizarro were at first appalled by the overwhelming danger which surrounded them. Concealing their agitation, however, they compelled Chiruca to send a message to each of the confederate caciques, inviting him to a secret conference, under pretence of giving him important information. The caciques came at the summons: they were thus taken one by one to the number of eighteen, and put in chains. Just at this juncture Peñalosa arrived with the thirty men who had remained with him at Tutibra. Their arrival was hailed with joy by their comrades, who had given them up for lost. Encouraged by this unexpected reinforcement, the Spaniards now attacked by surprise the main body of confederate Indians, who, being ignorant of the discovery of their plot and capture of the caciques, were awaiting the return of the latter in a state of negligent security.

Pizarro led the van, and set upon the enemy at daybreak with the old Spanish war-cry of Santiago! It was a slaughter rather than a battle, for the Indians were unprepared for resistance. Before sun-rise, seven hundred lay dead upon the field. Returning from the massacre, the commanders doomed the caciques who were in chains to be torn in pieces by the bloodhounds; nor was even Chiruca spared from this sanguinary sentence. Notwithstanding this bloody revenge, the vindictive spirit of the commanders was still unappeased, and they set off to surprise the village of a cacique named Biru, who dwelt on the eastern side of the Gulf of St. Michael. He was famed for valour and for cruelty: his dwelling was surrounded by the weapons and other trophies of those whom he had vanquished; and he was said never to give quarter.

The Spaniards assailed his village before day-break with fire and sword, and made dreadful havoc. Biru escaped from his burning habitation, rallied his people, kept up a galling fight thoughout the greater part of that day, and handled the Spaniards so roughly, that, when he drew off at night, they did not venture to pursue him, but returned right gladly from his territory. According to some of the Spanish writers, the kingdom of Peru derived its name from this warlike cacique, through a blunder of the early discoverers; the assertion, however, is believed to be erroneous.

The Spaniards had pushed their bloody revenge to an extreme, and were now doomed to suffer from the recoil. In the fury of their passions, they had forgotten that they were but a handful of men surrounded by savage nations. Returning wearied and disheartened from the battle with Biru, they were waylaid and assaulted by a host of Indians led on by the son of Chiruca. A javelin from his hand pierced one of the Spaniards through the breast and came out between the shoulders; several others were wounded, and the remainder were harassed by a galling fire kept up from among rocks and bushes.

Dismayed at the implacable vengeance they had aroused, the Spaniards hastened to abandon these hostile shores and make the best of their way back to Darien. The Indians, however, were not to be appeased by the mere departure of the intruders. They followed them perseveringly for seven days, hanging on their skirts, and harassing them by con-

tinual alarms. Morales and Pizarro, seeing the obstinacy of
their pursuit, endeavoured to gain a march upon them by
stratagem. Making large fires as usual one night about the
place of their encampment, they left them burning to deceive
the enemy while they made a rapid retreat. Among their
number was one poor fellow named Velasquez, who was so
grievously wounded that he could not walk. Unable to accompany his countrymen in their flight, and dreading to fall
into the merciless hands of the savages, he determined to
hang himself, nor could the prayers and even tears of his
comrades dissuade him from his purpose.

The stratagem of the Spaniards, however, was unavailing.
Their retreat was perceived, and at day-break, to their dismay, they found themselves surrounded by three squadrons
of savages. Unable, in their haggard state, to make head
against so many foes, they remained drawn up all day on the
defensive, some watching while others reposed. At night they
lit their fires and again attempted to make a secret retreat.
The Indians, however, were as usual on their traces, and
wounded several with arrows. Thus pressed and goaded, the
Spaniards became desperate, and fought like madmen, rushing upon the very darts of the enemy.

Morales now resorted to an inhuman and fruitless ex-
pedient to retard his pursuers. He caused several Indian
prisoners to be slain, hoping that their friends would stop to

lament over them; but the sight of their mangled bodies only increased the fury of the savages and the obstinacy of their pursuit.

For nine days were the Spaniards hunted in this manner about the woods and mountains, the swamps and fens, wandering they knew not whither, and returning upon their steps, until, to their dismay, they found themselves in the very place where, several days previously, they had been surrounded by the three squadrons.

Many now began to despair of ever escaping with life from this trackless wilderness, thus teeming with deadly foes. It was with difficulty their commanders could rally their spirits, and encourage them to persevere. Entering a thick forest they were again assailed by a band of Indians, but despair and fury gave them strength: they fought like wild beasts rather than like men, and routed the foe with dreadful carnage. They had hoped to gain a breathing time by this victory, but a new distress attended them. They got entangled in one of those deep and dismal marshes which abound on those coasts, and in which the wanderer is often drowned or suffocated. For a whole day they toiled through brake and bramble, and miry fen, with the water reaching to their girdles. At length they extricated themselves from the swamp, and arrived at the seashore. The tide was out, but was about to return, and on this coast it rises rapidly to a great height. Fearing to be overwhelmed by the rising surf, they hastened to climb a rock out of reach of the swelling waters. Here they threw themselves on the earth panting with fatigue and abandoned to despair. A savage wilderness filled with still more savage foes, was on one side, on the other the roaring sea. How were they to extricate themselves from these surrounding perils? While reflecting on their desperate situation, they heard the voices of Indians. On looking cautiously round, they beheld four canoes entering a neighbouring creek. A party was immediately despatched who came upon the savages by surprise, drove them into the woods, and seized upon the canoes. In these frail barks the Spaniards escaped from their perilous neighbourhood, and, traversing the Gulf of St. Michael, landed in a less hostile part, from whence they set out a second time, across the mountains.

It is needless to recount the other hardships they endured, and their further conflicts with the Indians; suffice it to say, after a series of almost incredible sufferings and disasters, they at length arrived in a battered and emaciated condition at Darien. Throughout all their toils and troubles, however, they had managed to preserve a part of the treasure they had gained in the islands; especially the pearls given them by the cacique of Isla Rica. These were objects of universal admiration. One of them was put up at auction, and bought by

Pedrarias, and was afterwards presented by his wife Doña Isabella de Bobadilla to the Empress, who, in return, gave her four thousand ducats.[74]

Such was the cupidity of the colonists, that the sight of these pearls and the reputed wealth of the islands of the Southern Sea, and the kingdoms on its borders, made far greater impression on the public mind, than the tale told by the adventurers of all the horrors they had passed; and every one was eager to seek these wealthy regions beyond the mountains.

CHAPTER XXIII

Unfortunate Enterprises of the Officers of Pedrarias.—
Matrimonial Compact between the Governor
and Vasco Nuñez.

IN NARRATING the preceding expedition of Morales and Pizarro, we have been tempted into what
may almost be deemed an episode, though it serves
to place in a proper light the lurking difficulties and
dangers which beset the expeditions of Vasco Nuñez to the
same regions, and his superior prudence and management in
avoiding them. It is not the object of this narrative, however, to record the general events of the colony under the
administration of Don Pedrarias Davila. We refrain, therefore, from detailing various expeditions set on foot by him to
explore and subjugate the surrounding country; and which,
being ignorantly or rashly conducted, too often ended in misfortune and disgrace. One of these was to the province of
Zenu, where gold was supposed to be taken in the rivers in
nets; and where the Bachelor Enciso once undertook to invade the sepulchres. A captain named Francisco Becerra
penetrated into this country at the head of one hundred and

eighty men, well armed and equipped, and provided with three pieces of artillery; but neither the commander nor any of his men returned. An Indian boy who accompanied them was the only one who escaped, and told the dismal tale of their having fallen victims to the assaults and stratagems and poisoned arrows of the Indians.

Another band was defeated by Tubanama, the ferocious cacique of the mountains, who bore as banners the bloody shirts of the Spaniards he had slain in former battles. In fine, the colony became so weakened by these repeated losses, and the savages so emboldened by success, that the latter beleaguered it with their forces, harassed it by assaults and ambuscades, and reduced it to great extremity. Such was the alarm in Darien, says the Bishop Las Casas, that the people feared to be burnt in their houses. They kept a watchful eye upon the mountains, the plains, and the very branches of the trees. Their imaginations were infected by their fears. If they looked toward the land, the long waving grass of the savannahs appeared to them to be moving hosts of Indians. If they looked towards the sea, they fancied they beheld fleets of canoes in the distance. Pedrarias endeavoured to prevent all rumours from abroad that might increase this fevered state of alarm; at the same time he ordered the smelting-house to be closed, which was never done but in time of war. This was done at the suggestion of the Bishop, who caused prayers to be put up, and fasts proclaimed, to avert the impending calamities.

While Pedrarias was harassed and perplexed by these complicated evils, he was haunted by continual apprehensions of the ultimate ascendency of Vasco Nuñez. He knew him to be beloved by the people, and befriended by the Bishop; and he had received proofs that his services were highly appreciated by the king. He knew also that representations had been sent home by him and his partizans, of the evils and abuses of the colony under the present rule, and of the necessity of a more active and efficient governor. He dreaded lest these representations should ultimately succeed; that he should be undermined in the royal favour, and Vasco Nuñez be elevated upon his ruins.

The politic bishop perceived the uneasy state of the governor's mind, and endeavoured, by means of his apprehensions, to effect that reconciliation which he had sought in vain to produce through more generous motives. He represented to him that his treatment of Vasco Nuñez was odious in the eyes of the people, and must eventually draw on him the displeasure of his sovereign. "But why persist," added he, "in driving a man to become your deadliest enemy, whom you may grapple to your side as your firmest friend? You have several daughters—give him one in marriage; you will then have for a son-in-law a man of merit and popularity, who is a hidalgo by birth, and a favourite of the king. You are advanced in life and infirm; he is in the prime and vigour of his days, and possessed of great activity. You can make him your lieutenant; and while you repose from your toils, he can carry on the affairs of the colony with spirit and enterprise; and all his achievements will redound to the advancement of your family and the splendour of your administration."

The governor and his lady were won by the eloquence of the bishop, and readily listened to his suggestions; and Vasco Nuñez was but too happy to effect a reconciliation on such flattering terms. Written articles were accordingly drawn up and exchanged, contracting a marriage between him and the eldest daughter of Pedrarias. The young lady was then in Spain, but was to be sent for, and the nuptials were to be celebrated on her arrival at Darien.

Having thus fulfilled his office of peace-maker, and settled, as he supposed, all feuds and jealousies on the sure and permanent foundation of family alliance, the worthy bishop departed shortly afterwards for Spain.

CHAPTER XXIV

Vasco Nuñez transports ships across the mountains to the Pacific Ocean.—[1516.]

BEHOLD Vasco Nuñez once more in the high career of prosperity! His most implacable enemy had suddenly been converted into his dearest friend; for the governor, now that he looked upon him as his son-in-law, loaded him with favours. Above all, he authorized him to build brigantines and make all the necessary preparations for his long desired expedition to explore the Southern Ocean. The place appointed for these purposes was the port of Careta, situated to the west of Darien; from whence there was supposed to be the most convenient route across the mountains. A town called Acla had been founded at this port; and the fortress was already erected, of which Lope de Olano was Alcalde; Vasco Nuñez was now empowered to continue the building of the town. Two hundred men were placed under his command to aid him in carrying his plans into execution, and a sum of money was advanced to him out of the royal treasury. His supply of funds, however, was not sufficient, but he received assistance from a

private source. There was a notary at Darien, named
Hernando de Aguello, a man of some consequence in the
community, and who had been one of the most furious op-
ponents of the unfortunate Nicuesa. He had amassed considerable property, and now embarked a great part of it in
the proposed enterprise, on condition, no doubt, of sharing
largely in its anticipated profits.

On arriving at Acla, Vasco Nuñez set to work to prepare
the materials of four brigantines that were to be launched
into the South Sea. The timber was felled on the Atlantic sea-
board; and was then, with the anchors and rigging, transported across the lofty ridge of mountains to the opposite
shores of the Isthmus. Several Spaniards, thirty Negroes,
and a great number of Indians were employed for the purpose. They had no other roads but Indian paths, straggling
through almost impervious forests, across torrents, and up
rugged defiles, broken by rocks and precipices. In this way
they toiled like ants up the mountains, with their ponderous
burthens, under the scorching rays of a tropical sun. Many
of the poor Indians sank by the way and perished under this
stupendous task. The Spaniards and Negroes, being of
hardier constitutions, were better able to cope with the incredible hardships to which they were subjected. On the
summit of the mountains a house had been provided for
their temporary repose. After remaining here a little time to

refresh themselves and gain new strength, they renewed their labours, descending the opposite side of the mountains until they reached the navigable part of a river, which they called the Balsas, and which flowed into the Pacific.

Much time and trouble, and many lives were expended on this arduous undertaking, before they had transported to the river sufficient timber for two brigantines; while the timber for the other two, and the rigging and munitions for the whole, yet remained to be brought. To add to their difficulties, they had scarcely begun to work upon the timber before they discovered that it was totally useless, being subject to the ravages of the worms from having been cut in the vicinity of salt water. They were obliged, therefore, to begin anew, and fell trees on the border of the river.

Vasco Nuñez maintained his patience and perseverance, and displayed admirable management under these delays and difficulties. Their supply of food being scanty, he divided his people, Spaniards, Negroes, and Indians, into three bands: one was to cut and saw the wood, another to bring the rigging and iron work from Acla, which was twenty-two leagues distant; and the third to forage the neighbouring country for provisions.

Scarcely was the timber felled and shaped for use when the rains set in, and the river swelled and overflowed its banks so suddenly, that the workmen barely escaped with their lives, by clambering into the trees; while the wood on which they had been working was either buried in sand or slime, or swept away by the raging torrent. Famine was soon added to their other distresses. The foraging party was absent and did not return with food; and the swelling of the river cut them off from that part of the country from whence they obtained their supplies. They were reduced, therefore, to such scarcity as to be fain to assuage their hunger with such roots as they could gather in the forests.

In this extremity the Indians bethought themselves of one of their rude and simple expedients. Plunging into the river they fastened a number of logs together with withes, and connected them with the opposite bank, so as to make a floating bridge. On this a party of the Spaniards crossed with great difficulty and peril, from the violence of the current, and the flexibility of the bridge, which often sank beneath them until the water rose above their girdles. On being safely landed they foraged the neighbourhood, and procured a supply of provisions sufficient for the present emergency.

When the river subsided the workmen again resumed their labours; a number of recruits arrived from Acla, bringing various supplies, and the business of the enterprise was pressed with redoubled ardour, until at length, after a series of incredible toils and hardships, Vasco Nuñez had the satisfaction to behold two of his brigantines floating on the river

Balsas. As soon as they could be equipped for sea, he embarked in them with as many Spaniards as they could carry;
and, issuing forth from the river, launched triumphantly on
the great ocean he had discovered.

We can readily imagine the exultation of this intrepid adventurer, and how amply he was repaid for all his sufferings,
when he first spread a sail upon that untraversed ocean, and
felt that the range of an unknown world was open to him.

There are points in the history of these Spanish discoveries of the western hemisphere, that make us pause with
wonder and admiration at the daring spirit of the men who
conducted them, and the appalling difficulties surmounted
by their courage and perseverence. We know few instances,
however, more striking than this piece-meal transportation,
across the mountains of Darien, of the first European ships
that ploughed the waves of the Pacific; and we can readily
excuse the boast of the old Castilian writers, when they exclaim, "that none but Spaniards could ever have conceived
or persisted in such an undertaking; and no commander in
the new world but Vasco Nuñez could have conducted it to a
successful issue."[75]

CHAPTER XXV

Cruise of Vasco Nuñez in the Southern Sea.—
Rumours from Acla.

THE first cruise of Vasco Nuñez was to the group of Pearl islands, on the principal one of which he disembarked the greater part of his crews, and despatched the brigantines to the mainland to bring off the remainder. It was his intention to construct the other two vessels of his proposed squadron at this island. During the absence of the brigantines he ranged the island with his men, to collect provisions, and to establish a complete sway over the natives. On the return of his vessels, and while preparations were making for the building of the others, he embarked with a hundred men, and departed on a reconnoitering cruise to the eastward, towards the region pointed out by the Indians as abounding in riches.

Having passed about twenty leagues beyond the Gulf of San Miguel, the mariners were filled with apprehension at beholding a great number of whales, which resembled a reef of rocks stretching far into the sea, and lashed by breakers. In an unknown ocean like this, every unusual object is apt to

inspire alarm. The seamen feared to approach these fancied
dangers in the dark; Vasco Nuñez anchored, therefore, for
the night, under a point of land, intending to continue in the
same direction on the following day. When the morning
dawned, however, the wind had changed, and was contrary;
whereupon he altered his course, and thus abandoned a
cruise, which, if persevered in, might have terminated in the
discovery of Peru! Steering for the mainland, he anchored on
that part of the coast governed by the cacique Chuchama,
who had massacred Bernardo Morales and his companions,
when reposing in his village. Here landing with his men,
Vasco Nuñez came suddenly upon the dwelling of the cacique. The Indians sallied forth to defend their homes, but
were routed with great loss; and ample vengeance was taken
upon them for their outrage upon the laws of hospitality.
Having thus avenged the death of his countrymen, Vasco
Nuñez re-embarked and returned to Isla Rica.

He now applied himself diligently to complete the building of his brigantines, despatching men to Acla to bring the
necessary stores and rigging across the mountains. While
thus occupied, a rumour reached him that a new governor
named Lope de Sosa was coming out from Spain to supersede
Pedrarias. Vasco Nuñez was troubled at these tidings. A new
governor would be likely to adopt new measures, or to have
new favourites. He feared, therefore, that some order might

come to suspend or embarrass his expedition; or that the command of it might be given to another. In his perplexity he held a consultation with several of his confidential officers.

After some debate, it was agreed among them that a trusty and intelligent person should be sent as a scout to Acla, under pretence of procuring munitions for the ships. Should he find Pedrarias in quiet possession of the government, he was to account to him for the delay of the expedition; to request that the time allotted to it might be extended, and to request reinforcements and supplies. Should he find, however, that a new governor was actually arrived, he was to return immediately with the tidings. In such case it was resolved to put to sea before any contrary orders could arrive, trusting eventually to excuse themselves on the plea of zeal and good intentions.

CHAPTER XXVI

*Reconnoitering expedition of Garabito.—Stratagem of
Pedrarias to entrap Vasco Nuñez.*

———————

THE person entrusted with the reconnoitering expedition to Acla was Andres Garabito, in whose fidelity and discretion Vasco Nuñez had implicit confidence. His confidence was destined to be fatally deceived. According to the assertions of contemporaries, this Garabito cherished a secret and vindictive enmity against his commander, arising from a simple but a natural cause. Vasco Nuñez had continued to have a fondness for the Indian damsel, daughter of the cacique Careta, whom he had received from her father as a pledge of amity. Some dispute arose concerning her on one occasion between him and Garabito, in the course of which he expressed himself in severe and galling language. Garabito was deeply mortified at some of his expressions, and, being of a malignant spirit, determined on a dastardly revenge. He wrote privately to Pedrarias, assuring him that Vasco Nuñez had no intention of solemnizing his marriage with his daughter, being completely under the influence of an Indian paramour; that he made use of the friendship of Pedrarias merely to further his own selfish views, intending, as soon as his ships were ready, to throw off all allegiance, and to put to sea as an independent commander.

This mischievous letter Garabito had written immediately after the last departure of Vasco Nuñez from Acla. Its effects upon the proud and jealous spirit of the governor may easily be conceived. All his former suspicions were immediately revived. They acquired strength during a long interval that elapsed without tidings being received from the expedition. There were designing and prejudiced persons at hand, who perceived and quickened these jealous feelings of the governor. Among these was the Bachelor Corral, who cherished a deep grudge against Vasco Nuñez for having once thrown him into prison for his factious conduct; and Alonzo de la Puente, the royal treasurer, whom Vasco Nuñez had affronted by demanding the re-payment of a loan. Such was the tempest that was gradually gathering in the factious little colony of Darien.

The subsequent conduct of Garabito gives much confirmation to the charge of perfidy that has been advanced against him. When he arrived at Acla he found that Pedrarias remained in possession of the government; for his intended successor had died in the very harbour. The conduct and conversation of Garabito was such as to arouse suspicions; he was arrested, and his papers and letters were sent to Pedrarias. When examined he readily suffered himself to be wrought upon by threats of punishment and promises of pardon, and revealed all that he knew, and declared still more that he suspected and surmised, of the plans and intentions of Vasco Nuñez.

The arrest of Garabito, and the seizure of his letters, produced a great agitation at Darien. It was considered a revival of the ancient animosity between the governor and Vasco Nuñez, and the friends of the latter trembled for his safety.

Hernando de Arguello, especially, was in great alarm. He had embarked the most of his fortune in the expedition, and the failure of it would be ruinous to him. He wrote to Vasco Nuñez informing him of the critical posture of affairs, and urging him to put to sea without delay. He would be protected at all events, he said, by the Jeronimite Fathers at San Domingo, who were at that time all-powerful in the new world, and who regarded his expedition as calculated to promote the glory of God as well as the dominion of the king.[76] This letter fell into the hands of Pedrarias, and convinced him of the existence of a dangerous plot against his authority. He immediately ordered Arguello to be arrested; and now devised means to get Vasco Nuñez within his power. While the latter remained on the shores of the South Sea with his brigantines and his band of hearty and devoted followers, Pedrarias knew that it would be in vain to attempt to take him by force. Dissembling his suspicions and intentions, therefore, he wrote to him in the most amicable terms, requesting him to repair immediately to Acla, as he wished to hold a conference with him about the impending expedition. Fearing, however, that Vasco Nuñez might suspect his motives and refuse to comply, he at the same time ordered Francisco Pizarro to muster all the armed force he could collect, and to seek and arrest his late patron and commander wherever he might be found.

So great was the terror inspired by the arrest of Arguello, and by the general violence of Pedrarias, that, though Vasco Nuñez was a favourite with the great mass of the people, no one ventured to warn him of the danger that attended his return to Acla.

CHAPTER XXVII

Vasco Nuñez and the Astrologer.—His return to Acla.

THE old Spanish writers who have treated of the fortunes of Vasco Nuñez, record an anecdote which is worthy of being cited, as characteristic of the people and the age. Among the motley crowd of adventurers lured across the ocean by the reputed wealth and wonders of the New world, was an Italian astrologer, a native of Venice, named Micer Codro. At the time that Vasco Nuñez held supreme sway at Darien, this reader of the stars had cast his horoscope, and pretended to foretell his destiny. Pointing one night to a certain star, he assured him that in the year in which he should behold that star in a part of the heavens which he designated, his life would be in imminent jeopardy; but should he survive this year of peril, he would become the richest and most renowned captain throughout the Indies.

Several years, it is added, had elapsed since this prediction was made; yet, that it still dwelt in the mind of Vasco Nuñez, was evident from the following circumstance. While waiting the return of his messenger, Garabito, he was on the

shore of Isla Rica one serene evening, in company with some
of his officers, when, regarding the heavens, he beheld the
fated star exactly in that part of the firmament which had
been pointed out by the Italian astrologer. Turning to his
companions, with a smile, "Behold," said he, "the wisdom
of those who believe in soothsayers, and, above all, in such
an astrologer, as Micer Codro! According to his prophecy, I
should now be in imminent peril of my life; yet, here I am,
within reach of all my wishes; sound in health, with four
brigantines and three hundred men at my command, and on
the point of exploring this great southern ocean."

At this fated juncture, says the chroniclers, arrived the
hypocritical letter of Pedrarias, inviting him to an interview
at Acla! The discreet reader will decide for himself what
credit to give to this anecdote, or rather, what allowance to
make for the little traits of coincidence gratuitously added
to the original fact by writers who delight in the marvellous.
The tenor of this letter awakened no suspicion in the breast
of Vasco Nuñez, who reposed entire confidence in the amity
of the governor as his intended father-in-law, and appears to
have been unconscious of anything in his own conduct that
could warrant hostility. Leaving his ships in command of
Francisco Compañon, he departed immediately to meet the
governor at Acla, unattended by any armed force.

The messengers who had brought the letter maintained at

first a cautious silence as to the events which had transpired at Darien. They were gradually won, however, by the frank and genial manners of Vasco Nuñez, and grieved to see so gallant a soldier hurrying into the snare. Having crossed the mountains and drawn near to Acla, their kind feelings got the better of their caution, and they revealed the true nature of their errand, and the hostile intentions of Pedrarias. Vasco Nuñez was struck with astonishment at the recital; but, being unconscious, it is said, of any evil intention, he could scarcely credit this sudden hostility in a man who had but recently promised him his daughter in marriage. He imagined the whole to be some groundless jealousy which his own appearance would dispel, and accordingly continued on his journey. He had not proceeded far, however, when he was met by a band of armed men, led by Francisco Pizarro. The latter stepped forward to arrest his ancient commander. Vasco Nuñez paused for a moment, and regarded him with a look of reproachful astonishment. "How is this, Francisco?" exclaimed he. "Is this the way you have been accustomed to receive me?" Offering no further remonstrance, he suffered himself quietly to be taken prisoner by his former adherent, and conducted in chains to Acla. Here he was thrown into prison, and Bartolome Hurtado, once his favourite officer, was sent to take command of his squadron.

CHAPTER XXVIII

Trial of Vasco Nuñez

DON PEDRARIAS concealed his exultation at the success of the stratagem by which he had ensnared his generous and confiding rival. He even visited him in prison, and pretended deep concern at being obliged to treat him with this temporary rigour, attributing it entirely to certain accusations lodged against him by the Treasurer Alonzo de la Puente, which his official situation compelled him to notice and investigate.

"Be not afflicted, however, my son!" said the hypocrite, "an investigation will, doubtless, not merely establish your innocence, but serve to render your zeal and loyalty towards your sovereign still more conspicuous."

While Pedrarias assumed this soothing tone towards his prisoner, he urged the Alcalde Mayor Espinosa to proceed against him with the utmost rigour of the law.

The charge brought against him of a treasonable conspiracy to cast off all allegiance to the crown, and to assume an independent sway on the borders of the Southern Sea, was principally supported by the confessions of Andres

Garabito. The evidence is also cited of a soldier, who stood
sentinel one night near the quarters of Vasco Nuñez on Isla
Rica, and who, being driven to take shelter from the rain
under the eaves of the house, overheard a conversation between that commander and certain of his officers, wherein
they agreed to put to sea with the squadron on their own
account, and to set the governor at defiance. This testimony,
according to Las Casas, arose from a misconstruction on the
part of the sentinel, who only heard a portion of their conversation, relating to their intention of sailing without waiting for orders, in case a new governor should arrive to
supersede Pedrarias.

The governor in the meantime informed himself from day
to day and hour to hour, of the progress of the trial, and,
considering the evidence sufficiently strong to warrant his
personal hostility, he now paid another visit to his prisoner,
and, throwing off all affectation of kindness, upbraided him
in the most passionate manner.

"Hitherto," said he, "I have treated you as a son, because I thought you loyal to your king, and to me as his
representative; but as I find you have meditated rebellion
against the crown of Castile, I cast you off from my affections, and shall henceforth treat you as an enemy."

Vasco Nuñez indignantly repelled the charge, and appealed to the confiding frankness of his conduct as a proof

of innocence. "Had I been conscious of my guilt," said he, "what could have induced me to come here and put myself into your hands? Had I meditated rebellion, what prevented me from carrying it into effect? I had four ships ready to weigh anchor, three hundred brave men at my command, and an open sea before me. What had I to do but to spread sail and press forward? There was no doubt of finding a land, whether rich or poor, sufficient for me and mine, far beyond the reach of your control. In the innocence of my heart, however, I came here promptly, at your mere request, and my reward is slander, indignity and chains!"

The noble and ingenuous appeal of Vasco Nuñez had no effect on the prejudiced feelings of the governor; on the contrary, he was but the more exasperated against his prisoner, and ordered that his irons should be doubled.

The trial was now urged by him with increased eagerness. Lest the present accusation should not be sufficient to effect the ruin of his victim, the old inquest into his conduct as governor, which had remained suspended for many years, was revived, and he was charged anew with the wrongs inflicted on the Bachelor Enciso, and with the death of the unfortunate Nicuesa.

Notwithstanding all these charges, the trial went on slowly, with frequent delays; for the Alcalde Mayor, Gaspar de Espinosa, seems to have had but little relish for the task assigned him, and to have needed frequent spurring from the eager and passionate governor. He probably considered the accused as technically guilty, though innocent of all intentional rebellion, but was ordered to decide according to the strict letter of the law. He therefore at length gave a reluctant verdict against Vasco Nuñez, but recommended him to mercy, on account of his great services, or entreated that, at least, he might be permitted to appeal. "No!" said the unrelenting Pedrarias, "if he has merited death, let him suffer death!" He accordingly condemned him to be beheaded. The same sentence was passed upon several of his officers, who were implicated in his alleged conspiracy; among these was Hernando de Arguello, who had written the letter to Vasco Nuñez, informing him of the arrest of his messenger, and advising him to put to sea, without heeding the hostility of Pedrarias. As to the perfidious informer Garabito, he was pardoned and set at liberty.

In considering this case as far as we are enabled, from the imperfect testimony that remains on record, we are inclined to think it one where passion and self interest interfered with the pure administration of justice. Pedrarias had always considered Vasco Nuñez as a dangerous rival, and, though his jealousy had been for some time lulled by looking on him as an intended son-in-law, it was revived by the suggestion that he intended to evade his alliance, and to dispute his authority. His exasperated feelings hurried him too far to retreat, and, having loaded his prisoner with chains and indignities, his death became indispensable to his own security.

For our own part, we have little doubt, that it was the fixed intention of Vasco Nuñez, after he had once succeeded in the arduous undertaking of transporting his ships across the mountains, to suffer no capricious order from Pedrarias, or any other governor, to defeat the enterprise which he had so long meditated, and for which he had so laboriously prepared. It is probable he may have expressed such general determination in the hearing of Garabito and of others of his companions. We can find ample excuse for such a resolution in his consciousness of his own deserts; his experience of past hinderances to his expedition, arising from the jealousy of others; his feeling of some degree of authority, from his office of Adelantado; and his knowledge of the favourable disposition and kind intentions of his sovereign towards him. We acquit him entirely of the senseless idea of rebelling against the crown; and suggest these considerations in palliation of any meditated disobedience of Pedrarias, should such a charge be supposed to have been substantiated.

CHAPTER XXIX

Execution of Vasco Nuñez.—[1517.]

IT WAS a day of gloom and horror at Acla, when Vasco Nuñez and his companions were led forth to execution. The populace were moved to tears at the unhappy fate of a man, whose gallant deeds had excited their admiration, and whose generous qualities had won their hearts. Most of them regarded him as the victim of a jealous tyrant; and even those who thought him guilty, saw something brave and brilliant in the very crime imputed to him. Such, however, was the general dread inspired by the severe measures of Pedrarias, that no one dared to lift up his voice, either in murmur or remonstrance.

The public crier walked before Vasco Nuñez, proclaiming, "This is the punishment inflicted by command of the king and his lieutenant, Don Pedrarias Davila, on this man, as a traitor and an usurper of the territories of the crown."

When Vasco Nuñez heard these words, he exclaimed indignantly, "It is false! never did such a crime enter my mind. I have ever served my king with truth and loyalty, and sought to augment his dominions."

These words were of no avail in his extremity, but they were fully believed by the populace.

The execution took place in the public square of Acla; and we are assured by the historian, Oviedo, who was in the colony at the time, that the cruel Pedrarias was a secret witness of the bloody spectacle, which he contemplated from between the reeds of the wall of a house, about twelve paces from the scaffold![77]

Vasco Nuñez was the first to suffer death. Having confessed himself and partaken of the sacrament, he ascended the scaffold with a firm step and a calm and manly demeanour; and laying his head upon the block, it was severed in an instant from his body. Three of his officers, Valderrabano, Botello, and Hernan Muños, were in like manner brought one by one to the block, and the day had nearly expired before the last of them was executed.

One victim still remained. It was Hernan de Arguello, who had been condemned as an accomplice, for having written the intercepted letter.

The populace could no longer restrain their feelings. They had not dared to intercede for Vasco Nuñez, knowing the implacable enmity of Pedrarias; but they now sought the governor, and throwing themselves at his feet, entreated that this man might be spared, as he had taken no active part in the alleged treason. The daylight, they said, was at an end, and it seemed as if God had hastened the night, to prevent the execution.

The stern heart of Pedrarias was not to be touched. "No," said he, "I would sooner die myself than spare one of them." The unfortunate Arguello was led to the block. The brief tropical twilight was past, and in the gathering gloom of the night the operations on the scaffold could not be distinguished. The multitude stood listening in breathless silence, until the stroke of the executioner told that all was accomplished. They then dispersed to their homes with hearts filled with grief and bitterness, and a night of lamentation succeeded to this day of horrors.

The vengeance of Pedrarias was not satisfied with the death of his victim: he confiscated his property and dishonoured his remains, causing his head to be placed upon a pole and exposed for several days, in the public square.[78]

Thus perished, in his forty-second year, in the prime and vigour of his days and the full career of his glory, one of the most illustrious and deserving of the Spanish discoverers— a victim of the basest and most perfidious envy.

How vain are our most confident hopes, our brightest triumphs! When Vasco Nuñez from the mountains of Darien, beheld the Southern Ocean revealed to his gaze, he considered its unknown realms at his disposal. When he had launched his ships upon its waters, and his sails were in a

manner flapping in the wind, to bear him in quest of the
wealthy empire of Peru, he scoffed at the prediction of the
astrologer, and defied the influence of the stars. Behold him
interrupted at the very moment of his departure; betrayed
into the hands of his most invidious foe; the very enterprise
that was to have crowned him with glory wrested into a
crime; and himself hurried to a bloody and ignominious
grave, at the foot, as it were, of the mountain from whence
he had made his discovery! His fate, like that of his renowned predecessor Columbus, proves, that it is sometimes
dangerous even to discern too greatly!

The Fortunes of
VALDIVIA AND HIS
COMPANIONS

IT WAS in the year 1512 that Valdivia, the regidor of Darien, was sent to Hispaniola by Vasco Nuñez de Balboa for reinforcements and supplies for the colony. He set sail in a caravel, and pursued his voyage prosperously until he arrived in sight of the island of Jamaica. Here he was encountered by one of the violent hurricanes which sweep those latitudes, and driven on the shoals and sunken rocks called the Vipers, since infamous for many a shipwreck. His vessel soon went to pieces, and Valdivia and his crew, consisting of twenty men, escaped with difficulty in the boat, without having time to secure a supply either of water or provisions. Having no sails, and their oars being scarcely fit for use, they were driven about for thirteen days, at the mercy of the currents of those unknown seas. During this time their sufferings from hunger and thirst were indescribable. Seven of their number perished, and the rest were nearly famished, when they were stranded on the eastern coast of Yucatan, in a province called Maya. Here they were set upon by the natives, who broke their boat in pieces, and carried them off captive to the cacique of the province, by whose orders they were mewed up in a kind of pen.

At first their situation appeared tolerable enough considering the horrors from which they had escaped. They were closely confined, it is true, but they had plenty to eat and drink, and soon began to recover flesh and vigour. In a little while, however, their enjoyment of this good cheer met with a sudden check, for the unfortunate Valdivia, and four of his companions, were singled out by the cacique, on account of their improved condition, to be offered up to his idols. The natives of this coast in fact were cannibals, devouring the flesh of their enemies and of such strangers as fell into their hands. The wretched Valdivia and his fellow victims, therefore, were sacrificed in the bloody temple of the idol, and their limbs afterwards served up at a grand feast held by the cacique and his subjects.

The horror of the survivers may be more readily imagined than described. Their hearts died within them when they heard the yells and howlings of the savages over their victims, and the still more horrible revelry of their cannibal orgies. They turned with loathing from the food set so abundantly before them, at the idea that it was but intended to fatten them for a future banquet.

Recovering from the first stupor of alarm, their despair lent them additional force. They succeeded in breaking, in the night, from the kind of cage in which they were confined, and fled to the depths of the forest. Here they wandered about forlorn, exposed to all the dangers and miseries of the wilderness; famishing with hunger, yet dreading to approach the haunts of men. At length their sufferings drove them forth from the woods into another part of the country, where they were again taken captive. The cacique of this province, however, was an enemy to the one from whom they had escaped, and of less cruel propensities. He spared their lives, and contented himself with making them slaves, exacting from them the severest labour. They had to cut and draw wood, to procure water from a distance, and to carry enormous burthens. The cacique died soon after their capture, and was succeeded by another called Taxmar. He was a chief of some talent and sagacity, but he continued the same rigorous treatment of the captives. By degrees they sank beneath the hardships of their lot, until only two were left; one of them a sturdy sailor named Gonzalo Guerrero, the other a kind of clerical adventurer named Jeronimo de Aguilar. The sailor had the good luck to be transferred to the service of the cacique of the neighbouring province of Chatemal, by whom he was treated with kindness. Being a thorough son of the ocean, seasoned to all weathers, and ready for any chance or change, he soon accommodated himself to his new situation, followed the cacique to the wars, rose by his hardihood and prowess to be a distinguished warrior, and succeeded in gaining the heart and hand of an Indian princess.

The other surviver, Jeronimo de Aguilar, was of a different complexion. He was a native of Ecija, in Andalusia, and had been brought up to the church, and regularly ordained, and shortly afterwards had sailed in one of the expeditions to San Domingo, from whence he had passed to Darien.

He proceeded in a different mode from that adopted by his comrade, the sailor, in his dealings with the Indians, and in one more suited to his opposite calling. Instead of playing the hero among the men, and the gallant among the women, he recollected his priestly obligations to humility and chastity. Accordingly, he made himself a model of meekness and obedience to the cacique and his warriors, while he closed his eyes to the charms of the infidel women. Nay, in the latter respect, he reinforced his clerical vows by a solemn promise to God to resist all temptations of the flesh, so he might be delivered out of the hands of these Gentiles.

Such were the opposite measures of the sailor and the saint, and they appear to have been equally successful. Aguilar, by his meek obedience to every order, however arbitrary and capricious, gradually won the good will of the cacique and his family. Taxmar, however, subjected him to many trials before he admitted him to his entire confidence. One day when the Indians, painted and decorated in warlike style, were shooting at a mark, a warrior, who had for some time fixed his eyes on Aguilar, approached suddenly and seized him by the arm. "Thou seest," said he, "the certainty of these archers; if they aim at the eye, they hit the eye—if at the mouth, they hit the mouth—what wouldest thou think, if thou were to be placed instead of the mark, and they were to shoot at and miss thee?"

Aguilar secretly trembled lest he should be the victim of some cruel caprice of the kind. Dissembling his fears, however, he replied with great submission, "I am your slave, and you may do with me as you please; but you are too wise to destroy a slave who is so useful and obedient." His answer pleased the cacique, who had secretly sent this warrior to try his humility.

Another trial of the worthy Jeronimo was less stern and fearful indeed, but equally perplexing. The cacique had remarked his unexampled discretion with respect to the sex, but doubted his sincerity. After laying many petty temptations in his way, which Jeronimo resisted with the self denial of a saint, he at length determined to subject him to a fiery ordeal. He accordingly sent him on a fishing expedition accompanied by a buxom damsel of fourteen years of age:

they were to pass the night by the seaside, so as to be ready to fish at the first dawn of day, and were allowed but one hammock to sleep in. It was an embarrassing predicament—not apparently to the Indian beauty, but certainly to the scrupulous Jeronimo. He remembered, however, his double vow, and, suspending his hammock to two trees, resigned it to his companion; while, lighting a fire on the seashore, he stretched himself before it on the sand. It was, as he acknowledged, a night of fearful trial, for his sandy couch was cold and cheerless, the hammock warm and tempting; and the infidel damsel had been instructed to assail him with all manner of blandishments and reproaches. His resolution, however, though often shaken, was never overcome; and the morning dawned upon him still faithful to his vow.

The fishing over, he returned to the residence of the cacique, where his companion, being closely questioned, made known the triumph of his self-denial before all the people. From that time forward he was held in great respect; the cacique especially treated him with unlimited confidence, entrusting to him the care, not merely of his house, but of his wives, during his occasional absence.

Aguilar now felt ambitious of rising to greater consequence among the savages, but this he knew was only to be done by deeds of arms. He had the example of the sturdy seaman,

Gonzalo Guerrero, before his eyes, who had become a great captain in the province in which he resided. He entreated Taxmar therefore to entrust him with bow and arrows, buckler and war club, and to enrol him among his warriors. The cacique complied. Aguilar soon made himself expert at his new weapons, signalised himself repeatedly in battle, and, from his superior knowledge of the arts of war, rendered Taxmar such essential service, as to excite the jealousy of some of the neighbouring caciques. One of them remonstrated with Taxmar for employing a warrior who was of a different religion, and insisted that Aguilar should be sacrificed to their gods. "No," replied Taxmar, "I will not make so base a return for such signal services: surely the gods of Aguilar must be good, since they aid him so effectually in maintaining a just cause."

The cacique was so incensed at this reply that he assembled his warriors and marched to make war upon Taxmar. Many of the counsellors of the latter urged him to give up the stranger who was the cause of this hostility. Taxmar, however, rejected their counsel with disdain and prepared for battle. Aguilar assured him that his faith in the Christian's God would be rewarded with victory; he, in fact, concerted a plan of battle which was adopted. Concealing himself, with a chosen band of warriors, among thickets and herbage, he suffered the enemy to pass by in making their attack. Taxmar and his host pretended to give way at the first onset. The foe rushed heedlessly in pursuit; whereupon Aguilar and his ambuscade assaulted them in the rear. Taxmar turned upon them in front; they were thrown in confusion, routed with great slaughter, and many of their chiefs taken prisoners. This victory gave Taxmar the sway over the land, and strengthened Aguilar more than ever in his good graces.

Several years had elapsed in this manner, when, in 1517, intelligence was brought to the province of the arrival on the neighbouring coast of great vessels of wonderful construction, filled with white and bearded men, who fought with thunder and lightning. It was, in fact, the squadron of Francisco Hernandez de Cordova, then on a voyage of discovery. The tidings of this strange invasion spread consternation through the country, heightened, if we may credit the old Spanish writers, by a prophecy current among the savages of these parts, and uttered in former times by a priest named Chilam Cambal, who foretold that a white and bearded people would come from the region of the rising sun, who would overturn their idols and subjugate the land.

The heart of Jeronimo de Aguilar beat quick with hope when he heard of European ships at hand; he was distant from the coast, however, and perceived that he was too closely watched by the Indians to have any chance of escape.

Dissembling his feelings, therefore, he affected to hear of the ships with perfect indifference, and to have no desire to join the strangers. The ships disappeared from the coast, and he remained disconsolate at heart, but was regarded with increased confidence by the natives.

His hopes were again revived in the course of a year or two by the arrival on the coast of other ships, which were those commanded by Juan de Grijalva, who coasted Yucatan in 1518; Aguilar, however, was again prevented by the jealous watchfulness of the Indians from attempting his escape, and when this squadron left the coast he considered all chance of deliverance at an end.

Seven years had gone by since his capture, and he had given up all hopes of being restored to his country and friends, when, in 1519, there arrived one day at the village three Indians, natives of the small island of Cozumel, which lies a few leagues in the sea, opposite the eastern coast of Yucatan. They brought tidings of another visit of white bearded men to their shores, and one of them delivered a letter to Aguilar, which, being entirely naked, he had concealed it in the long tresses of his hair which were bound round his head.

Aguilar received the letter with wonder and delight, and read it in presence of the cacique and his warriors. It proved to be from Hernando Cortes, who was at that time on his

great expedition, which ended in the conquest of Mexico.
He had been obliged by stress of weather to anchor at the
island of Cozumel, where he learned from the natives, that
several white men were detained in captivity among the
Indians on the neighbouring coast of Yucatan. Finding it
impossible to approach the mainland with his ships, he prevailed upon three of the islanders, by means of gifts and
promises, to venture upon an embassy among their cannibal
neighbours, and to convey a letter to the captive white men.
Two of the smallest caravels of the squadron were sent
under the command of Diego de Ordas, who was ordered
to land the three messengers at the point of Cotoche, and
to wait there eight days for their return.

The letter brought by these envoys informed the Christian captives of the force and destination of the squadron of
Cortes, and of his having sent the caravels to wait for them
at the point of Cotoche, with a ransom for their deliverance,
inviting them to hasten and join him at Cozumel.

The transport of Aguilar on first reading the letter, was
moderated when he reflected on the obstacles that might
prevent him from profiting by his chance of deliverance. He
had made himself too useful to the cacique to hope that he
would readily give him his liberty, and he knew the jealous
and irritable nature of the savages too well not to fear that
even an application for leave to depart might draw upon

him the severest treatment. He endeavoured, therefore, to operate upon the cacique through his apprehensions. To this end he informed him that the piece of paper which he held in his hand brought him a full account of the mighty armament that had arrived on the coast. He described the number of the ships and various particulars concerning the squadron, all which were amply corroborated by the testimony of the messengers. The cacique and his warriors were astonished at this strange mode of conveying intelligence from a distance, and regarded the letter as something mysterious and supernatural. Aguilar went on to relate the tremendous and superhuman powers of the people in these ships, who, armed with thunder and lightning, wreaked destruction on all who displeased them, while they dispensed inestimable gifts and benefits on such as proved themselves their friends. He, at the same time spread before the cacique various presents brought by the messengers, as specimens of the blessings to be expected from the friendship of the strangers. The intimation was effectual. The cacique was filled with awe at the recital of the terrific powers of the white men, and his eyes were dazzled by the glittering trinkets displayed before him. He entreated Aguilar, therefore, to act as his embassador and mediator, and to secure him the amity of the strangers.

Aguilar saw with transport the prospect of a speedy

deliverance. In this moment of exultation, he bethought himself of the only surviving comrade of his past fortunes, Gonsalo Guerrero, and, sending the letter of Cortes to him, invited him to accompany him in his escape. The sturdy seaman was at this time a great chieftain in his province, and his Indian bride had borne him a numerous progeny. His heart, however, yearned after his native country, and he might have been tempted to leave his honours and dignities, his infidel wife and half savage offspring behind him, but an insuperable, though somewhat ludicrous, obstacle presented itself to his wishes. Having long since given over all expectation of a return to civilized life, he had conformed to the customs of the country, and had adopted the external signs and decorations that marked him as a warrior and a man of rank. His face and hands were indelibly painted or tattooed; his ears and lips were slit to admit huge Indian ornaments, and his nose was drawn down almost to his mouth by a massy ring of gold, and a dangling jewel.

Thus curiously garbled and disfigured, the honest seaman felt, that however he might be admired in Yucatan, he should be apt to have the rabble at his heels in Spain. He made up his mind, therefore, to remain a great man among the savages, rather than run the risk of being shown as a man-monster at home.

Finding that he declined accompanying him, Jeronimo de

Aguilar set off for the point of Cotoche, escorted by three Indians. The time he had lost in waiting for Guerrero had nearly proved fatal to his hopes, for when he arrived at the point, the caravels sent by Cortes had departed, though several crosses of reeds set up in different places gave tokens of the recent presence of Christians.

The only hope that remained, was that the squadron of Cortes might yet linger at the opposite island of Cozumel; but how was he to get there? While wandering disconsolately along the shore, he found a canoe, half buried in sand and water, and with one side in a state of decay; with the assistance of the Indians he cleaned it, and set it afloat, and on looking further he found the stave of a hogshead which might serve for a paddle. It was a frail embarkation in which to cross an arm of the sea, several leagues wide, but there was no alternative. Prevailing on the Indians to accompany him, he launched forth in the canoe and coasted the mainland until he came to the narrowest part of the strait, where it was but four leagues across; here he stood directly for Cozumel, contending, as well as he was able, with a strong current, and at length succeeded in reaching the island.

He had scarce landed when a party of Spaniards, who had been lying in wait, rushed forth from their concealment, sword in hand. The three Indians would have fled, but

Aguilar reassured them, and, calling out to the Spaniards in their own language, assured them that he was a Christian. Then, throwing himself upon his knees, and raising his eyes, streaming with tears to heaven, he gave thanks to God for having restored him to his countrymen.

The Spaniards gazed at him with astonishment: from his language he was evidently a Castilian, but to all appearance he was an Indian. He was perfectly naked; wore his hair braided round his head in the manner of the country, and his complexion was burnt by the sun to a tawny colour. He had a bow in his hand, a quiver at his shoulder, and a network pouch at his side in which he carried his provisions.

The Spaniards proved to be a reconnoitering party, sent out by Cortes to watch the approach of the canoe, which had been descried coming from Yucatan. Cortes had given up all hopes of being joined by the captives, the caravel having waited the allotted time at Cotoche, and returned without news of them. He had in fact made sail to prosecute his voyage, but fortunately one of his ships had sprung a leak, which had obliged him to return to the island.

When Jeronimo de Aguilar and his companions arrived in the presence of Cortes, who was surrounded by his officers, they made a profound reverence, squatted on the ground, laid their bows and arrows beside them, and touching their right hands, wet with spittle on the ground, rubbed them about the region of the heart, such being their sign of the most devoted submission.

Cortes greeted Aguilar with a hearty welcome, and raising him from the earth, took from his own person a large yellow mantle lined with crimson, and threw it over his shoulders. The latter, however, had for so long a time gone entirely naked, that even this scanty covering was at first almost insupportable, and he had become so accustomed to the diet of the natives, that he found it difficult to reconcile his stomach to the meat and drink set before him.

When he had sufficiently recovered from the agitation of his arrival among Christians, Cortes drew from him the particulars of his story, and found that he was related to one of his own friends, the licentiate Marcos de Aguilar. He treated him, therefore, with additional kindness and respect, and retained him about his person to aid him as an interpreter in his great Mexican expedition.

The happiness of Jeronimo de Aguilar at once more being restored to his countrymen, was doomed to suffer some alloy from the disasters that had happened in his family. Peter Martyr records a touching anecdote of the effect that had been produced upon his mother by the tidings of his misfortune. A vague report had reached her in Spain, that her son had fallen into the hands of cannibals. All the horrible tales that circulated in Spain concerning the treatment of these savages to their prisoners rushed to her imagination, and she went distracted. Whenever she beheld roasted meat, or flesh upon the spit, she would fill the house with her out-cries. "Oh wretched mother! oh most miserable of women!" would she exclaim, "behold the limbs of my murdered son."[79]

It is to be hoped that the tidings of his deliverance had a favourable effect upon her intellects, and that she lived to rejoice at his after fortunes. He served Hernando Cortes with great courage and ability throughout his Mexican con-quests, acting sometimes as a soldier, sometimes as inter-preter and embassador to the Indians, and in reward of his fidelity, and services, was appointed regidor, or civil gov-ernor of the city of Mexico.

MICER CODRO, THE
ASTROLOGER

𝕿HE fate of the Italian astrologer, Micer Codro, who predicted the end of Vasco Nuñez, is related by the historian Oviedo, with some particulars that border upon the marvelous. It appears that, after the death of his patron, he continued for several years rambling about the New World, in the train of the Spanish discoverers; but intent upon studying the secrets of its natural history, rather than searching after its treasures.

In the course of his wanderings he was once coasting the shores of the Southern ocean, in a ship commanded by one Geronimo de Valenzuela, from whom he received such cruel treatment as to cause his death, though, what the nature of the treatment was, we are not precisely informed.

Finding his end approaching, the unfortunate astrologer addressed Valenzuela in the most solemn manner: "Captain," said he, "you have caused my death by your cruelty; I now summon you to appear with me, within a year, before the judgment seat of God!"

The captain made a light and scoffing answer, and treated his summons with contempt.

They were then off the coast of Veragua, near the verdant islands of Zebaco, which lie at the entrance of the Gulf of Paria. The poor astrologer gazed wistfully with his dying eyes upon the green and shady groves, and entreated the pilot or mate of the caravel to land him on one of the islands, that he might die in peace. "Micer Codro," replied the pilot, "those are not islands but points of land: there are no islands hereabout."

"There are, indeed," replied the astrologer, "two good and pleasant islands, well watered, and near to the coast, and within them is a great bay with a harbour. Land me, I pray you, upon one of these islands, that I may have comfort in my dying hour."

The pilot, whose rough nature had been touched with pity for the condition of the unfortunate astrologer, listened to his prayer, and conveyed him to the shore, where he found the opinion he had given of the character of the coast to be correct. He laid him on the herbage in the shade, where the poor wanderer soon expired. The pilot then dug a grave at the foot of a tree, where he buried him with all possible decency, and carved a cross on the bark to mark the grave.

Some time afterwards, Oviedo, the historian, was on the island with this very pilot, who showed him the cross on the tree, and gave his honest testimony to the good character and worthy conduct of Micer Codro. Oviedo, as he regarded the nameless grave, passed the eulogium of a scholar upon the poor astrologer: "He died," said he, "like Pliny, in the discharge of his duties, travelling about the world to explore the secrets of nature." According to his account the prediction of Micer Codro held good with respect to Valenzuela, as it had in the case of Vasco Nuñez. The captain died within the term in which he had summoned him to appear before the tribunal of God![80]

JUAN PONCE DE LEON

CONQUEROR OF PORTO RICO, AND DISCOVERER OF FLORIDA

CHAPTER I

Reconnoitering Expedition of Juan Ponce de Leon to the Island of Boriquen.—[1508.]

MANY years had elapsed since the discovery and colonization of Hayti, yet its neighbouring island of Boriquen, or as the Spaniards called it, St. Juan (since named Porto Rico), remained unexplored. It was beautiful to the eye as beheld from the sea, having lofty mountains clothed with forest trees of prodigious size and magnificent foliage. There were broad fertile valleys also, always fresh and green; for the frequent showers and abundant streams in these latitudes, and the absence of all wintry frost, produce a perpetual verdure. Various ships had occasionally touched at the island, but their crews had never penetrated into the interior. It was evident, however, from the number of hamlets and scattered houses, and the smoke rising in all directions from

among the trees, that it was well peopled. The inhabitants
still continued to enjoy their life of indolence and freedom,
unmolested by the ills that overwhelmed the neighbouring
island of Hayti. The time had arrived, however, when they
were to share the common lot of their fellow savages, and
to sink beneath the yoke of the white man.

At the time when Nicholas de Ovando, Governor of
Hispaniola, undertook to lay waste the great province of
Higuey, which lay at the eastern end of Hayti, he sent as
commander of part of the troops a veteran soldier, named
Juan Ponce de Leon. He was a native of Leon in Spain, and
in his boyhood had been page to Pedro Nuñez de Guzman,
Señor of Toral.[81] From an early age he had been schooled
to war, and had served in the various campaigns against the
Moors of Granada. He accompanied Columbus in his second voyage in 1493, and was afterwards, it is said, one of
the partizans of Francisco Roldan, in his rebellion against
the admiral. Having distinguished himself in various battles
with the Indians, and acquired a name for sagacity as well
as valour, he received a command subordinate to Juan de
Esquibel in the campaign against Higuey, and seconded his
chief so valiantly in that sanguinary expedition, that, after
the subjugation of the province, he was appointed to the
command of it, as lieutenant of the Governor of Hispaniola.

Juan Ponce de Leon had all the impatience of quiet life

and the passion for exploit of a veteran campaigner. He had not been long in the tranquil command of his province of Higuey, before he began to cast a wistful eye towards the green mountains of Boriquen. They were directly opposite, and but twelve or fourteen leagues distant, so as to be distinctly seen in the transparent atmosphere of the tropics. The Indians of the two islands frequently visited each other, and in this way Juan Ponce received the usual intelligence, that the mountains he had eyed so wistfully abounded with gold. He readily obtained permission from Governor Ovando to make an expedition to this island, and embarked in the year 1508, in a caravel, with a few Spaniards, and several Indian interpreters and guides.

After an easy voyage, he landed on the woody shores of the island, near to the residence of the principal cacique, Agueybana. He found the chieftain seated in patriarchal style under the shade of his native groves, and surrounded by his family, consisting of his mother, step-father, brother and sister, who vied with each other in paying homage to the strangers. Juan Ponce, in fact, was received into the bosom of the family, and the cacique exchanged names with him, which is the Indian pledge of perpetual amity. Juan Ponce also gave Christian names to the mother and step-father of the cacique, and would fain have baptized them, but they declined the ceremony, though they always took a pride in the names thus given them.

In his zeal to gratify his guests, the cacique took them to various parts of the island. They found the interior to correspond with the external appearance. It was wild and mountainous, but magnificently wooded, with deep rich valleys fertilized by limpid streams. Juan Ponce requested the cacique to reveal to him the riches of the island. The simple Indian showed him his most productive fields of Yuca, the groves laden with the most delicious fruit, the sweetest and purest fountains, and the coolest runs of water.

Ponce de Leon heeded but little these real blessings, and demanded whether the island produced no gold. Upon this the cacique conducted him to two rivers, the Manatuabon and the Zebuco, where the very pebbles seemed richly veined with gold, and large grains shone among the sand through the limpid water. Some of the largest of these were gathered by the Indians and given to the Spaniards. The quantity thus procured confirmed the hopes of Juan Ponce; and leaving several of his companions in the house of the hospitable cacique he returned to Hayti to report the success of his expedition. He presented the specimens of gold to the Governor Ovando, who assayed them in a crucible. The ore was not so fine as that of Hispaniola, but, as it was supposed to exist in greater quantities, the Governor determined on the subjugation of the island, and confided the enterprise to Juan Ponce de Leon.

CHAPTER II

Juan Ponce aspires to the government of Porto Rico.—
[1509.]

THE natives of Boriquen were more warlike than those of Hispaniola; being accustomed to the use of arms from the necessity of repelling the frequent invasions of the Caribs. It was supposed, therefore, that the conquest of their island would be attended with some difficulty, and Juan Ponce de Leon made another, and as it were, a preparatory visit, to make himself acquainted with the country, and with the nature and resources of the inhabitants. He found the companions whom he had left there on this former visit, in good health and spirits, and full of gratitude towards the cacique Agueybana who had treated them with undiminished hospitality. There appeared to be no need of violence to win the island from such simple hearted and confiding people. Juan Ponce flattered himself with the hopes of being appointed to its government by Ovando, and of bringing it peaceably into subjection. After remaining some time on the island, he returned to San Domingo to seek the desired appointment,

326

but to his surprise, found the whole face of affairs had changed during his absence.

His patron, the Governor Ovando, had been recalled to Spain, and Don Diego Columbus, son of the renowned discoverer, appointed in his place to the command at San Domingo. To add to the perplexities of Juan Ponce, a cavalier had already arrived from Spain, empowered by the king to form a settlement and build a fortress on the island of Porto Rico. His name was Christoval de Sotomayor; he was brother to the Count of Camina, and had been secretary to Philip I. surnamed the Handsome, king of Castile and father of Charles V.

Don Diego Columbus was highly displeased with the act of the king in granting these powers to Sotomayor, as it had been done without his knowledge and consent, and of course in disregard of his prerogative, as viceroy, to be consulted as to all appointments made within his jurisdiction. He refused, therefore, to put Sotomayor in possession of the island. He paid as little respect to the claims of Juan Ponce de Leon, whom he regarded with an ungracious eye as a favourite of his predecessor Ovando. To settle the matter effectually, he exerted what he considered his official and hereditary privilege, and chose officers to suit himself, appointing one Juan Ceron to the government of Porto Rico, and Miguel Diaz to serve as his lieutenant.[82]

Juan Ponce de Leon and his rival candidate, Christoval de Sotomayor, bore their disappointment with a good grace. Though the command was denied them, they still hoped to improve their fortunes in the island, and accordingly joined the crowd of adventurers that accompanied the newly appointed governor.

New changes soon took place in consequence of the jealousies and misunderstandings between king Ferdinand and the admiral as to points of privilege. The former still seemed disposed to maintain the right of making appointments without consulting Don Diego, and exerted it in the present instance; for, when Ovando, on his return to Spain, made favourable representation of the merits of Juan Ponce de Leon, and set forth his services in exploring Porto Rico, the king appointed him governor of that island, and signified specifically that Don Diego Columbus should not presume to displace him.

CHAPTER III

*Juan Ponce rules with a strong hand.—Exasperation of the
Indians.—Their experiment to prove whether
the Spaniards were mortal.*

JUAN PONCE DE LEON assumed the command
of the island of Boriquen in the year 1509. Being
a fiery high-handed old soldier, his first step was
to quarrel with Juan Ceron and Miguel Diaz, the
ex-governor and his lieutenant, and to send them prisoners
to Spain.[83]

He was far more favourable to his late competitor, Christoval de Sotomayor. Finding him to be a cavalier of noble
blood and high connexions, yet void of pretension, and of
most accommodating temper, he offered to make him his
lieutenant, and to give him the post of Alcalde Mayor, an
offer which was very thankfully accepted.

The pride of rank, however, which follows a man even
into the wilderness, soon interfered with the quiet of Sotomayor; he was ridiculed for descending so much below his
birth and dignity, as to accept a subaltern situation to a
simple gentleman in the island which he had originally

aspired to govern. He could not withstand these sneers, but resigned his appointment, and remained in the island as a private individual; establishing himself in a village where he had a large repartimiento or allotment of Indians assigned to him by a grant from the king.

Juan Ponce fixed his seat of government in a town called Caparra, which he founded on the northern side of the island, about a league from the sea, in a neighbourhood supposed to abound in gold. It was in front of the port called Rico, which subsequently gave its name to the island. The road to the town was up a mountain, through a dense forest, and so rugged and miry that it was the bane of man and beast. It cost more to convey provisions and merchandize up this league of mountain than it had to bring them from Spain.

Juan Ponce, being firmly seated in his government, began to carve and portion out the island, to found towns, and to distribute the natives into repartimientos, for the purpose of exacting their labour.

The poor Indians soon found the difference between the Spaniards as guests, and the Spaniards as masters. They were driven to despair by the heavy tasks imposed upon them; for to their free spirits and indolent habits, restraint and labour were worse than death. Many of the most hardy and daring proposed a general insurrection, and a massacre of their oppressors; the great mass, however, were deterred by the belief that the Spaniards were supernatural beings and could not be killed.

A shrewd and sceptical cacique named Brayoan, determined to put their immortality to the test. Hearing that a young Spaniard named Salzedo, was passing through his lands, he sent a party of his subjects to escort him, giving them secret instructions how they were to act. On coming to a river they took Salzedo on their shoulders to carry him across, but, when in the midst of the stream, they let him fall, and, throwing themselves upon him, pressed him under water until he was drowned. Then dragging his body to the shore, and still doubting his being dead, they wept and howled over him, making a thousand apologies for having fallen upon him, and kept him so long beneath the surface.

The cacique Brayoan came to examine the body and pronounced it lifeless; but the Indians, still fearing it might possess lurking immortality and ultimately revive, kept watch over it for three days, until it showed incontestible signs of putrefaction.

Being now convinced that the strangers were mortal men like themselves, they readily entered into a general conspiracy to destroy them.[84]

CHAPTER IV

Conspiracy of the Caciques.—Fate of Sotomayor.

THE prime mover of the conspiracy among the natives was Agueybana, brother and successor to the hospitable cacique of the same name, who had first welcomed the Spaniards to the island, and who had fortunately closed his eyes in peace, before his native groves were made the scenes of violence and oppression. The present cacique had fallen within the repartimiento of Don Christoval de Sotomayor, and, though treated by that cavalier with kindness, could never reconcile his proud spirit to the yoke of vassalage.

Agueybana held secret councils with his confederate caciques, in which they concerted a plan of operations. As the Spaniards were scattered about in different places, it was agreed that, at a certain time, each cacique should despatch those within his province. In arranging the massacre of those within his own domains, Agueybana assigned to one of his inferior caciques the task of surprising the village of Sotomayor, giving him 3000 warriors for the purpose. He was to assail the village in the dead of the night, to set fire to the houses, and to slaughter all the inhabitants. He proudly, however, reserved to himself the honour of killing Don Christoval with his own hand.

Don Christoval had an unsuspected friend in the very midst of his enemies. Being a cavalier of gallant appearance and amiable and courteous manners, he had won the affections of an Indian princess, the sister of the cacique Agueybana. She had overheard enough of the war-council of her brother and his warriors to learn that Sotomayor was in danger. The life of her lover was more precious in her eyes than the safety of her brother and her tribe; hastening, therefore, to him, she told him all that she knew or feared, and warned him to be upon his guard. Sotomayor appears to have been of the most easy and incautious nature, void of all evil and deceit himself, and slow to suspect anything of the kind in others. He considered the apprehension of the princess, as dictated by her fond anxiety, and neglected to profit by her warning.

He received, however, about the same time, information from a different quarter, tending to the same point. A Spaniard, versed in the language and customs of the natives, had observed a number gathering together one evening, painted and decorated as if for battle. Suspecting some lurking mischief, he stripped and painted himself in their manner, and, favoured by the obscurity of the night, succeeded in mingling among them undiscovered. They were assembled round a fire performing one of their mystic war-dances, to the chant of an Areyto or legendary ballad. The strophes and responses treated of revenge and slaughter, and repeatedly mentioned the death of Sotomayor.

The Spaniard withdrew unperceived, and hastened to apprise Don Christoval of his danger. The latter still made light of these repeated warnings; revolving them, however, in his mind in the stillness of the night, he began to feel some uneasiness, and determined to repair in the morning to Juan Ponce de Leon, in his stronghold at Caparra. With his fated heedlessness, or temerity, however, he applied to Agueybana for Indians to carry his baggage, and departed slightly armed, and accompanied by but three Spaniards, although he had to pass through close and lonely forests, where he would be at the mercy of any treacherous or lurking foe.

The cacique watched the departure of his intended victim and set out shortly afterwards, dogging his steps at a distance through the forest, accompanied by a few chosen warriors. Agueybana and his party had not proceeded far when they met a Spaniard named Juan Gonzalez, who spoke the Indian language. They immediately assailed him and wounded him in several places. He threw himself at the feet of the cacique, imploring his life in the most abject terms. The chief spared him for the moment, being eager to make sure of Don Christoval. He overtook that incautious cavalier in the very heart of the woodland, and stealing silently upon him burst forth suddenly with his warriors from the covert of the thickets, giving the fatal war whoop. Before Sotomayor could put himself upon his guard a blow from the war club of the cacique felled him to the earth, when he was quickly despatched by repeated blows. The four Spaniards who accompanied him shared his fate, being assailed, not merely by the warriors who had come in pursuit of them, but by their own Indian guides.

When Agueybana had glutted his vengeance on this unfortunate cavalier, he returned in quest of Juan Gonzalez. The latter, however, had recovered sufficiently from his wounds to leave the place where he had been assailed, and, dreading the return of the savages, had climbed into a tree and concealed himself among the branches. From thence, with trembling anxiety he watched his pursuers as they searched all the surrounding forest for him. Fortunately they did not think of looking up into the trees, but, after beating the bushes for some time, gave up the search. Though he saw them depart, yet he did not venture from his concealment until the night had closed; he then descended from the tree and made the best of his way to the residence of certain Spaniards, where his wounds were dressed. When this was done he waited not to take repose, but repaired by a circuitous route to Caparra, and informed Juan Ponce de

Leon of the danger he supposed to be still impending over Sotomayor, for he knew not that the enemy had accomplished his death. Juan Ponce immediately sent out forty men to his relief. They came to the scene of massacre, where they found the body of the unfortunate cavalier, partly buried, but with the feet out of the earth.

In the meantime the savages had accomplished the destruction of the village of Sotomayor. They approached it unperceived, through the surrounding forest, and entering it in the dead of the night, set fire to the straw-thatched houses, and attacked the Spaniards as they endeavoured to escape from the flames.

Several were slain at the onset, but a brave Spaniard, named Diego de Salazar, rallied his countrymen, inspirited them to beat off the enemy, and succeeded in conducting the greater part of them, though sorely mangled and harassed, to the stronghold of the Governor at Caparra. Scarcely had these fugitives gained the fortress, when others came hurrying in from all quarters, bringing similar tales of conflagration and massacre. For once a general insurrection, so often planned in savage life, against the domination of the white men, was crowned with success. All the villages founded by the Spaniards had been surprised, about a hundred of their inhabitants destroyed, and the survivers driven to take refuge in a beleaguered fortress.

CHAPTER V

War of Juan Ponce with the cacique Agueybana.

J UAN PONCE DE LEON might now almost be considered a governor without territories and a general without soldiers. His villages were smoking ruins, and his whole force did not amount to a hundred men, several of whom were disabled by their wounds. He had an able and implacable foe in Agueybana, who took the lead of all the other caciques, and even sent envoys to the Caribs of the neighbouring islands, entreating them to forget all ancient animosities and to make common cause against these strangers—the deadly enemies of the whole Indian race. In the meantime the whole of this wild island was in rebellion, and the forests around the fortress of Caparra, rang with the whoops and yells of the savages, the blasts of their war conchs, and the stormy roaring of their drums.

Juan Ponce was a staunch and wary old soldier and not easily daunted. He remained grimly ensconced within his fortress, from whence he despatched messengers in all haste to Hispaniola, imploring immediate assistance. In the

337

meantime he tasked his wits to divert the enemy and to keep them at bay. He divided his little force into three bodies of about thirty men each, under the command of Diego Salazar, Miguel de Toro, and Luis de Anasco, and sent them out alternately to make sudden surprises and assaults, to form ambuscades, and to practise the other stratagems of partizan warfare, which he had learnt in early life, in his campaigns against the Moors of Granada.

One of his most efficient warriors was a dog named Berezillo, renowned for courage, strength and sagacity. It is said that he could distinguish those of the Indians who were allies, from those who were enemies of the Spaniards. To the former he was docile and friendly, to the latter fierce and implacable. He was the terror of the natives, who were unaccustomed to powerful and ferocious animals, and did more service in this wild warfare, than could have been rendered by several soldiers. His prowess was so highly appreciated that his master received for him the pay, allowance and share of booty, assigned to a cross-bow man, which was the highest stipend given."[85]

At length the stout old cavalier Juan Ponce was reinforced in his stronghold, by troops from Hispaniola, whereupon he sallied forth boldly to take revenge upon those who had thus held him in a kind of durance. His foe Agueybana was at that time encamped in his own territories with more

than five thousand warriors, but in a negligent unwatchful
state, for he knew nothing of the reinforcements of the
Spaniards, and supposed Juan Ponce shut up with his handful of men in Caparra. The old soldier, therefore, took him
completely by surprise, and routed him with great slaughter.
Indeed it is said the Indians were struck with a kind of
panic when they saw the Spaniards as numerous as ever,
notwithstanding the number they had massacred. Their belief in their immortality revived, they fancied that those
whom they had slain had returned to life, and they de-
spaired of victory over beings who could thus arise with
renovated vigour from the grave.

Various petty actions and skirmishes afterwards took
place, in which the Indians were defeated. Agueybana, however, disdained this petty warfare, and stirred up his countrymen to assemble their forces, and by one grand assault
to decide the fate of themselves and their island. Juan Ponce
received secret tidings of their intent, and of the place where
they were assembling. He had at that time barely eighty
men at his disposal, but then they were cased in steel and
proof against the weapons of the savages. Without stopping
to reflect, the high-mettled old cavalier put himself at their
head and led them through the forest in quest of the foe.

It was nearly sunset when he came in sight of the Indian
camp, and the multitude of warriors assembled there made

him pause, and almost repent of his temerity. He was as shrewd, however, as he was hardy and resolute. Ordering some of his men in the advance to skirmish with the enemy he hastily threw up a slight fortification with the assistance of the rest. When it was finished he withdrew his forces into it and ordered them to keep merely on the defensive. The Indians made repeated attacks, but were as often repulsed with loss. Some of the Spaniards, impatient of this covert warfare, would sally forth in open field with pike and cross-bow, but were called back within the fortification by their wary commander.

The cacique Agueybana was enraged at finding his host of warriors thus baffled and kept at bay by a mere handful of Spaniards. He beheld the night closing in, and feared that in the darkness the enemy would escape. Summoning his choicest warriors round him, therefore, he led the way in a general assault, when, as he approached the fortress he received a mortal wound from an arquebus and fell dead upon the spot.

The Spaniards were not aware at first of the importance of the chief whom they had slain. They soon surmised it, however, from the confusion that ensued among the enemy, who bore off the body with great lamentations, and made no further attack.

The wary Juan Ponce took advantage of the evident

distress of the foe, to draw off his small forces in the night, happy to get out of the terrible jeopardy into which a rash confidence had betrayed him. Some of his fiery spirited officers would have kept the field in spite of the overwhelming force of the enemy. "No, no," said the shrewd veteran; "it is better to protract the war than to risk all upon a single battle."

While Juan Ponce de Leon was fighting hard to maintain his sway over the island, his transient dignity was overturned by another power, against which the prowess of the old soldier was of no avail. King Ferdinand had repented of the step he had ill-advisedly taken, in superseding the governor and lieutenant governor, appointed by Don Diego Columbus. He became convinced, though rather tardily, that it was an infringement of the rights of the admiral, and that policy, as well as justice, required him to retract it. When Juan Ceron and Miguel Diaz, therefore, came prisoners to Spain, he received them graciously, conferred many favours on them to atone for their rough ejectment from office, and finally, after some time, sent them back, empowered to resume the command of the island. They were ordered, however, on no account to manifest rancour or ill will against Juan Ponce de Leon, or to interfere with any property he might hold, either in houses, lands, or Indians; but on the contrary, to cultivate the most friendly understanding with him. The king also wrote to the hardy veteran explaining to him, that this restitution of Ceron and Diaz had been determined upon in council, as a mere act of justice due to them, but was not intended as a censure upon his conduct, and that means should be sought to indemnify him for the loss of his command.

By the time the governor and his lieutenant reached the island, Juan Ponce had completed its subjugation. The death of the island champion, the brave Agueybana, had in fact been a death blow to the natives, and shows how much, in savage warfare, depends upon a single chieftain. They never made head of war afterwards; but, dispersing among their forests and mountains, fell gradually under the power of the Spaniards. Their subsequent fate was like that of their neighbours of Hayti. They were employed in the labour of the mines, and in other rude toils so repugnant to their nature that they sank beneath them, and, in a little while, almost all the aboriginals disappeared from the island.

CHAPTER VI

Juan Ponce de Leon hears of a wonderful country and miraculous fountain.

JUAN PONCE DE LEON resigned the command of Porto Rico with tolerable grace. The loss of one wild island and wild government was of little moment, when there was a new world to be shared out, where a bold soldier like himself, with sword and buckler, might readily carve out new fortunes for himself. Beside, he had now amassed wealth to assist him in his plans, and, like many of the early discoverers, his brain was teeming with the most romantic enterprises. He had conceived the idea that there was yet a third world to be discovered, and he hoped to be the first to reach its shores, and thus to secure a renown equal to that of Columbus.

While cogitating these things, and considering which way he should strike forth in the unexplored regions around him, he met with some old Indians who gave him tidings of a country which promised, not merely to satisfy the cravings of his ambition, but to realize the fondest dreams of the poets. They assured him that, far to the north, there existed

a land abounding in gold and in all manner of delights;
but, above all, possessing a river of such wonderful virtue
that whoever bathed in it would be restored to youth! They
added, that in times past, before the arrival of the Spaniards, a large party of the natives of Cuba had departed
northward in search of this happy land and this river of
life, and, having never returned, it was concluded that they
were flourishing in renovated youth, detained by the pleasures of that enchanting country.

Here was the dream of the Alchymist realized! one had
but to find this gifted land and revel in the enjoyment of
boundless riches and perennial youth! nay, some of the ancient Indians declared that it was not necessary to go so
far in quest of these rejuvenating waters, for that, in a
certain island of the Bahama group, called Bimini, which
lay far out in the ocean, there was a fountain possessing
the same marvelous and inestimable qualities.

Juan Ponce de Leon listened to these tales with fond
credulity. He was advancing in life, and the ordinary term
of existence seemed insufficient for his mighty plans. Could
he but plunge into this marvellous fountain or gifted river,
and come out with his battered, war-worn body restored to
the strength and freshness and suppleness of youth, and his
head still retaining the wisdom and knowledge of age, what

enterprises might he not accomplish in the additional course of vigorous years insured to him!

It may seem incredible, at the present day, that a man of years and experience could yield any faith to a story which resembles the wild fiction of an Arabian tale; but the wonders and novelties breaking upon the world in that age of discovery almost realised the illusions of fable, and the imaginations of the Spanish voyagers had become so heated that they were capable of any stretch of credulity.

So fully persuaded was the worthy old cavalier of the existence of the region described to him, that he fitted out three ships at his own expense to prosecute the discovery, nor had he any difficulty in finding adventurers in abundance ready to cruise with him in quest of this fairy-land.[86]

CHAPTER VII

*Cruise of Juan Ponce de Leon in search of the Fountain
of Youth.*—[1512.]

IT WAS on the third of March, 1512, that Juan Ponce
sailed with his three ships from the Port of St.
Germain in the island of Porto Rico. He kept for
some distance along the coast of Hispaniola, and
then, stretching away to the northward, made for the Bahama islands, and soon fell in with the first of the group.
He was favoured with propitious weather and tranquil seas,
and glided smoothly with wind and current along that verdant archipelago, visiting one island after another, until, on
the fourteenth of the month, he arrived at Guanahani, or
St. Salvador's, where Christopher Columbus had first put
his foot on the shores of the new world. His inquiries for
the island of Bimini were all in vain, and as to the fountain
of youth, he may have drank of every fountain, and river,
and lake, in the archipelago, even to the salt pools of Turk's
island, without being a whit the younger.

Still he was not discouraged; but, having repaired his
ships, he again put to sea and shaped his course to the

north-west. On Sunday, the 27th of March, he came in sight of what he supposed to be an island, but was prevented from landing by adverse weather. He continued hovering about it for several days, buffeted by the elements, until, in the night of the second of April, he succeeded in coming to anchor under the land in thirty degrees eight minutes of latitude. The whole country was in the fresh bloom of spring; the trees were gay with blossoms, and the fields covered with flowers; from which circumstance, as well as from having discovered it on Palm Sunday (Pascua Florida), he gave it the name of Florida, which it retains to the present day. The Indian name of the country was Cautio.[87]

Juan Ponce landed, and took possession of the country in the name of the Castilian Sovereigns. He afterwards continued for several weeks ranging the coasts of this flowery land, and struggling against the gulf-stream and the various currents which sweep it. He doubled Cape Cañaveral, and reconnoitered the southern and eastern shores without suspecting that this was a part of Terra Firma. In all his attempts to explore the country, he met with resolute and implacable hostility on the part of the natives, who appeared to be a fierce and warlike race. He was disappointed also in his hopes of finding gold, nor did any of the rivers or fountains which he examined possess the rejuvenating virtue. Convinced, therefore, that this was not the promised land of Indian tradition, he turned his prow homeward on the 14th of June, with the intention in the way of making one more attempt to find the island of Bimini.

In the outset of his return he discovered a group of islets abounding with sea-fowl and marine animals. On one of them his sailors, in the course of a single night, caught one hundred and seventy turtles, and might have taken many more, had they been so inclined. They likewise took fourteen sea wolves, and killed a vast quantity of pelicans and other birds. To this group Juan Ponce gave the name of the Tortugas, or turtles, which they still retain.

Proceeding in his cruise, he touched at another group of islets near the Lucayos, to which he gave the name of La Vieja, or the Old Woman group, because he found no inhabitant there but one old Indian woman.[88] This ancient sybil he took on board his ship to give him information about the labyrinth of islands into which he was entering, and perhaps he could not have had a more suitable guide in the eccentric quest he was making. Notwithstanding her pilotage, however, he was exceedingly baffled and perplexed in his return voyage among the Bahama islands, for he was forcing his way as it were against the course of nature, and encountering the currents which sweep westward along these islands, and the trade-wind which accompanies them. For a long time he struggled with all kinds of difficulties and dangers; and was obliged to remain upwards of a month in one of the islands to repair the damages which his ship had suffered in a storm.

Disheartened at length by the perils and trials with which nature seemed to have beset the approach to Bimini, as to some fairy island in romance, he gave up the quest in person, and sent in his place a trusty captain, Juan Perez de Ortubia, who departed in one of the other ships, guided by the experienced old woman of the isles, and by another Indian. As to Juan Ponce, he made the best of his way back to Porto Rico, where he arrived infinitely poorer in purse and wrinkled in brow, by this cruise after inexhaustible riches and perpetual youth.

He had not been long in port when his trusty envoy, Juan Perez, likewise arrived. Guided by the sage old woman, he had succeeded in finding the long-sought-for Bimini. He described it as being large, verdant, and covered with beautiful groves. There were crystal springs and limpid streams in abundance, which kept the island in perpetual verdure, but none that could restore to an old man the vernal greenness of his youth.

Thus ended the romantic expedition of Juan Ponce de Leon. Like many other pursuits of a chimera, it terminated in the acquisition of a substantial good. Though he had failed in finding the fairy fountain of youth, he had discovered in place of it the important country of Florida.[89]

CHAPTER VIII

Expedition of Juan Ponce against the Caribs.—His Death.—[1514.]

JUAN PONCE DE LEON now repaired to Spain to make a report of his voyage to King Ferdinand. The hardy old cavalier experienced much raillery from the witlings of the court on account of his visionary voyage, though many wise men had been as credulous as himself at the outset. The king, however, received him with great favour, and conferred on him the title of Adelantado of Bimini and Florida, which last was as yet considered an island. Permission was also granted him to recruit men either in Spain or in the colonies for a settlement in Florida; but he deferred entering on his command for the present, being probably discouraged and impoverished by the losses in his last expedition, or finding a difficulty in enlisting adventurers. At length another enterprise presented itself. The Caribs had by this time become a terror to the Spanish inhabitants of many of the islands, making descents upon the coasts and carrying off captives, who it was supposed were doomed to be devoured by these cannibals. So frequent were their invasions of the island of Porto Rico, that it was feared they would ultimately oblige the Spaniards to abandon it.

At length King Ferdinand, in 1514, ordered that three ships, well armed and manned, should be fitted out in Seville, destined to scour the islands of the Caribs, and to free the seas from those cannibal marauders. The command of the Armada was given to Juan Ponce de Leon, from his knowledge in Indian warfare, and his varied and rough experience which had mingled in him the soldier with the sailor. He was instructed in the first place to assail the Caribs of those islands most contiguous and dangerous to Porto Rico, and then to make war on those of the coast of Terra Firma, in the neighbourhood of Carthagena. He was afterwards to take the captaincy of Porto Rico, and to attend to the repartimientos or distributions of the Indians in conjunction with a person to be appointed by Diego Columbus.

The enterprise suited the soldier-like spirit of Juan Ponce de Leon, and the gallant old cavalier set sail full of confidence in January, 1515, and steered direct for the Caribbees, with a determination to give a wholesome castigation to the whole savage Archipelago. Arriving at the island of Guadaloupe, he cast anchor, and sent men on shore for wood and water, and women to wash the clothing of the crews, with a party of soldiers to mount guard.

Juan Ponce had not been as wary as usual, or he had to deal with savages unusually adroit in warfare. While the people were scattered carelessly on shore, the Caribs rushed forth from an ambuscade, killed the greater part of the men, and carried off the women to the mountains.

This blow at the very outset of his vaunted expedition sank deep into the heart of Juan Ponce, and put an end to all his military excitement. Humbled and mortified, he set sail for the island of Porto Rico, where he relinquished all further prosecution of the enterprise, under pretext of ill health, and gave the command of the squadron to a captain named Zuñiga; but it is surmised that his malady was not so much of the flesh as of the spirit. He remained in Porto Rico as governor; but, having grown testy and irritable through vexations and disappointments, he gave great offence, and caused much contention on the island by positive and strong-handed measures, in respect to the distributions of the Indians.

He continued for several years in that island, in a state of growling repose, until the brilliant exploits of Hernando Cortes, which threatened to eclipse the achievements of all the veteran discoverers, roused his dormant spirit.

Jealous of being cast in the shade in his old days, he determined to sally forth on one more expedition. He had heard that Florida, which he had discovered, and which he had hitherto considered a mere island, was part of Terra Firma, possessing vast and unknown regions in its bosom. If so, a grand field of enterprise lay before him, wherein he might make discoveries and conquests to rival, if not surpass, the far-famed conquest of Mexico.

Accordingly in the year 1521, he fitted out two ships at the island of Porto Rico, and embarked almost the whole of his property in the undertaking. His voyage was toilsome and tempestuous, but at length he arrived at the wished-for land. He made a descent upon the coast with a great part of his men, but the Indians sallied forth with unusual valour to defend their shores. A bloody battle ensued, several of the Spaniards were slain, and Juan Ponce was wounded by an arrow, in the thigh. He was borne on board his ship, and finding himself disabled for further action, set sail for Cuba, where he arrived ill in body and dejected in heart.

He was of an age where there is no longer prompt and healthful reaction either mental or corporeal. The irritations of humiliated pride and disappointed hope, exasperated the fever of his wound, and he died soon after his arrival at the island. "Thus fate," says one of the quaint old Spanish writers, "delights to reverse the schemes of man. The discovery that Juan Ponce flattered himself was to lead to a means of perpetuating his life, had the ultimate effect of hastening his death."

It may be said, however, that he has at least attained the shadow of his desire, since, though disappointed in extending the natural term of his existence, his discovery has ensured a lasting duration to his name.

The following epitaph was inscribed upon his tomb, which does justice to the warrior qualities of the stout old cavalier.

> Mole sub hac fortis requiescat ossa Leonis,
> Qui vicit factis nomina magna suis.

It has thus been paraphrased in Spanish by the Licentiate Juan de Castellanos.

> Aqueste lugar estrecho
> Es sepulchro del varon,
> Que en el nombre fue Leon,
> Y mucho mas en el hecho.

"In this sepulchre rest the bones of a man, who was a lion by name, and still more by nature."

APPENDIX

A VISIT TO PALOS

---

*[The following narrative was actually commenced, by the author
of this work, as a letter to a friend, but unexpectedly swelled
to its present size. He has been induced to insert it here
from the idea that many will feel the same curiosity to know
something of the present state of Palos and its inhabitants
that led him to make the journey.]*

Seville, 1828.

SINCE I last wrote to you I have made, what I
may term, an American Pilgrimage, to visit the
little port of Palos in Andalusia, where Columbus fitted out his ships, and whence he sailed
for the discovery of the New World. Need I tell you how
deeply interesting and gratifying it has been to me? I had
long meditated this excursion as a kind of pious, and if I
may so say, filial duty of an American, and my intention
was quickened when I learnt that many of the edifices mentioned in the history of Columbus still remained in nearly
the same state in which they existed at the time of his
sojourn at Palos, and that the descendants of the intrepid
Pinzons, who aided him with ships and money, and sailed

357

with him in the great voyage of discovery, still flourished in the neighborhood.

The very evening before my departure from Seville on the excursion, I heard that there was a young gentleman of the Pinzon family studying law in the city. I got introduced to him, and found him of most prepossessing appearance and manners. He gave me a letter of introduction to his father, Don Juan Fernandez Pinzon, resident of Moguer, and the present head of the family.

As it was in the middle of August, and the weather intensely hot, I hired a calesa for the journey. This is a two-wheeled carriage, resembling a cabriolet, but of the most primitive and rude construction; the harness is profusely ornamented with brass, and the horse's head decorated with tufts and tassels and dangling bobs of scarlet and yellow worsted. I had, for calasero, a tall, long-legged Andalusian, in short jacket, little round-crowned hat, breeches decorated with buttons from the hip to the knees, and a pair of russet leather bottinas or spatterdashes. He was an active fellow, though uncommonly taciturn for an Andalusian, and strode along beside his horse, rousing him occasionally to greater speed by a loud malediction or a hearty thwack of his cudgel.

In this style I set off late in the day to avoid the noontide heat, and after ascending the lofty range of hills that

borders the great valley of the Guadalquiver, and having
a rough ride among their heights, I descended about twilight
into one of those vast, silent, melancholy plains, frequent
in Spain, where I beheld no other signs of life than a roaming flock of bustards, and a distant herd of cattle, guarded
by a solitary herdsman, who, with a long pike planted in
the earth, stood motionless in the midst of the dreary landscape, resembling an Arab of the desert. The night had
somewhat advanced when we stopped to repose for a few
hours at a solitary venta or inn, if it might be so called,
being nothing more than a vast low-roofed stable, divided
into several compartments for the reception of the troops
of mules and arrieros (or carriers) who carry on the internal
trade of Spain. Accommodation for the traveller there was
none—not even for a traveller so easily accommodated as
myself. The landlord had no food to give me, and as to a
bed, he had none but a horse cloth, on which his only child,
a boy of eight years old, lay naked on the earthen floor.
Indeed the heat of the weather and the fumes from the
stables made the interior of the hovel insupportable, so I
was fain to bivouac on my cloak on the pavement at the
door of the venta, where, on waking after two or three hours
of sound sleep, I found a contrabandista (or smuggler)
snoring beside me, with his blunderbuss on his arm.

I resumed my journey before break of day, and had made

several leagues by ten o'clock, when we stopped to breakfast, and to pass the sultry hours of midday in a large village, from whence we departed about four o'clock, and,
after passing through the same kind of solitary country,
arrived just after sunset at Moguer. This little city (for at
present it is a city) is situated about a league from Palos,
of which place it has gradually absorbed all the respectable
inhabitants, and, among the number, the whole family of
the Pinzons.

So remote is this little place from the stir and bustle of
travel, and so destitute of the show and vainglory of this
world, that my calesa as it rattled and jingled along the
narrow and ill-paved streets caused a great sensation; the
children shouted and scampered along by its side, admir-
ing its splendid trappings of brass and worsted, and gazing
with reverence at the important stranger who came in so
gorgeous an equipage.

I drove up to the principal posada, the landlord of which
was at the door. He was one of the very civilest men in the
world, and disposed to do everything in his power to make
me comfortable; there was only one difficulty, he had neither
bed nor bed-room in his house. In fact, it was a mere venta
for muleteers, who are accustomed to sleep on the ground
with their mule cloths for beds and pack-saddles for pillows.
It was a hard case, but there was no better posada in the

place. Few people travel for pleasure or curiosity in these out-of-the-way parts of Spain, and those of any note are generally received into private houses. I had travelled sufficiently in Spain to find out that a bed, after all, is not an article of indispensable necessity, and was about to bespeak some quiet corner where I might spread my cloak, when fortunately the landlord's wife came forth. She could not have a more obliging disposition than her husband, but then— God bless the women!—they always know how to carry their good wishes into effect. In a little while a small room, about ten feet square, that had formed a thoroughfare between the stables and a kind of shop or bar room, was cleared of a variety of lumber, and I was assured that a bed should be put up there for me. From the consultations I saw my hostess holding with some of her neighbour gossips, I fancied the bed was to be a kind of piece-meal contribution among them for the credit of the house.

As soon as I could change my dress, I commenced the historical researches which were the object of my journey, and inquired for the abode of Don Juan Fernandez Pinzon. My obliging landlord himself volunteered to conduct me thither, and I set off full of animation at the thoughts of meeting with the lineal representative of one of the coadjutors of Columbus.

A short walk brought us to the house, which was most respectable in its appearance, indicating easy, if not affluent circumstances. The door, as is customary in Spanish villages, during summer, stood wide open. We entered with the usual salutation or rather summons, "Ave Maria!" A trim Andalusian handmaid answered to the call, and, on our inquiring for the master of the house, led the way across a little patio or court, in the centre of the edifice, cooled by a fountain surrounded by shrubs and flowers, to a back court or terrace, likewise set out with flowers, where Don Juan Fernandez was seated with his family, enjoying the serene evening in the open air.

I was much pleased with his appearance. He was a venerable old gentleman, tall and somewhat thin, with fair complexion and grey hair. He received me with great urbanity, and on reading the letter from his son, appeared struck with surprise to find I had come quite to Moguer, merely to visit the scene of the embarkation of Columbus; and still more so on my telling him, that one of my leading objects of curiosity was his own family connexion; for it would seem that the worthy cavalier had troubled his head but little about the enterprizes of his ancestors.

I now took my seat in the domestic circle and soon felt myself quite at home, for there is generally a frankness in the hospitality of Spaniards that soon puts a stranger at his ease beneath their roof. The wife of Don Juan Fernandez was extremely amiable and affable, possessing much of that

natural aptness for which the Spanish women are remarkable. In the course of conversation with them I learnt, that
Don Juan Fernandez, who is seventy-two years of age, is the
eldest of five brothers, all of whom are married, have numerous offspring, and live in Moguer and its vicinity, in nearly
the same condition and rank of life as at the time of the discovery. This agreed with what I had previously heard, respecting the families of the discoverers. Of Columbus no lineal
and direct descendant exists; his was an exotic stock that
never took deep and lasting root in the country; but the race of
the Pinzons continues to thrive and multiply in its native soil.

While I was yet conversing, a gentleman entered, who
was introduced to me as Don Luis Fernandez Pinzon, the
youngest of the brothers. He appeared to be between fifty
and sixty years of age, somewhat robust, with fair complexion and grey hair, and a frank and manly deportment.
He is the only one of the present generation that has followed the ancient profession of the family; having served
with great applause as an officer of the royal navy, from
which he retired, on his marriage, about twenty-two years
since. He is the one, also, who takes the greatest interest
and pride in the historical honours of his house, carefully
preserving all the legends and documents of the achievements and distinctions of his family, a manuscript volume
of which he lent me for my inspection.

Don Juan now expressed a wish that, during my residence in Moguer, I would make his house my home. I endeavoured to excuse myself, alleging, that the good people at the po- sada had been at such extraordinary trouble in preparing quarters for me, that I did not like to disappoint them. The worthy old gentleman undertook to arrange all this, and, while supper was preparing, we walked together to the posada. I found that my obliging host and hostess had in- deed exerted themselves to an uncommon degree. An old rickety table had been spread out in a corner of the little room as a bedstead, on top of which was propped up a grand *cama de luxo*, or state bed, which appeared to be the admiration of the house. I could not, for the soul of me, appear to under-value what the poor people had prepared with such hearty good will, and considered such a triumph of art and luxury; so I again entreated Don Juan to dispense with my sleeping at his house, promising most faithfully to make my meals there while I should stay at Moguer, and as the old gentleman understood my motives for declining his invitation, and felt a good humoured sympathy in them, we readily arranged the matter. I returned therefore with Don Juan to his house, and supped with his family. During the repast a plan was agreed upon for my visit to Palos, and to the convent of La Rabida, in which Don Juan volun- teered to accompany me and be my guide, and the following day was allotted to the expedition. We were to breakfast at a hacienda, or country seat, which he possessed in the vicinity of Palos, in the midst of his vineyards, and were to dine there on our return from the convent. These arrangements being made, we parted for the night; I returned to the posada highly gratified with my visit, and slept soundly in the extraordinary bed which, I may almost say, had been invented for my accommodation.

On the following morning, bright and early, Don Juan Fernandez and myself set off in the calesa for Palos. I felt apprehensive at first, that the kind-hearted old gentleman, in his anxiety to oblige, had left his bed at too early an hour, and was exposing himself to fatigues unsuited to his age. He laughed at the idea, and assured me that he was an early riser, and accustomed to all kinds of exercise on horse and foot, being a keen sportsman, and frequently passing days together among the mountains on shooting expeditions, taking with him servants, horses, and provisions, and living in a tent. He appeared, in fact, to be of an active habit, and to possess a youthful vivacity of spirit. His cheerful disposition rendered our morning drive extremely agreeable; his urbanity was shown to every one whom we met on the road; even the common peasant was saluted by him with the appellation of *caballero*, a mark of respect ever gratifying to the poor but proud Spaniard, when yielded by a superior.

As the tide was out we drove along the flat grounds bordering the Tinto. The river was on our right, while on our left
was a range of hills, jutting out into promontories, one beyond the other, and covered with vineyards and fig trees.
The weather was serene, the air soft and balmy, and the
landscape of that gentle kind calculated to put one in a quiet
and happy humour. We passed close by the skirts of Palos,
and drove to the hacienda, which is situated at some little
distance from the village, between it and the river. The
house is a low stone building, well white-washed, and of great
length; one end being fitted up as a summer residence, with
saloons, bed-rooms, and a domestic chapel; and the other as
a bodega or magazine for the reception of the wine produced
on the estate.

The house stands on a hill, amidst vineyards, which are
supposed to cover a part of the site of the ancient town of
Palos, now shrunk to a miserable village. Beyond these vineyards, on the crest of a distant hill, are seen the white walls
of the convent of La Rabida rising above a dark wood of pine
trees.

Below the hacienda flows the river Tinto, on which Columbus embarked. It is divided by a low tongue of land, or
rather the sand bar of Saltes, from the river Odiel, with
which it soon mingles its waters, and flows on to the ocean.
Beside this sand bar, where the channel of the river runs

deep, the squadron of Columbus was anchored, and from hence he made sail on the morning of his departure.

The soft breeze that was blowing scarcely ruffled the surface of this beautiful river; two or three picturesque barks, called mysticks, with long latine sails were gliding down it. A little aid of the imagination might suffice to picture them as the light caravels of Columbus, sallying forth on their eventful expedition, while the distant bells of the town of Huelva, which were ringing melodiously, might be supposed as cheering the voyagers with a farewell peal.

I cannot express to you what were my feelings on treading the shore which had once been animated by the bustle of departure, and whose sands had been printed by the last footstep of Columbus. The solemn and sublime nature of the event that had followed, together with the fate and fortunes of those concerned in it, filled the mind with vague yet melancholy ideas. It was like viewing the silent and empty stage of some great drama when all the actors had departed. The very aspect of the landscape, so tranquilly beautiful, had an effect upon me, and as I paced the deserted shore by the side of a descendant of one of the discoverers, I felt my heart swelling with emotions and my eyes filling with tears.

What surprised me was to find no semblance of a seaport; there was neither wharf nor landing-place—nothing but a naked river bank, with the hulk of a ferry-boat, which I was told carried passengers to Huelva, lying high and dry on the sands, deserted by the tide. Palos, though it has doubtless dwindled away from its former size, can never have been important as to extent and population. If it possessed warehouses on the beach, they have disappeared. It is at present a mere village of the poorest kind, and lies nearly a quarter of a mile from the river, in a hollow among hills. It contains a few hundred inhabitants, who subsist principally by labouring in the fields and vineyards. Its race of merchants and mariners are extinct. There are no vessels belonging to the place, nor any show of traffic, excepting at the season of fruit and wine, when a few mysticks and other light barks anchor in the river to collect the produce of the neighbourhood. The people are totally ignorant and it is probable that the greater part of them scarce know even the name of America. Such is the place from whence sallied forth the enterprise for the discovery of the western world!

We were now summoned to breakfast in a little saloon of the hacienda. The table was covered with natural luxuries produced upon the spot—fine purple and muscatel grapes from the adjacent vineyard, delicious melons from the garden, and generous wines made on the estate. The repast was heightened by the genial manners of my hospitable host, who appeared to possess the most enviable cheerfulness of spirit and simplicity of heart.

After breakfast we set off in the calesa to visit the Convent of La Rabida, which is about half a league distant. The road, for a part of the way, lay through the vineyards, and was deep and sandy. The calasero had been at his wit's end to conceive what motive a stranger like myself, apparently travelling for mere amusement, could have in coming so far to see so miserable a place as Palos, which he set down as one of the very poorest places in the whole world; but this additional toil and struggle through deep sand to visit the old Convent of La Rabida, completed his confusion—"Hombre!" exclaimed he, "es una ruina! no hay mas que dos frailes!"— "Zounds! why it's a ruin! there are only two friars there!" Don Juan laughed, and told him that I had come all the way from Seville precisely to see that old ruin and those two friars. The calasero made the Spaniard's last reply when he is perplexed—he shrugged his shoulders and crossed himself.

After ascending a hill and passing through the skirts of a straggling pine wood, we arrived in front of the convent. It stands in a bleak and solitary situation, on the brow of a rocky height or promontory, overlooking to the west a wide range of sea and land, bounded by the frontier mountains of Portugal, about eight leagues distant. The convent is shut out from a view of the vineyard of Palos by the gloomy forest of pines which I have mentioned, which cover the promontory to the east, and darken the whole landscape in that direction.

There is nothing remarkable in the architecture of the convent; part of it is Gothic, but the edifice, having been frequently repaired, and being whitewashed, according to a universal custom in Andalusia, inherited from the Moors, it has not that venerable aspect which might be expected from its antiquity.

We alighted at the gate where Columbus, when a poor pedestrian, a stranger in the land, asked bread and water for his child! As long as the convent stands, this must be a spot calculated to awaken the most thrilling interest. The gate remains apparently in nearly the same state as at the time of his visit, but there is no longer a porter at hand to administer to the wants of the wayfarer. The door stood wide open, and admitted us into a small court yard. From thence we passed through a Gothic portal into the chapel, without seeing a human being. We then traversed two interior cloisters, equally vacant and silent, and bearing a look of neglect and dilapidation. From an open window we had a peep at what had once been a garden, but that had also gone to ruin; the walls were broken and thrown down; a few shrubs, and a scattered fig-tree or two were all the traces of cultivation that remained. We passed through the long dormitories, but the cells were shut up and abandoned; we saw no living thing except a solitary cat stealing across a distant corridor, which fled in a panic at the unusual sight of strangers. At length, after patrolling nearly the whole of the empty building to the echo of our own footsteps, we came to where the door of a cell, being partly open, gave us the sight of a monk within, seated at a table writing. He rose and received us with much civility, and conducted us to the superior, who was reading in an adjacent cell. They were both rather young men, and, together with a noviciate and a lay-brother, who officiated as cook, formed the whole community of the convent.

Don Juan Fernandez communicated to them the object of my visit, and my desire also to inspect the archives of the convent to find if there was any record of the sojourn of Columbus. They informed us that the archives had been entirely destroyed by the French. The younger monk, however, who had perused them, had a vague recollection of various particulars concerning the transactions of Columbus at Palos, his visit to the convent, and the sailing of his expedition. From all that he cited, however, it appeared to me that all the information on the subject contained in the archives, had been extracted from Herrera and other well known authors. The monk was talkative and eloquent, and soon diverged from the subject of Columbus, to one which he considered of infinitely greater importance;—the miraculous image of the Virgin possessed by their convent, and known by the name of "Our Lady of La Rabida." He gave us a history of the wonderful way in which the image had been found buried in the earth, where it had lain hidden for ages, since the time of the conquest of Spain by the Moors; the disputes between the convent and different places in the neighbourhood for the possession of it; the marvellous protection it extended to the adjacent country, especially in preventing all madness, either in man or dog, for this malady was anciently so prevalent in this place as to gain it the appellation of La Rabida, by which it was originally called; a name which, thanks to the beneficent influence of the Virgin, it no longer merited or retained. Such are the legends and reliques with which every convent in Spain is enriched,which are zealously cried up by the monks, and devoutly credited by the populace.

Twice a year on the festival of our Lady of La Rabida, and on that of the patron saint of the order, the solitude and silence of the convent are interrupted by the intrusion of a swarming multitude, composed of the inhabitants of Moguer, of Huelva, and the neighbouring plains and mountains. The open esplanade in front of the edifice resembles a fair, the adjacent forest teems with the motley throng, and the image of our Lady of La Rabida is borne forth in triumphant procession.

While the friar was thus dilating upon the merits and renown of the image, I amused myself with those day dreams, or conjurings of the imagination to which I am a little given.

As the internal arrangements of convents are apt to be the same from age to age, I pictured to myself this chamber as the same inhabited by the guardian, Juan Perez de Marchena at the time of the visit of Columbus. Why might not the old and ponderous table before me be the very one on which he displayed his conjectural maps, and expounded his theory of a western route to India? It required but another stretch of the imagination to assemble the little conclave around the table; Juan Perez the friar, Garci Fernandez the physician, and Martin Alonzo Pinzon the bold navigator, all listening with wrapped attention to Columbus, or to the tale of some old seaman of Palos, about islands seen in the western parts of the ocean.

The friars, as far as their poor means and scanty knowledge extended, were disposed to do everything to promote the object of my visit. They showed us all parts of the convent, which, however, has little to boast of, excepting the historical associations connected with it. The library was reduced to a few volumes, chiefly on ecclesiastical subjects, piled promiscuously in the corner of a vaulted chamber, and covered with dust. The chamber itself was curious, being the most ancient part of the edifice, and supposed to have formed part of a temple in the time of the Romans.

We ascended to the roof of the convent to enjoy the extensive prospect it commands. Immediately below the

promontory on which it is situated, runs a narrow but toler-
ably deep river, called the Domingo Rubio, which empties
itself into the Tinto. It is the opinion of Don Luis Fernandez
Pinzon, that the ships of Columbus were careened and fitted
out in this river, as it affords better shelter than the Tinto,
and its shores are not so shallow. A lonely bark of a fisherman
was lying in this stream, and not far off, on a sandy point,
were the ruins of an ancient watch-tower. From the roof of
the convent, all the windings of the Odiel and the Tinto were
to be seen, and their junction into the main stream, by which
Columbus sallied forth to sea. In fact the convent serves as a
landmark, being, from its lofty and solitary situation, visible
for a considerable distance to vessels coming on the coast.
On the opposite side I looked down upon the lonely road,
through the wood of pine trees, by which the zealous guardian of the convent, Fray Juan Perez departed at midnight
on his mule, when he sought the camp of Ferdinand and
Isabella in the Vega of Granada, to plead the project of
Columbus before the queen.

Having finished our inspection of the convent, we prepared
to depart, and were accompanied to the outward portal by
the two friars. Our calesero brought his rattling and rickety
vehicle for us to mount; at sight of which one of the monks
exclaimed, with a smile, "Santa Maria! only to think! A
calesa before the gate of the convent of La Rabida!" And,

indeed, so solitary and remote is this ancient edifice, and so simple is the mode of living of the people in this bye-corner of Spain, that the appearance of even a sorry calesa might well cause astonishment. It is only singular that in such a bye-corner the scheme of Columbus should have found intelligent listeners and coadjutors, after it had been discarded, almost with scoffing and contempt, from learned universities and splendid courts.

On our way back to the hacienda, we met Don Rafael, a younger son of Don Juan Fernandez, a fine young man about twenty-one years of age, and who, his father informed me, was at present studying French and mathematics. He was well mounted on a spirited grey horse, and dressed in the Andalusian style, with the little round hat and jacket. He sat his horse gracefully, and managed him well. I was pleased with the frank and easy terms on which Don Juan appeared to live with his children. This I was inclined to think his favourite son, as I understood he was the only one that partook of the old gentleman's fondness for the chase, and that accompanied him in his hunting excursions.

A dinner had been prepared for us at the hacienda, by the wife of the capitaz, or overseer, who, with her husband, seemed to be well pleased with this visit from Don Juan, and to be confident of receiving a pleasant answer from the good humoured old gentleman whenever they addressed him. The dinner was served up about two o'clock, and was a most agreeable meal. The fruits and wines were from the estate, and were excellent; the rest of the provisions were from Moguer, for the adjacent village of Palos is too poor to furnish anything. A gentle breeze from the sea played through the hall, and tempered the summer heat. Indeed I do not know when I have seen a more enviable spot than this country retreat of the Pinzons. Its situation on a breezy hill, at no great distance from the sea, and in a southern climate, produces a happy temperature, neither hot in summer nor cold in winter. It commands a beautiful prospect, and is surrounded by natural luxuries. The country abounds with game, the adjacent river affords abundant sport in fishing, both by day and night, and delightful excursions for those fond of sailing. During the busy seasons of rural life, and especially at the joyous period of vintage, the family pass some time here, accompanied by numerous guests, at which times, Don Juan assured me, there was no lack of amusements, both by land and water.

When we had dined, and taken the siesta, or afternoon nap, according to the Spanish custom in summer time, we set out on our return to Moguer, visiting the village of Palos in the way. Don Gabriel had been sent in advance to procure the keys of the village church, and to apprise the curate of our wish to inspect the archives. The village consists principally of two streets of low white-washed houses. Many of the inhabitants have very dark complexions, betraying a mixture of African blood.

On entering the village, we repaired to the lowly mansion of the curate. I had hoped to find him some such personage as the curate in Don Quixote, possessed of shrewdness and information in his limited sphere, and that I might gain some anecdotes from him concerning his parish, its worthies, its antiquities, and its historical events. Perhaps I might have done so at any other time, but, unfortunately, the curate was something of a sportsman, and had heard of some game among the neighbouring hills. We met him just sallying forth from his house, and, I must confess, his appearance was picturesque. He was a short, broad, sturdy, little man, and had doffed his cassock and broad clerical beaver, for a short jacket and a little round Andalusian hat; he had his gun in hand, and was on the point of mounting a donkey which had been led forth by an ancient withered handmaid. Fearful of being detained from his foray, he accosted my companion the moment he came in sight. "God preserve you, Señor Don Juan! I have received your message, and have but one answer to make. The archives have all been destroyed. We have no trace of anything you seek for—nothing—nothing. Don Rafael has the keys of the church. You can examine it at your leisure—Adios, caballero!" With these words the galliard little curate mounted his donkey, thumped his ribs with the butt end of his gun, and trotted off to the hills.

On our way to the church we passed by the ruins of what had once been a fair and spacious dwelling, greatly superior to the other houses of the village. This, Don Juan informed me, was an old family possession, but since they had removed from Palos it had fallen to decay for want of a tenant. It was probably the family residence of Martin Alonzo or Vicente Yañez Pinzon, in the time of Columbus.

We now arrived at the church of St. George, in the porch of which, Columbus first proclaimed to the inhabitants of Palos the order of the sovereigns, that they should furnish him with ships for his great voyage of discovery. This edifice has lately been thoroughly repaired, and, being of solid mason work, promises to stand for ages, a monument of the discoverers. It stands outside of the village, on the brow of a hill, looking along a little valley toward the river. The remains of a Moorish arch prove it to have been a mosque in former times; just above it, on the crest of the hill, is the ruin of a Moorish castle.

I paused in the porch and endeavoured to recall the interesting scene that had taken place there, when Columbus, accompanied by the zealous friar, Juan Perez, caused the public notary to read the royal order in presence of the astonished alcaldes, regidors, and alguazils; but it is difficult to conceive the consternation that must have been struck into so remote a little community, by this sudden apparition of an entire stranger among them, bearing a command that they should put their persons and ships at his disposal, and sail with him away into the unknown wilderness of the ocean.

The interior of the church has nothing remarkable, excepting a wooden image of St. George vanquishing the Dragon, which is erected over the high altar, and is the admiration of the good people of Palos, who bear it about the streets in grand procession on the anniversary of the saint. This group existed in the time of Columbus, and now flourishes in renovated youth and splendour, having been newly painted and gilded, and the countenance of the saint rendered peculiarly blooming and lustrous.

Having finished the examination of the church, we resumed our seats in the calesa and returned to Moguer. One thing only remained to fulfil the object of my pilgrimage. This was to visit the chapel of the Convent of Santa Clara. When Columbus was in danger of being lost in a tempest on his way home from his great voyage of discovery, he made a vow, that should he be spared, he would watch and pray one whole night in this chapel; a vow which he doubtless fulfilled immediately after his arrival.

My kind and attentive friend, Don Juan, conducted me to the convent. It is the wealthiest in Moguer, and belongs to a

sisterhood of Franciscan nuns. The chapel is large, and ornamented with some degree of richness, particularly the part
about the high altar, which is embellished by magnificent
monuments of the brave family of the Puerto Carreros, the
ancient lords of Moguer, and renowned in Moorish warfare.
The alabaster effigies of distinguished warriors of that house,
and of their wives and sisters, lie side by side, with folded
hands, on tombs immediately before the altar, while others
recline in deep niches on either side. The night had closed in
by the time I entered the church, which made the scene more
impressive. A few votive lamps shed a dim light about the
interior; their beams were feebly reflected by the guilded
work of the high altar, and the frames of the surrounding
paintings, and rested upon the marble figures of the warriors
and dames lying in the monumental repose of ages. The
solemn pile must have presented much the same appearance
when the pious discoverer performed his vigil, kneeling before this very altar, and praying and watching throughout
the night, and pouring forth heart-felt praises for having
been spared to accomplish his sublime discovery.

I had now completed the main purpose of my journey,
having visted the various places connected with the story of
Columbus. It was highly gratifying to find some of them so
little changed though so great a space of time had inter-
vened; but in this quiet nook of Spain, so far removed from

the main thoroughfares, the lapse of time produces but few violent revolutions. Nothing, however, had surprised and gratified me more than the continued stability of the Pinzon family. On the morning after my excursion to Palos, chance gave me an opportunity of seeing something of the interior of most of their households. Having a curiosity to visit the remains of a Moorish castle, once the citadel of Moguer, Don Fernandez undertook to show me a tower which served as a magazine of wine to one of the Pinzon family. In seeking for the key we were sent from house to house of nearly the whole connexion. All appeared to be living in that golden mean equally removed from the wants and superfluities of life, and all to be happily interwoven by kind and cordial habits of intimacy. We found the females of the family generally seated in the patios, or central courts of their dwellings, beneath the shade of awnings and among shrubs and flowers. Here the Andalusian ladies are accustomed to pass their mornings at work, surrounded by their handmaids, in the primitive, or rather, oriental style. In the porches of some of the houses I observed the coat of arms, granted to the family by Charles V. hung up like a picture in a frame. Over the door of Don Luis, the naval officer, it was carved on an escutcheon of stone, and coloured. I had gathered many particulars of the family also from conversation with Don Juan, and from the family legend lent me by Don Luis. From all that I could learn, it would appear that the lapse of nearly three centuries and a half has made but little change in the condition of the Pinzons. From generation to generation they have retained the same fair standing and reputable name throughout the neighbourhood, filling offices of public trust and dignity, and possessing great influence over their fellow citizens by their good sense and good conduct. How rare is it to see such an instance of stability of fortune in this fluctuating world, and how truly honourable is this hereditary respectability, which has been secured by no titles or entails, but perpetuated merely by the innate worth of the race! I declare to you that the most illustrious descents of mere titled rank could never command the sincere respect and cordial regard with which I contemplated this staunch and enduring family, which for three centuries and a half has stood merely upon its virtues.

As I was to set off on my return to Seville before two o'clock, I partook of a farewell repast at the house of Don Juan, between twelve and one, and then took leave of his household with sincere regret. The good old gentleman, with the courtesy, or rather the cordiality of a true Spaniard, accompanied me to the posada to see me off. I had dispensed but little money in the posada—thanks to the hospitality of the Pinzons—yet the Spanish pride of my host and hostess seemed pleased that I had preferred their humble chamber, and the scanty bed they had provided me, to the spacious mansion of Don Juan; and when I expressed my thanks for their kindness and attention, and regaled mine host with a few choice cigars, the heart of the poor man was overcome. He seized me by both hands and gave me a parting benediction, and then ran after the calasero to enjoin him to take particular care of me during my journey.

Taking a hearty leave of my excellent friend Don Juan, who had been unremitting in his attentions to me to the last moment, I now set off on my wayfaring, gratified to the utmost with my visit, and full of kind and grateful feelings towards Moguer and its hospitable inhabitants.

MANIFESTO OF ALONZO DE OJEDA

[The following curious formula, composed by learned divines in Spain, was first read aloud by the friars in the train of Alonzo de Ojeda as a prelude to his attack on the savages of Carthagena; and was subsequently adopted by the Spanish discoverers in general, in their invasions of the Indian countries.]

I ALONZO DE OJEDA, servant of the high and mighty kings of Castile and Leon, civilizers of barbarous nations, their messenger and captain, notify and make known to you, in the best way I can, that God our Lord one and eternal, created the heavens and the earth, and one man and one woman, from whom you, and we, and all the people of the earth were and are descendants, procreated, and all those who shall come after us; but the vast number of generations which have proceeded from them, in the course of more than five thousand years that have elapsed since the creation of the world, made it necessary that some of the human race should disperse in one direction

384

and some in another, and that they should divide themselves
into many kingdoms and provinces, as they could not sustain and preserve themselves in one alone. All these people
were given in charge, by God our Lord, to one person, named
Saint Peter, who was thus made Lord and superior of all the
people of the earth, and head of the whole human lineage,
whom all should obey, wherever they might live, and whatever might be their law, sect or belief; he gave him also the
whole world for his service and jurisdiction, and though he
desired that he should establish his chair in Rome, as a place
most convenient for governing the world, yet he permitted
that he might establish his chair in any other part of the
world, and judge and govern all the nations, Christians,
Moors, Jews, Gentiles, and whatever other sect or belief
might be. This person was denominated Pope, that is to say,
admirable, supreme, father and guardian, because he is
father and governor of all mankind. This holy father was
obeyed and honoured as lord, king, and superior of the
universe by those who lived in his time, and, in like manner,
has been obeyed and honoured by all those who have been
elected to the Pontificate, and thus it has continued unto the
present day, and will continue until the end of the world.

One of these Pontiffs of whom I have spoken, as lord of
the world, made a donation of these islands and continents,
of the ocean, sea, and all that they contain, to the Catholic

kings of Castile, who, at that time were Ferdinand and Isabella of glorious memory, and to their successors, our sovereigns, according to the tenor of certain papers drawn up for the purpose, (which you may see if you desire.) Thus his majesty is king and sovereign of these islands and continents by virtue of the said donation; and as king and sovereign, certain islands, and almost all to whom this has been notified, have received his majesty, and have obeyed and served and do actually serve him. And, moreover, like good subjects, and with good will, and without any resistance or delay, the moment they were informed of the foregoing, they obeyed all the religious men sent among them to preach and teach our Holy Faith; and these of their free and cheerful will, without any condition or reward, became Christians, and continue so to be. And his majesty received them kindly and benignantly, and ordered that they should be treated like his other subjects and vassals: you also, are required and obliged to do the same. Therefore, in the best manner I can, I pray and entreat you, that you consider well what I have said, and that you take whatever time is reasonable to understand and deliberate upon it, and that you recognise the church for sovereign and superior of the universal world, and the supreme Pontiff, called Pope, in her name, and his majesty in his place, as superior and sovereign king of the islands and Terra Firma, by virtue of the said donation; and that you consent that these religious fathers declare and preach to you the foregoing; and if you shall so do, you will do well; and will do that to which you are bounden and obliged; and his majesty, and I in his name, will receive you with all due love and charity, and will leave you, your wives and children, free from servitude, that you may freely do with these and with yourselves whatever you please, and think proper, as have done the inhabitants of the other islands. And besides this, his majesty will give you many privileges and exemptions, and grant you many favours. If you do not do this, or wickedly and intentionally delay to do so, I certify to you, that, by the aid of God, I will powerfully invade and make war upon you in all parts and modes that I can, and will subdue you to the yoke and obedience of the church and of his majesty: and I will take your wives and children and make slaves of them, and sell them as such, and dispose of them as his majesty may command; and I will take your effects and will do you all the harm and injury in my power, as vassals who will not obey or receive their sovereign, and who resist and oppose him. And I protest that the deaths and disasters which may in this manner be occasioned, will be the fault of yourselves and not of his majesty, nor of me, nor of these cavaliers who accompany me. And of what I here tell you and require of you, I call upon the notary here present to give me his signed testimonial.

THE END

NOTES

1. Vespucci, Vespuchy.
2. Ojeda is pronounced in Spanish Oheda, with a strong aspiration of the *h*.
3. Varones Ilustres, por F. Pizarro y Orellana, p. 41. Las Casas, Hist. Ind. l. i. c. 82.
4. Pizarro. Varones Ilustres.
5. Navarrete, t. ii. Document, cxiii.
6. Navarrete. Collec. Viag. t. iii. p. 4.
7. Navarrete. t. iii. p. 5.
8. Viages de Vespucci. Navarrete. t. iii. p. 211.
9. There is some discrepance in the early accounts of this battle, as to the time and place of its occurrence. The author has collated the narratives of Vespucci, Las Casas, Herrera, and Peter Martyr, and the evidence given in the law-suit of Diego Columbus, and has endeavoured as much as possible to reconcile them.
10. Vespucci.—Letter to Lorenzo de Pier Francisco de Medicis.
11. Navarrete, t. iii. p. 8. Idem, pp. 107, 108.

It is worthy of particular mention that Ojeda, in his report of his voyage to the Sovereigns, informed them of his having met with English voyagers in the vicinity of Coquibacoa, and that the Spanish government attached such importance to his information as to take measures to prevent any intrusion into those parts by the English. It is singular that no record should exist of this early and extensive expedition of English navigators. If it was undertaken in the service of the Crown, some document might be found concerning it among the archives of the reign of Henry VII. The English had already discovered the continent of North America. This had been done in 1497, by John Cabot, a Venetian, accompanied by his son Sebastian, who was born in Bristol. They sailed under a license of Henry VII., who was to have a fifth of the profits of the voyage. On the 24th of June they discovered Newfoundland, and afterwards coasted the continent quite to Florida, bringing back to England a valuable cargo and several of the natives. *This was the first discovery of the mainland of America.* The success of this expedition may have prompted the one which Ojeda encountered in the neighbourhood of Coquibacoa.

12. Pronounced Ninyo. The Ñ in Spanish is always pronounced as if followed by the letter *y*.

13. Testimony of Bastides in the law suit of Diego Columbus.

14. Las Casas. Hist. Ind. lib. i. c. 171.

15. Navarrete, t. iii. p. 14.

16. Peter Martyr. Other historians give a different date for their arrival. Herrera says Feb. 6.

17. Navarrete. Collect. t. iii. p. 11. Herrera, d. i. l. iv. c. v.

18. Navarrete, vol. iii. See Doc. No. 7: where Vicente Yañez Pinzon petitions for redress.

19. On the 5th of September, 1501, a royal permission was given to Vicente Yañez Pinzon to colonize and govern the lands he had discovered, beginning a little north of the river Amazon, and extending to Cape St. Augustine. The object of the government in this permission was to establish an outpost and a resolute commander on this southern frontier, that should check any intrusions the Portuguese might make in consequence of the accidental discovery of a part of the coast of Brazil by Pedro Alvarez Cabral, in 1500. The subsequent arrangement of a partition line between the two countries prevented the necessity of this precaution, and it does not appear that Vicente Yañez Pinzon made any second voyage to those parts.

In 1506 he undertook an expedition in company with Juan Diaz de Solis, a native of Lebrija, the object of which was to endeavour to find the strait or passage supposed by Columbus to lead from the Atlantic to a southern ocean. It was necessarily without success, as was also another voyage made by them, for the same purpose, in 1508. As no such passage exists, no blame could attach to those able navigators for being foiled in the object of their search.

In consequence of the distinguished merits and services of the Pinzon family they were raised, by the emperor Charles V., to the dignity of a Hidalguia, or nobility, without any express title, and a coat of arms was granted them, on which were emblazoned three caravels, with a hand at the stern pointing to an island covered with savages. This coat of arms is still maintained by the family, who have added to it the motto granted to Columbus, merely substituting the name of Pinzon for that of the Admiral,

A Castile y a Leon,
Nuevo Mundo dio Pinzon.

20. Navarrete. Collec. t. iii.

21. Navarrete, t. iii. document x.

22. Hist. Gen. de Viages. Herrera, Hist. Ind.

23. Peter Martyr gives the following weighty testimony to the knowledge and skill of this excellent seamen:—"Of the Spaniards, as many as thought themselves to have any knowledge of what pertained to measure the land and sea, drew cardes (charts) on parchment as concerning these navigations. Of all others they most esteem them which Juan de la Cosa, the companion of Ojeda, and another pilot, called Andres Morales, had set forth, and this, as well for the great experience which both had, (*to whom these tracks were as well known as the chambers of their own houses,*) as also that they were thought to be cunninger in that part of cosmography which teacheth the description and measuring of the sea."

P. Martyr, Decad. ii. c. 10.

24. Equivalent to 10,650 dollars of the present day.

25. Francisco Pizarro was a native of Truxillo in Estremadura. He was the illegitimate fruit of an amour between Gonsalvo Pizarro, a veteran captain of infantry, and a damsel in low life. His childhood was passed in grovelling occupations incident to the humble condition of his mother, and he is said to have been a swineherd. When he had sufficiently increased in years and stature he enlisted as a soldier. His first campaigns may have been against the Moors in the war of Granada. He certainly served in Italy under the banner of the Great Captain, Gonsalvo of Cordova. His roving spirit then induced him to join the bands of adventurers to the New World. He was of ferocious courage, and, when engaged in any enterprise, possessed an obstinate perseverance that was neither to be deterred by danger, weakened by fatigue and hardship, or checked by repeated disappointment. After having conquered the great kingdom of Peru, he was assassinated, at an advanced age in 1541, defending himself bravely to the last.

26. Las Casas. Hist. Ind. l. ii. c. 57. MS.

27. The reader will find the complete form of this curious manifesto in the appendix.

28. The picture here given is so much like romance, that the author quotes his authority at length.—"Llegaron adonde havia, junto al agua de la mar, unos Manglares, que son arboles, que siempre nacen, i crecen i permanecen dentro del agua de la mar, con grandes raices, asidas, i enmarañadas unas con otras, i alli metido, i escondido hallaron à Alonso de Ojeda, con su espada en la mano, i la rodela en las espaldas, i en ella sobre trecientas señales de flechazos. Estabo descaido de hambre, que no podia hechar de si la habla; i si no fuera tan robusto, aunque chico de cuerpo, fuera muerto."

Las Casas. l. ii. c. 58. MS. Herrara, Hist. Ind. D. l. I. vii. c. xv.

29. Las Casas ubi. sup.

30. Las Casas, *ubi sup.*

31. Equivalent to 37,281 dollars of the present day.
32. Herrera, Hist. Ind. D. 1. l. vii. c. xvi.
33. Charlevoix, ut sup. p. 293.
34. Las Casas, Hist. Ind. lib. ii, c. 59. MS.
35. Hist. S. Domingo, lib. iv.
36. Herrera. Decad. 1. l. viii. c. 3.
37. Las Casas, Hist. Ind. l. ii. c. 60. MS.
38. Las Casas, Hist. Ind. c. 61, MS.—Herrera, Hist. Ind. d. i. l. ix., c. xv.
39. Las Casas, ubi sup.
40. Charlevoix, Hist. S. Doming.
41. Herrera, Hist. Ind. D. i. and viii. c. 2.
42. Herrera, Hist. Ind. d. 1. l. vii. c. 10.

43. The above anecdote is related by the Bachelor Enciso himself, in a geographical work entitled *Suma de Geographia*, which he published in Seville, in 1519. As the reply of the poor savages contains something of natural logic we give a part of it as reported by the Bachelor. "Respondieron me: que en lo que dezia que no avia sino un dios y que este governaba el cielo y la tierra y que era señor de todo que les parecia y que asi debia ser: pero que en lo que dezia que el papa era señor de todo el universo en lugar de dios y que el avia fecho merced de aquella tierra al rey de Castilla; dixeron que el papa debiera estar boracho quando lo hizo, pues daba lo que no era suyo, y que el rey que pedia y tomava tal merced debia ser algun loco pues pedia lo que era de otros," &c.

44. Equivalent to a present sum of 53,259 dollars.

45. The harbour of Nombre de Dios continued for a long time to present traces of the sufferings of the Spaniards. We are told by Herrera, that several years after the time here mentioned, a band of eighty Spanish soldiers, commanded by Gonzalo de Badajos, arrived at the harbour with an intention of penetrating into the interior. They found there the ruined fort of Nicuesa, together with sculls and bones, and crosses erected on heaps of stones, dismal mementos of his followers who had perished of hunger; the sight of which struck such horror and dismay into the hearts of the soldiers that they would have abandoned their enterprise, had not their intrepid captain immediately sent away the ships, and thus deprived them of the means of retreating. Herrera, d. 11. l. i.

46. Las Casas, Hist. Ind. l. ii. c. 68.
47. Las Casas, *ut sup.* c. 68.
48. P. Martyr, D. 3. c. vi.
49. P. Martyr, decad. 3. c. vi. Idem. d. 7. c. x.

50. In recording this expedition, the author has followed the old Spanish narratives, written when the face of the country was but little known, and he was much perplexed to reconcile the accounts given of numerous streams with the rivers laid down on modern maps. By a clear and judicious explanation, given in the recent work of Don Manuel Josef Quintana, it appears that the different streams explored by Vasco Nuñez and Colmenares were all branches of one grand river, which, descending from the mountains of the interior, winds about in crystal streams among the plains and morasses bordering the bottom of the great gulf of Darien, and discharges itself by various mouths into the gulf. In fact, the stream which ran by the infant city of Santa Maria de la Antigua was but one of its branches, a fact entirely unknown to Vasco Nuñez and his companions.

51. Oviedo, Hist. Indies, p. 2. c. 3. MS.

52. Herrera, Hist. Ind. d. 1. l. x. c. 1.

53. Peter Martyr, in his third Decade, makes mention of these negroes in the following words:—"About two days' journey distant from Quaraqua is a region inhabited only by black moors, exceeding fierce and cruel. It is supposed that in time past certain black moors sailed thither out of Ethiopia, to rob, and that by shipwreck, or some other chance, they were driven to these mountains." As Martyr lived and wrote at the time, he of course related the mere rumour of the day, which all subsequent accounts have disproved. The other historians who mentioned the circumstance, have probably repeated it from him. It must have risen from some misrepresentation, and is not entitled to credit.

54. Vidas de Espanoles Célebres, por Don Manuel Josef Quintana. Tom. ii. p. 40.

55. Herrera, Hist. Ind. d. i. l. x. c. 2.

56. Many of the foregoing particulars are from the unpublished volume of Oviedo's History of the Indias.

57. Oviedo, Hist. Gen. p. 2. MS.

58. P. Martyr, d. iii. c. 2.

59. Herrera, d. i. l. x. c. 4.

60. Oviedo, Hist. Gen. Part II. c. 4. MS.

61. By the English historians he has generally been called Davila.

62. Oviedo, l. ii. c. 7. MS.

63. This was the same Marchioness de Moya, who during the war of Granada, while the court and royal army were encamped before Malaga, was mistaken for the queen by a Moorish fanatic, and had nearly fallen beneath his dagger.

64. P. Martyr, decad. 3, chap. iii, Lok's translation.
65. P. Martyr, decad. 3. c. iii, Lok's translation.
66. Oviedo, Hist. Ind. p. 2. c. 8.
67. P. Martyr, decad. 3. c. vi.
68. Herrera, decad. 2. l. i. c. 2.
69. P. Martyr.
70. P. Martyr, decad. 7, c. 10.
71. Oviedo, part 2. c. 9. MS. Oviedo, the historian, was present at this consultation, and says that he wrote down the opinions given on the occasion, which the parties signed with their proper hands.
72. Oviedo, part 2. c. 9. MS.
73. Herrera, d. 2. l. i. c. iv. P. Martyr, d. 3. c. x.
74. Herrera, Hist. Ind. d. 2, l. i. c. 4.
75. Herrera, d. 2. l. ii. c. 1 1.
76. In consequence of the eloquent representations made to the Spanish government by the venerable Las Casas, of the cruel wrongs and oppressions practised upon the Indians in the colonies, the Cardinal Ximenes, in 1516, sent out three Jeronimite Friars, chosen for their zeal and abilities, clothed with full powers to inquire into and remedy all abuses, and to take all proper measures for the good government, religious instruction, and effectual protection of the natives. The exercise of their powers at San Domingo made a great sensation in the new world, and, for a time, had a beneficial effect in checking the oppressive and licentious conduct of the colonists.
77. Oviedo, Hist. Ind. p. 2. c. 9. MS.
78. Oviedo, ubi sup.
79. P. Martyr, decad. 4, c. 6.
80. Vide Oviedo, Hist. Gen. l. xxxix. c. 2.
81. Incas, Garcilaso de la Vega, Hist. Florida, t. iv. c. 37.
82. If the reader has perused the history of Columbus, he may remember the romantic adventure of this Miguel Diaz with a female cacique, which led to the discovery of the gold mines of Hayna, and the founding of the city of San Domingo.
83. Herrera, decad. 1. l. vii. c. 13.
84. Herrera, decad. 1. l. viii. c. 13.
85. This famous dog was killed some years afterwards by a poisoned arrow, as he was swimming in the sea in pursuit of a Carib Indian. He left, however, a numerous progeny and a great name behind him; and his merits and exploits were long a favourite theme among the Spanish colonists. He was father to the

renowned Leoncico, the faithful dog of Vasco Nuñez, which resembled him in looks and equalled him in prowess.

86. It was not the credulous minds of voyagers and adventurers alone that were heated by these Indian traditions and romantic fables. Men of learning and eminence were likewise beguiled by them: witness the following extract from the second decade of Peter Martyr, addressed to Leo X., then Bishop of Rome:—

"Among the islands on the north side of Hispaniola there is one about 325 leagues distant, as they say which have searched the same, in the which is a continual spring of running water, of such marvellous virtue that the water thereof being drunk, perhaps with some diet, maketh olde men young again. And here I must make protestation to your holiness not to think this to be said lightly or rashly, for they have so spread this rumour for a truth throughout all the court, that not only all the people, but also many of them whom wisdom or fortune hath divided from the common sort, think it to be true; but, if you will ask my opinion herein, I will answer that I will not attribute so great power to nature, but that God hath no lesse reserved this prerogative to himself than to search the hearts of men," &c.—P. Martyr, D. 2. c. 10, Lok's translation.

87. Herrera, Hist. Ind. d. 1. l. ix, c. 10.

88. Herrera, d. 1. l. ix.

89. The belief of the existence, in Florida, of a river like that sought by Juan Ponce, was long prevalent among the Indians of Cuba, and the caciques were anxious to discover it. That a party of the natives of Cuba once went in search of it, and remained there, appears to be a fact, as their descendants were afterwards to be traced among the people of Florida. Las Casas says, that even in his days, many persisted in seeking this mystery, and some thought that the river was no other than that called the Jordan, at the point of St. Helena; without considering that the name was given to it by the Spaniards in the year 1520, when they discovered the land of Chicora.